Alan Bairner

Sport, Nationalism, and Globalization

EUROPEAN AND NORTH AMERICAN PERSPECTIVES

STATE UNIVERSITY OF NEW YORK PRESS

Cover photo: PhotoDisc

Published by
State University of New York Press, Albany

For information, address State University of New York Press,
90 State Street, Suite 700, Albany, NY 12207

Production by Judith Block
Marketing by Anne M. Valentine
Composition by Doric Lay Publishers

Library of Congress Cataloging-in-Publication Data

Bairner, Alan.
    Sport, nationalism, and globalization : European and North American
perspectives / Alan Bairner.
       p.   cm. — (SUNY series in national identities)
    Includes bibliographical references and index.
    ISBN 0-7914-4911-4 (alk. paper) — ISBN 0-7914-4912-2 (pbk. : alk. paper)
    1. Nationalism and sports—North America.   2. Nationalism and sports—
Europe. I. Title. II. Series.

GV706.34 .B25 2001
306.4'83'094—dc21

                                               00-032980

10 9 8 7 6 5 4 3 2 1

In memory of my parents

SANDY BAIRNER (1917–1993)
RETA BARCLAY (1917–1991)

contents

introduction

SPORT AND NATIONALITY

Sport and nationalism are arguably two of the most emotive issues in the modern world. Both inspire intense devotion and frequently lead to violence. Furthermore, their fortunes are often linked. Sport is frequently a vehicle for the expression of nationalist sentiment to the extent that politicians are all too willing to harness it for such disparate, even antithetical, purposes as nation building, promoting the nation-state, or giving cultural power to separatist movements. Ironically, however, at the start of a new millennium both the relationship between sport and national identity and the fate of the nation (especially the nation-state) itself are being seriously questioned. Globalizing impulses are thought to be diminishing the significance of national identity in general while simultaneously weakening the link beween sport and expressions of nationalism. As this book shows, however, although the process known as globalization has clearly had an impact on them, the relationship beween sport, national identity and nationalism remains as strong as ever.

While attempting to identify the character of his nation, former British Conservative Prime Minister John Major chose the game of cricket as being quintessentially English. But what did this mean? Is cricket the English national sport? It certainly cannot be regarded as such in terms of the numbers who play and watch it. The implication of Major's claim, however, is that cricket reflects the principal values of the nation in ways that other, more popular sports do not. Clearly his claim was inspired by nostalgia for an older England in which more people did, in fact, play and watch cricket. Nevertheless, it prompted thoughts about the relationship between sport and national identity just as earlier comments had by another Conservative politician, Norman Tebbit, which suggested in regard to the identity of ethnic minorities in Britain, that a "cricket test" should be applied. Do members of these groups support the English cricket team? Or do they favor the test match playing representatives of their places of ethnic origin, particularly India, Pakistan, and the West Indies? The implication of Tebbit's claim was obvious. One way of becoming a true citizen of the nation would be to support the national sports teams. This presupposes, of course, that the identity and territorial integrity of the nation are uncontested. However, relations between sport and national identity, as this book reveals, vary markedly according to the status of particular nations.

Tebbit and Major are by no means the only modern politicians to have seen a link between sport and national identity. Similar issues arose concerning the soccer team selected by France to compete on home soil in the World Cup Finals of 1998. Jean-Marie Le Pen, leader of the National Front, had complained that it was artificial to choose players from abroad and seek to present them as making up an authentically French team (*Economist*, 18 July 1998). The reference was to players such as Zinedine Zidane (born in Marseilles of Algerian parentage), Lilian Thuram (from Guadeloupe), Christian Karembeu (a Kanak from New Caledonia), Marcel Desailly (born in Ghana), and so on. Ironically two of these players, Zidane and Desailly, were the star performers in the final against Brazil, which resulted in France's first-ever World Cup triumph. Although this was never likely to eradicate racism overnight, or weaken Le Pen's electoral support base, it did raise questions about what it means to be French—questions that might be answered eventually in such a way as to raise the status of ethnic minority groups within France. Conversely, the performance of a player such as Zidane was clearly a source of pride for young North Africans who used the World Cup Finals to promote their own separate identity. As a result, cultural diversity rather than assimilation is likely to be the long-term achievement of the multiracial harmony demonstrated by the French team. Few commentators pointed out that ethnic diversity in the French national team is nothing new. As Marks (1999) observes, "The main difference is that this diversity of origin is now embraced in the positive light of multicultural integration" (55).

Also in the summer of 1998, the British press made much of the fact that Muttiah Muralitharan, the spin bowler who effectively won the test match for Sri Lanka against England, is a Tamil (*Guardian*, 1 September 1998). But what point was being made? Was he a Tamil who had deserted his people to play for the enemy? Was he seeking to use his undoubted cricketing prowess to promote Tamil political demands? Does he think of himself as Sri Lankan first and Tamil second? Or maybe he simply wants to ply his trade at the highest possible level, which in this instance means playing test match cricket for Sri Lanka irrespective either of his identity or his political beliefs. If one could ask Murali about these things no doubt the truth might even unfold to reveal a complex amalgam of all of these feelings. The point is that we must always delve deeper if we are to understand the relationship between sport and national identity, and arguably we should each begin with our own personal story.

A Boy's Story

Having grown up in central Scotland in the 1950s, some of my most vivid memories revolve around two of the world's most popular sports, soccer and golf. In regard to the former, two fixtures were of particular significance. The first was the twice yearly meeting of Glasgow's great rivals—Celtic and Rangers, the so-called Old Firm—and the second was the annual match between the national sides of Scotland and England. My own hometown soccer team was Dunfermline Athletic and, in a sense, the Old Firm rivalry need not have concerned me at all. Yet I was conscious from an early age that this was about more than soccer. The games played between these two clubs were bound up with questions of identity, and it seemed as if everyone in Scotland had to take a side even if they usually supported another, smaller club. In this regard, I chose, not for the last time in my life it has to be said, to be perverse.

Although I was being brought up as a Protestant and Rangers were the "Protestant" team, I always found myself siding with their traditional rivals. Celtic was the team that carried with them the hopes of Scotland's Catholic underdogs, most of whom traced their ancestry back to Irish immigrants. Naturally, I was not fully aware of this political dimension at the time. Almost certainly, the Celtic colors and the green and white hoops of their shirts had simply caught the eye of a young boy. But gradually I became aware that other members of my family disliked Rangers too and, in particular, the type of Protestantism that so many of the club's fans appeared to represent. As a result, I was introduced as a child to the complexities of the relationship between sport and identity. The rivalry between Scotland and England, on the other hand, created no such difficulties.

Each year, the soccer season reached its climax when the two oldest rivals in the international game met at either Hampden Park in Glasgow or London's Wembley Stadium. Seldom did any of my young friends or I attend these matches but, from an early age, we were acutely aware of their significance. Special editions of the Saturday sports newspapers, which normally did not appear until the early evening, were available on the morning of the big match between Scotland and the "Auld Enemy." I can still see the pink or green pages on which appeared photographs of the players who would represent their respective countries later that day. I had seen some of them in the flesh playing for Celtic or Rangers or even some of Scotland's less internationally renowned clubs. Others, of course, including nearly all of the English team, were unfamiliar faces who consequently looked different from our players. In this way the idea of difference became entangled with feelings of animosity and conflict. In addition, the match itself became interwoven in the popular imagination with stories, both real and invented, about the historical relationship between the two competing nations.

We were the underdogs, the plucky fighters, one of whose national heroes, Robert Bruce, had derived inspiration from a spider and had taught us all that we should try, try, and try again. The English, on the other hand, were arrogant. Their country was larger and more powerful than ours and they deserved to be taken down a peg or two. We also knew that the Wembley game was particularly important. Thousands of Scots made the biennial pilgrimage to the British (but not in this case the nation's) capital to see their sporting representatives take on the mighty English in their own lair and seek revenge for English military incursions north of the border in years gone by. Scottish fans had traditionally saved money so that they could attend this fixture, even at a time when it was still relatively unusual to go to away games. Victory allowed Scots to feel good about themselves. Defeat meant a period of introspection and low self-esteem as the nation wallowed in collective despair.

It was only when I went to live in England many years later that I came to realize that the English did not see the rivalry in anything like the same light that the Scots did. I had to listen to English friends tell me that in their national team's absence from World Cup Finals, they would be supporting Scotland. It was unthinkable that Scots would behave as charitably if the roles were reversed. On one occasion, when England won the Wembley game by five goals to one, I was almost afraid to go out for fear of the ritual humiliation that lay ahead of me. When I finally did summon the courage to go into a local bar, the game was not mentioned and I gradually realized that hardly any of my fellow drinkers had even watched the live television coverage. Of course, had England been playing Germany, Brazil, or Italy, they would have watched. But Scotland was a different proposition. This was a game they expected to win and upon the final result of which, in any case, very little depended. In this way, I came to realize something else about sporting nationalism, above all the extent to which it is inextricably linked to broader political and cultural power relations. As junior partners in the United Kingdom, Scots needed the sporting contest with England as an element in a constant struggle to maintain a separate identity. The English, on the other hand, as the main exponents of Britishness, were more interested in contests with the outside world as opposed to those within the boundaries of the United Kingdom.

When the summer came, of course, soccer was set to one side. For most Scots, this presented problems as, unlike the English, we did not have a strong cricketing tradition to fall back on. Golf, however, has always had a special place in the affections of Scottish sports lovers not least because of the, admittedly unauthenticated, claim that the game was first played in Scotland. In my own family, interest in golf was considerable. My father had grown up in St. Andrews and had played the game to a high level from an early age. Uncles and aunts were also golfers. Furthermore, as my grandparents still lived in the traditional home of golf, I often spent summer holidays close to the famous Old Course and the Royal and Ancient clubhouse.

Looking back on these years, I now realize that I was being exposed to very different ideas about the links between sport and identity than those sustained by soccer. The big annual occasion was the Open Championship. We would never have called it the British Open for the simple reason that it was the true Open. It was played on a Scottish links course more regularly than on English soil, and this we regarded as natural since we had invented the game and continued to regard it as belonging to all Scots and not merely to the privileged few. Yet this was the extent of the sporting nationalism that surrounded the Open. I do not recall being concerned by the fact that Scots did not do particularly well in the competition. In this instance, our self-esteem was adequately fuelled by the sight of the world's greatest golfers coming to our country. At some stage during the 1950s, I met the Open champion, A. D. (Bobby) Locke, perhaps the best putter to have played the game, at the home of my aunt and uncle. At the time, I was unaware of the significance of this event and more or less took it for granted that such things happen in life. Now I recognize that I had been given an insight into the globalization of sport and its implications. Not only was Locke sitting in a small apartment on the east coast of Scotland rather that at home in South Africa, he was also a hero figure. Meeting one of Scotland's leading golfers would not have meant as much to my family as none of them had acquired a status comparable with Locke's. We were learning something about sport's place in the global village and also about the fact that our sporting heroes need not always be from our own nation. When winter returned, of course, the old identities reasserted themselves, which, in my case at least, meant being contrary on the question of the rivalry between Celtic and Rangers and unashamedly and unquestionably Scottish with regard to the ongoing struggle against the Auld Enemy.

Naturally, as I was growing up I did not interpret any of these sporting experiences in terms of globalization or the construction and reproduction of national identities. Sport in those days was all about having fun and it was only much later that I began to realize the importance of understanding its social, cultural, and political implications. The main catalyst for this growing awareness of sport's wider significance was working on my doctoral thesis on the political theory of Antonio Gramsci. Not only did Gramsci's own work encourage me to recognize the political nature of various forms of culture, but I was also fortunate enough to have as my research supervisor at the University of Hull the late R. N. (Bob) Berki, who in the course of preparing numerous highly regarded monographs on different aspects of political philosophy, never forgot that he was a soccer fan. Many of his earliest memories were of watching the Budapest team Ferencvaros and his love of the game remained closely linked to his Hungarian identity.

It was some years later, when I came to work at the Ulster Polytechnic (later to become part of the University of Ulster) that the ideas I had acquired in Hull began to be translated into more serious thoughts about the possibility of actually studying sport. In this I was greatly helped by the fact that a colleague at the time was John Sugden who had already travelled the road from mainstream social science to the sociology of sport and who gave me an excellent introduction to the main debates and also the key figures in what was for me totally virgin territory. Both John and I were also assisted by having come to work in Northern Ireland where it had become immediately apparent to us that the interrelationship between sport and identity was even more pronounced than we had previously experienced in Scotland, England, or even the United States, where John had written his doctoral thesis on the subculture of boxing. As a consequence, we were able to develop our ideas by studying the local sporting culture. My continuing interest in the place of sport in Irish society is reflected in the contents of two of the chapters that follow. In this regard, I am grateful to those loyalist and republican political prisoners in HM Prison Maze (or Long Kesh) for the countless insights into Irish (and Northern Irish in the case of the loyalists) sport during a series of discussions I held in the prison from 1996–1998 in a scheme organized by the Probation Board for Northern Ireland and supported by the Community Relations Council. Thanks are also owed to members of the probation service based at the Maze, particularly Michael Winnington, for encouragement and support.

Having become increasingly involved in researching and, in due course, teaching the sociology and politics of sport, I was fortunate enough to meet many other researchers in the field. Both their written work and their informal advice have made a major contribution to my understanding of sport and national identity in various parts of the world. They are too numerous for me to mention individually but some have been too influential for me not to record their help.

As regards Canada, I have learned much from conversations with Anouk Bélanger, Normand Bourgeois, Christine Dallaire, Peter Donnelly, Jean Harvey, Laura Robinson, Kevin Walmsley, David Whitson, and

Kevin Young. John Hoberman, Bill Morgan and Don Sabo, among others, have influenced my thinking about sport in the United States. Jan Lindroth has been my main mentor in terms of Swedish sport, and evenings spent discussing sport and life with him and his wife, Karin, in their Stockholm apartment have been a consistent source of happy and instructive memories. From fans of AIK I have acquired very different perspectives on sport in Sweden. Closer to home, Pete Shirlow has given me great encouragement together with new academic insights while John Sugden has continued to share ideas with me about sport and much else besides. Grant Jarvie and Graham Walker first gave me an opportunity to write about Scottish sport and have subsequently helped me to further develop my ideas. I have also been given useful advice at different times by Lincoln Allison, Paul Darby, Eric Dunning, John Horne, Alan Tomlinson, and Jennifer Hargreaves. At the University of Ulster, many of my closest colleagues, both in the Faculty of Humanities and in the School of Leisure and Tourism, have at different times influenced my thinking about sport. We have not always agreed but I trust that they have found the exchanges as helpful and stimulating as I have. I should also acknowledge the insights provided by my students over many years as well as by the many sports players and fans whom I count among my friends.

For financial support, I owe a debt of gratitude to the British Academy for funding two research visits to Sweden and to the Research Committee of the Faculty of Humanities in the University of Ulster for consistently supporting my work over a number of years.

With particular reference to this project, I wish to thank Tom Wilson both for suggesting that this study might be an appropriate addition to the State University of New York Press's National Identities series and also for his subsequent advice which was invaluable. My gratitude is also owed to Zina Lawrence and Nancy Ellegate at SUNY Press for their encouragement and forbearance during this project's long gestation period, to Kristin Milavec for her guidance at the production stage and to Alan V. Hewat for his copyediting skills.

Finally, I must acknowledge the influence of my parents, to whose memory this book is dedicated. My father instilled in me from an early age a love of sport that has remained a constant part of my life. He himself played a number of sports to a relatively high standard. Unable to emulate his achievements, I have joined the ranks of those who talk about sport and hopefully thereby have carried on a family tradition, albeit by a different route. Although my words may contribute to sexist stereotyping, I would have to say that my mother's role was largely to tolerate and at times to acquiesce in my enthusiasm for sport. To that extent, and because of her love of reading, she would have been pleased to see the publication of this work. That its central subject matter is sport would probably not have surprised her although she might have thought to herself that it is surely about time that I grew up.

CONTENT

The book begins with a discussion of national identity. There is also some exploration of the concept of globalization since it has been regarded by some as posing a threat to the nation and to nationalism. There follows a discussion of these ideas as they relate specifically to the academic study of sport. Subsequent chapters consist of a range of case studies of specific nations and/or nationalities. Given the restricted number of examples that are discussed in the book, it is impossible to do full justice to the range of experiences that are linked to the relationship between sport and national identity. Instead, these chapters should be read as a collection of essays, each of which highlights particular facets of the relationship as it manifests itself in a specific nationality and thereby seeks to shed light on the relationship more generally.

One national identity that is not the subject of a case study here although it is intimately bound up with sport and is clearly relevant to the book's major concerns is that of the English. However, the modern sporting revolution that began in England provides a large part of the context in which the sporting nationalisms that form the main subject matter of this book can best be understood. In particular, the analysis of the relationship between sport and the construction of Ulster unionist identities is dependent on an understanding of the emergence of a British (or English) sporting culture (Hargreaves 1986; Holt 1989; Mason 1988). In addition, each of the other sporting nationalities that are discussed are formed, to varying degrees, in response to or as a consequence of foundations laid in England.

The chapters conform to a uniform pattern inasmuch as each attempts to explain the precise relationship between sport and a particular national identity. Some consideration is also given in all the chapters to the question of whether or not globalization has had any measurable impact on that relationship. The research approach is eclectic. It makes use of direct observation, participant observation, and historical study in much the same way as has been advocated by figurational sociologists (Dunning 1999). Some of the case studies are more historically based than others. Some rely more heavily than others on firsthand experience especially where secondary literature is relatively sparse. Regardless of the approach, however, two concerns always take center stage. First, there is the role sport has played in the construction and reproduction of the relevant national identity. Attention is paid to the ways in which the search for a sporting nationalism either succeeds in disguising fundamental identity divisions that result from major cleavages in society, including race, ethnicity, and gender, or, conversely, comes into conflict with these divisions to such a degree that it becomes impossible to speak of a cohesive sporting nationalism at all. This is not to imply that national identities and other forms of identity are necessarily mutually exclusive. However, each of the case studies reveals, albeit to varying degrees, that the successful creation of a national identity centered around sport is rendered particularly problematic by the fact that sport is so closely interwoven with other sources of identity formation.

Consideration is also given in most of the chapters to the status of nationalism in terms of the perceived demise of the nation-state. In turn, this particular concern leads on to the second question that runs through the book as a whole. Each chapter considers the extent to which globalizing tendencies in sport undermine the specific identities under discussion. This also involves examining ways in which nationalist resistance to globalization through sport has manifested itself and with what degree of success. The final chapter revisits the original theoretical discussion and examines it within the empirical context provided by the case studies of specific nationalities. It is intended that this closing discussion, together with earlier sections of the book, will provide readers with insights into the general links between sport and national identities, as well as offering scholars firmer foundations upon which to construct their own analyses of this relationship as it manifests itself in other nations.

chapter one

National Identity, Globalization, and Sport

SPORT, NATIONALISM, AND NATIONALITY

It is virtually self-evident that identities are formed in a number of different locations and social practices. As Preston (1997) observes, "Identity is not a single homogeneous stock of traits, images and habits" (4). One important arena for the construction of certain identities (masculinity, for example, or social class) is sport (Jones 1988; Messner 1992; Messner and Sabo 1990). Specifically, sport is clearly linked to the construction and reproduction of the national identities of many people. But how precisely does that process develop? Furthermore, to what extent is the linkage between sport and national identity likely to be weakened as a result of major transformations in global society? In other areas of identity politics we might anticipate change. For example, will sport in the future have less influence in terms of gendered power relations as increasing numbers of women win their fight to play with the boys? How far will the cause of racial integration be furthered by way of multiracial teams in a range of sports? Is it likely that various "sport for all" mechanisms will ensure that in the future all people will have access to all sports irrespective of their socioeconomic status? In each of these areas, of course, there remains considerable room for skepticism as to the likelihood of real change. One theory, however, that is put forward with a greater degree of confidence suggests that, as a result of the process known as globalization, the relationship between sport and *national* identity is self-evidently unravelling to reveal an increasingly homogeneous global sporting culture. The theoretical underpinnings of this particular proposition will

1

be discussed in the later stages of this chapter. But first it is important to say a little more at the general level about the relationship between sport, nationalism, and national identities.

At a range of major sporting events, fans arrive waving their national flags and with their faces painted in national colors. Seldom do they favor more transnational emblems and insignia. While some fans of the European players in golf's Ryder Cup unfurl the flag of the European Union, many persist in waving their national flags despite the multinational composition of the European team. Rarely do fans wave the colors of sport's major sponsors, except when their names appear on the shirts of a club or a national team. Indeed, although competitors promote their sponsors by wearing certain clothing and using specific equipment, they continue to wave national flags to celebrate victories even, for example, in Grand Prix athletics events where, in practical terms, they are representing only themselves, although technically they remain affiliated in the course of the event to a national federation. Formula One motor racing provides an exception to this general rule, with supporters of Ferrari celebrating the achievements of their team's drivers by waving flags emblazoned with the manufacturer's emblem. Even in this instance, however, the purpose of the exercise is at least quasi-national in that it salutes an Italian car maker.What kind of nationalism is being celebrated in these different examples? To be able to answer that it is necessary first to explore theories of nationalism and national identity in the modern era.

NATION, NATIONALISM, AND NATIONALITY

The nation itself is one of the most discussed concepts in modern social and political thought. Its precise character has been subjected to a wide variety of interpretations, with language, ethnicity, geography, religion, and shared experience all having been cited as fundamental determinants. The picture is clouded still further by the fact that the nation-state, the most universal form of political organization in the modern world, is not always coterminous with the nation, particularly as defined by nationalists. Moreover, key distinctions recur throughout the analysis that follows—between civic and ethnic nationalism, for example, and also between secessionist, unificatory and expansionist nationalist movements—and each of these must be understood if one is to develop a full appreciation of the interaction between sport and national identity in particular social formations.

Forms of nationalism differ markedly from each other. As Kamenka (1993) observes, "Nationalism, it is widely recognized, has a positive side and a negative side: it can be democratic or authoritarian, backward-looking or forward-looking, socialist or conservative, secular or religious, generous or chauvinist" (85). There are also major disagreements concerning the origins of nations, nationalism, and nationalities. Are they natural phenomena? Or are they products of the imagination and, if so, what factors prompted their intellectual construction? It is impossible to do justice to all of the interpretations of nationalism in a brief discussion such as this. It is important, however, to identify key elements in contemporary discourses on nationalism in order that we may be able to better understand the theoretical and political contexts within which sport and national identities interact.

"As all commentators on nations and nationalism agree," writes Canovan (1996), "this is a subject on which it is extraordinarily hard to get a conceptual grip" (50). Dunn (1994) offers a distinction between the "nation," membership in which is secured through birth ties, and the "state," for which we require legal membership. This is inadequate, however, for a true understanding of the complex relationships between nationality and politics. More useful is the distinction between "ethnic" and "civic" nationalisms, both of which can provide the basis for the formation and maintenance of a nation-state. Clearly, this distinction, in part, reflects a desire, particularly on the part of nationalists themselves, to separate good from evil. However, it is also analytically valuable in its own right since it forces us to consider the precise limits of specific national identities. Ethnic nationalist discourse is very close to assumptions about the primordial and, therefore, natural origins of the nation. It is also often bound up with language and, in some instances, race. It is generally regarded as being unenlightened and exclusive in its political aspirations. Either one belongs or one does not. Membership is not a movable feast. As Smith (1995) observes, "It is often assumed that the intrusion of ethnic elements and sentiments of collective belonging into the life of the nation inevitably breeds exclusiveness and intolerance, and that ethnic closure is the chief basis of many of the current national conflicts that afflict the world" (100).

Civic nationalism, on the other hand, is thought to have emerged with the largely artificial creation of nations and nation-states primarily during the nineteenth century. It celebrates citizenship within particular political entities as opposed to membership in supposedly natural human associations. As a consequence, civic nationalism is inclusive. Subject to immigration controls, anyone can become a member of the civic nation, at least in principle. In between these two extremes lies "social" nationalism. According to Kellas (1991), "This type of nationalism stresses the shared sense of national identity, community and culture, but outsiders can join the nation if they identify with it and adopt its social characteristics" (52). In practice, there is substantial overlap between these different nationalisms. For example, Smith (1995) suggests that it is inappropriate to assert a clear separation in practice between "civic" and "ethnic" nationalism. In fact, "modern nations are simultaneously and necessarily civic and ethnic" (99). Moreover, Smith (1995) is concerned with the moral judgments often made about these types of nationalism. He argues that:

> Not only ethnic but also civic nationalisms may demand the eradication of minority cultures and communities qua communities, on the common assumption, shared by Marxists and liberals, not just of equality through uniformity, but that "high cultures" and "great nations" are necessarily of greater value than "low" cultures and small nations or *ethnies*. (101)

As has been argued elsewhere, therefore, it is important to avoid falling into the trap of regarding self-proclaimed civic nationalists as the good guys of nationalist history and ethnic nationalists as the men and women who wear the black hats (Bairner, 1999). Kamenka (1993) makes a further distinction, between "cultural" and "political" nationalism, and notes that some of the founders of the former, Johann Gottfried von Herder, for example, were deeply distrustful of the latter. According to Smith (1995), however, "The idea that nationalism can be 'returned' to any sphere, even that of culture, is both naive and fundamentally misconceived" (13). As with much else in the study of nationalism and nationality, the relationship between culture and politics can only properly be understood by examining specific examples of the nationalist experience.

How the politics of particular nations are packaged depends to a considerable degree on specific circumstances rather than some deep-rooted commitment to one or other version of the ideology. It is necessary, therefore, to distinguish also between different sorts of nationalist movements as well as between various accounts of the nation. Many studies of nationalist politics are concerned with movements engaged in nation-building activities. Even these, however, assume different forms. In some cases, the nationalism involved is of a separatist type. The aim is to establish a new nation free from an existing empire or multinational state. The idea of this new nation is premised on a sense of social or ethnic national identity that can only find true political accommodation when freed from an unacceptable set of political arrangements. In other instances, the nation-building process seeks to create a nation-state by bringing together disparate regions, tribes, and other premodern social or political formations. Frequently this demands a civic approach to nationalism whereby the people become citizens of the new nation-state while often retaining a sense of identity located elsewhere. In addition, all established nation-states are involved in nationalist political activity to varying degrees. Thus, nationalist politics are implicated in the promotion of existing states and in attempts to engage in territorial expansion.

Although these various forms of nationalist political activity are very different, they share certain assumptions (e.g., about the existence of the nation) and rely, to a greater or lesser degree, on telling stories about the past, constructing national mythologies, and, in some cases, inventing traditions. Moreover, although national identities are partially rooted in the human imagination, the "imagined communities," to use Benedict Anderson's phrase (Anderson 1991), that emerge have some foundation in reality as well as at the level of consciousness. As Canovan (1996) suggests, "The cliché that nations depend on consciousness therefore needs to be qualified by the observation that this sort of imagined community is not constituted simply by individual choice in the way that (say) there may be an imagined community of supporters of a football [soccer] team or fans of a pop group" (56). The point is well made although one might question the extent to which some fans may feel that they have had any genuine choice in the matter of selecting a soccer team to follow. In addition, myth making and the invention of tradition are certainly important elements in the construction of national identities (Hobsbawm and Ranger 1983). Indeed, since the role of myth features prominently in the linkage of national identity to sport, it is worth saying a little more about this aspect of nationalist politics.

Nationalism and nationalists are frequently criticized for their over-reliance on myths about who they are and where they come from. What are presented as "facts" are simply untrue. Seeking to defend nationalism from what he regards as unfair criticism, Archard (1995) argues that "national myths are neither fables nor allegories" (475). Rather, "They are intended to be believed in their presented form and for what they actually claim to have been the case." They are myths "to the extent that they misrepresent what is actual for a purpose." Archard notes "the impermeability of national myths to intellectual criticism" (477). "They are deeply rooted within popular cultures," he argues, "and insofar as they do serve important practical purposes, they will continue to be accepted as true" (477–478). Those popular traditions that sustain national myths do, of course, change over time. In addition, the myths themselves deserve criticism when they either lead to harmful consequences or are perpetuated as a result of artificially sustained ignorance or are used to enforce a morally unacceptable state of affairs. However, when we are confronted by myths about national sporting traditions, it is important that we recognize that the myths are not bad simply by virtue of their being myths. Of course, we would also do well to examine the precise ways in which these myths are used and with what ramifications.

But what if all of this discussion is irrelevant to the changing world in which we live? We are told, primarily by hard-line advocates of the globalization thesis, that we live in a postnationalist world. Distinctive identities, including those centered on the nation, are everywhere being eroded. Indeed, it is a mark of civilization that this should be so. One wonders if this is borne out by the facts. As Smith (1995) observes, "In the era of globalisation, we find ourselves caught in a maelstrom of conflicts over political identities and ethnic fragmentation" (2). Nevertheless, it remains necessary to consider those arguments that point toward ever-increasing homogenization and the creation of a global culture.

NATIONAL IDENTITY AND GLOBALIZATION

According to Holton (1998), "Globalization has, over the past decade, become a major feature of commentaries on contemporary social life" (1). Underlying all the manifestations of globalization, as Holton suggests, "is the key idea of one single world or human society, in which all regional, national, and local elements are tied together in one interdependent whole" (2). Some commentators regard globalization, understood in this way, as a negative phenomenon that represents "the dominance of Western economic and cultural interests over the rest of the world" (Holton 1998, 2). Others see this same development in a positive, even triumphalist, light. Both types of commentator appear united, however, in the belief that the process described as globalization is both inevitable and all-consuming. There are, of course, pockets of resistance of which nationalism is one of the more potent. But even such a historically vital force as this is presented as being doomed in the face of the onward march of a homogeneous, global society.

However, it can also be argued that those very forces, which are thought by some to be leading toward homogenization, actually produce quite different consequences. Thus, the interpretation that informs the analysis to follow suggests that the resilience of national sentiment is as much a result of processes commonly gathered together under the title of globalization as a futile reaction to them. As the case studies that make up the bulk of the book suggest, the persistence of nationalism as a political force and, even more significantly, the identity politics of formerly submerged nationalities and ethnic groups have actually been facilitated by those developments that are increasingly subsumed under the heading of globalization. To that extent, this book, and specifically this opening chapter, addresses the idea of globalization for the simple reason that the concept has provided a theoretical context in which much of the recent debate on the links between sport, national identities, and international politics has been taking place. There is no implicit suggestion that the process described by the term *globalization* has successfully eradicated either completely or in part the central role of nationality in the contemporary world.

The main focus of the book is on national identity as opposed to globalization, and its ultimate objective is to explain the relationship between sport and national identity in a selection of societies, each of which has of course been affected to a greater or lesser degree by forces associated with globalization. Nevertheless, it is important to consider the development of the concept of globalization and to come to terms with the various ways in which it has been employed to understand the contemporary world, not least because, as has been suggested by Waters (1995), "[G]lobalization may be *the* concept of the 1990s" (1) and is likely to remain with us well into the next millennium.

According to Giddens (1991), "The emergence of globalised orders . . . means that the world we live 'in' today is different from that of previous ages" (225). Elsewhere, he comments (1990) on the way in which the relations between local and distant social forms and events have become stretched. Globalization, he claims, "refers to that stretching process, in so far as the modes of connection between different social contexts or regions become networked across the earth's surface as a whole" (64). For Featherstone and Lash (1995), globalization became "the successor to the debates on modernity and postmodernity in the understanding of sociocultural change and as the central thematic for social theory" (1).

There are always problems involved in using fashionable ideas such as globalization. As one of the concept's leading exponents, Roland Robertson (1990), observes, there is a danger that it becomes "an intellectual 'play-zone'—a site for the expression of residual social—theoretical interests, interpretive indulgence, or the display of world—ideological references" (16). However, Robertson himself has become implicated in the intellectual wrangles that may well have served to diminish the status of the concept as an analytical tool with which to make more sense of the contemporary world. For example, Giddens and he have adopted very different positions with reference to the relationship between globalization and modernity. Robertson (1995) writes of the need to avoid "the weaknesses of the proposition that globalization is simply a consequence of modernity" (27). Giddens (1990), on the other hand, argues that modernity "is inherently globalising" and that this is apparent "in some of the most basic characteristics of modern institutions, including particularly their disembeddedness and reflexivity" (63). Elsewhere, he refers to "the globalising tendencies of modernity" and argues that "the globalization of social activity which modernity has served to bring about is in some ways a process of the development of genuinely world-wide ties such as those involved in the global nation-state system or the international division of labour" (Giddens 1991, 21).

In fact, there is little reason why theorists should disagree so profoundly about the nature of the relationship between globalization and

modernity. It is evident that globalizing tendencies have been in operation certainly since the beginning of the modern era. What is described
as the process of globalization has quickened in pace in the contemporary era, thereby throwing into some doubt traditional and long-held
ideas about time and space. Given earlier global linkages, however,
whether this means that we are now witnessing an entirely novel phenomenon is open to doubt. What remains to be seen is whether the
greater speed and broader impact of the current phase of globalization
mean that the process is more complete than ever before. As a result, it
would place in jeopardy earlier sources of identity formation, including
the nation. One's response to the likelihood of this scenario will naturally depend on how one understands the nature of globalization and
what one considers to be its ramifications. In this sense, the relationship
of the concept to the premodern, to modernity or, even, to postmodernity is largely irrelevant.

The question of whether or not globalization has an agency, which
also divides opinion, is far less irrelevant. For many of those who do discern a determining agent, their subsequent analysis is interwoven with
Marxist or neo-Marxist claims that globalization is rooted in the capitalist economic process. Globalization theories, which owe less to Marxism,
argue that although certain elements of the phenomenon are intended,
most are accidental and are certainly beyond the control of individuals,
states, or even economic systems.

What emerges is that there is no single globalization theory to which
all of its proponents have been able to sign up. As Pieterse (1995) points
out, "In social science there are as many conceptualizations of globalization as there are disciplines" (45). Thus, economic theory spawns the idea
of a global economy and international relations the notion of a global
political order. Sociology refers to a world society. Historians speak of a
world history. Cultural studies offer us a sense of global communications
and worldwide cultural homogenization. According to Pieterse (1995),
"*All* the approaches and themes are relevant if we view globalization as
a multidimensional process which, like all significant social processes,
unfolds in multiple realms of existence simultaneously" (45). Thus, some
theorists are reduced to talking about globalizations rather than globalization and see this concept as an open-ended synthesis of a variety of
interdisciplinary approaches (Pieterse 1995). In the light of this apparent
confusion, it would be foolish to begin this study by adopting a single
definition of globalization. It is more useful instead to isolate a key
dichotomy that emerges in various discussions of the subject.

According to Appadurai (1990), "The central problem of today's global
interactions is the tension between cultural homogenization and cultural
heterogenization" (295). Pieterse (1995) notes that "the most common

interpretations of globalization are the ideas that the world is becoming more uniform and standardized, through a technological, commercial and cultural synchronization emanating from the west, and that globalization is tied up with modernity" (45). Similarly as Robertson (1995) observes, "Much of the talk about globalization has tended to assume that it is a process which overrides locality, including large-scale locality such as is exhibited in the various ethnic nationalisms which have seemingly arisen in various parts of the world in recent years" (26). Furthermore, according to Robertson (1995), "There is a widespread tendency to regard this problematic as straightforwardly involving a polarity, which assumes its most acute form in the claim that we live in a world of local assertions against globalising trends, a world in which the very idea of locality is sometimes cast as a form of opposition or resistance to the hegemonically global . . ." (29). Thus, we are confronted by a world in which multinational (or transnational) capitalism, a global media and international organizations of various sorts create an increasingly homogeneous world which is challenged only periodically by pockets of resistance.

One of the most common approaches to the dichotomy between homogenization and heterogenization has been to equate globalization with the triumphant march of world capitalism and, indeed, with the worldwide hegemonic domination of American cultural forms. Thus, Featherstone (1993) writes that "the assumption that all particularities, local cultures, would eventually give way under the relentless modernizing force of American cultural imperialism, implied that all particularities were linked together as a symbolic hierarchy" (170). In this way, globalization becomes known by alternative names: Americanization, Coca-colonization, McDonaldization. Since we all consume American fast food and soft drinks, listen to American music, watch American films and television programs, and dress in American-style clothing, we become more and more like Americans and, thus, more and more like each other. According to Barber (*Independent*, 29 August 1998), "Global culture is American." "McWorld," as he describes it, "represents an American push into the future animated by onrushing economic, technological, and ecological forces that demand integration and uniformity and that mesmerises people everywhere with fast music, fast computers, and fast food—MTV, Macintosh, and McDonald's—pressing nations into one homogeneous global culture, one McWorld tied together by communications, information, entertainment and commerce."

But this is to further simplify what actually happens in the real world. For example, in certain countries, particularly those in the Islamic world, there has been overt resistance to the wholesale adoption of American fashions and tastes. Even Barber (*Independent*, 29 August, 1998) admits that "McWorld does take on the cultures of the cultures it swallows up."

thus the pop music accented with reggae and Latino rhythms in the
Los Angeles *barrio*, Big Macs served with French wine in Paris or made
with Bulgarian beef in eastern Europe, Mickey speaking French at
Euro Disney. (*Independent*, 29 August 1998)

But, according to Barber, "in the end, MTV and McDonald's are US cultural icons, seemingly innocent Trojan-American horses nosing their way
into other nations' cultures." The result is "a global consumer society
composed not of tribesmen—too commercially challenged to shop; nor of
citizens—too civically engaged—but of consumers."

Now, of course, it is undeniable that American commodities have an
international appeal. Despite long-term protectionist habits, however, the
Americans have also been increasingly exposed to the habits and cultural
preferences of other countries. Indeed, given the domestic history of the
United States, it would be difficult to argue that the Big Mac is more distinctively American than pizza, chow mein, fajitas, or kebabs. One recognizes also that the cross-fertilization of musical styles is an increasingly
international phenomenon and that, while fashion has become more and
more global, there is no indication that this has involved only the adoption of an American dress sense in the rest of the world. Westernization
as opposed to Americanization might seem a more appropriate description of what has been taking place but even this would be to overlook the
influence of non-Western societies on social and cultural developments in
the United States itself as well as in other Western countries.

According to Robertson (1995), therefore, "There is no good reason,
other than recently established convention in some quarters, to define
globalization largely in terms of homogenization" (34). He suggests that
"it makes no sense to define the global as if the global excludes the local"
(34). Indeed, for Robertson (1995), "The debate about global homogenization versus heterogenization should be transcended" (27). As a consequence, there can emerge a more subtle analysis of what is often so
loosely described as the globalization process. For Robertson (1995), "It is
not a question of *either* homogenization or heterogenization, but rather of
the ways in which both of these two tendencies have become features of
life across much of the late twentieth-century world" (27). Thus, a more
sophisticated approach now tends to dominate the debate. There remains
some uncertainty, however, concerning the extent to which globalization
is ultimately a homogenizing project.

Appadurai (1990) argues that "the globalization of culture is not the
same as its homogenization, but globalization involves the use of a variety of instruments of homogenization" (307). As a result, he suggests that
"the central feature of global culture today is the politics of the mutual
effort of sameness and difference to cannibalize one another and thus to
proclaim their successful hijacking of the twin Enlightenment ideas of the

triumphantly universal and the resiliently particular" (307–308). In his excellent summary of the more sophisticated attempts to conceptualize globalization, Appadurai (1990) writes that "the critical point is that both sides of the coin of global cultural process today are products of the infinitely varied mutual contest of sameness and difference on a stage characterised by radical disjunctures between different sorts of global flows and the uncertain landscapes created in and through these disjunctures" (308). Waters (1995) sheds further light on this approach when he notes that "a globalized culture is chaotic rather than orderly—it is integrated and connected so that the meanings of its components are 'relativized' to one another but it is not unified or centralized" (136). Thus, according to Waters (1995), "Globalization does not necessarily imply homogenization or integration" (136). It is characterized instead by cultural flows, which themselves may be multidirectional processes, by hybridization and creolization. To understand the relevance of these theories, however, it is useful to examine how they relate to real social practices and in this particular discussion to sport. This is not merely in order that the theories can be either endorsed or rejected but also to take into account the fact that sports sociologists and sport itself have themselves made important contributions to the general debate.

GLOBALIZATION AND SPORT

It has been argued that the organizational infrastructure for the globalization of sport has been in existence for some time. Jarvie and Maguire (1994) suggest that "dominant, emergent and residual patterns of sport and leisure practices are closely intertwined with globalization processes" (230). What this means, however, depends to a considerable degree on one's understanding of globalization in general. According to Houlihan (1994), "Globalisation, as related to sport, is . . . most evident and significant in providing governments with a further medium through which to conduct international politics" (200–201). Whether or not it also indicates a move in the direction of homogenization, however, is another matter. As Houlihan (1994) observes, "At the deeper level of facilitating the internalization of capitalist and consumerist values within local communities globalization is also successful, though it is extremely difficult to identify the extent to which sport has been a primary vehicle for propagation of these values" (201). Indeed, it can be argued that sports sociologists have been prominent in the struggle to ensure that the globalization process should not become identified with a relentless and irresistible surge toward total homogenization.

Maguire (1994), in particular, has added much to our understanding through his discussion on " diminishing contrasts" and "increasing varieties." Adopting the more sophisticated view of globalization, Maguire argues that "global processes are multidirectional, involve a series of power balances, and have *neither* the hidden hand of progress *nor* some overarching conspiracy guiding them" (401). According to Maguire, "There is no *single* global flow" (402). As a consequence, "Competing and distinctive cultures are thus involved in an infinitely varied, mutual contest of *sameness* and *difference* across different figurational fields" (402). The result is neither cultural homogeneity nor chaotic cultural diversity. Rather, for Maguire, "In highlighting issues of homogeneity, and the mutual contest of sameness and difference in global cultural flows, the analysis can be developed with reference to the twin figurational concepts of diminishing contrasts and increasing varieties" (402). According to Maguire (1999), "Globalization can therefore be understood in terms of attempts by more established groups to control and regulate access to global flows and also in terms of how indigenous peoples both resist these processes and recycle their own cultural products" (93). Holton (1998) arrives at a similar conclusion when he writes that "the global repertoire is not . . . to be seen as a consumer paradise or a life-enhancing intercultural smörgåsbord, but neither is it a demonic system of top-down system domination" (185). It is impossible to apply either homogenization or polarization or, indeed, hybridization with complete accuracy. Moreover, it is only when we begin to examine specific examples of contemporary social life that we can begin to fully appreciate the complexity of what is actually taking place.

For example, it is important to resist some of the implications of concepts such as "McDonaldization" and "Cocacolonization." Global processes have not created a universe in which everyone drinks Coca-Cola and eats Big Macs with increasingly fewer dietary alternatives on offer. It is true, of course, that these products are available in more parts of the world on an ever-increasing basis and this represents a clear example of the concept of diminishing contrasts. To suggest, however, that this represents the triumph of Americanization and the arrival of a homogeneous global culinary culture is surely nonsensical. The fact is that more and more foods are becoming accessible in even the remotest parts of the world. Few countries, at least in the developed world, offer only indigenous cuisine. Instead, they offer Big Macs but also menus inspired by the culinary traditions of a vast range of cultures. Indeed, even in the United States the idea of a nation eating nothing but burgers is an absurdity. In terms of food and drink, most of the world's citizens, including many even in the developing world, are offered greater variety than ever before. But to what extent does Maguire's analysis hold true for sport as well?

As Donnelly (1996) remarks, "The spread of cultural forms from one apparent source to many places has a long history" (243). There is a question mark, however, as to whether this represents the product of cultural imperialism that spreads from dominant powers to subordinate satellites or alternatively a process of cultural exchange in which some countries may be more influential than others but none has total power (Tomlinson 1991). Sport emerges as a cultural form that can be exported and/or exchanged from the eighteenth century onward with Britain and its expanding empire playing a pivotal role. Not only countries in the British Empire itself but many others with which the British did business took up the various games, which were codified in the course of the British sporting revolution (Guttmann 1994). As some of the chapters in this book reveal, there was resistance to this tendency toward British sporting imperialism. In some countries, such as the United States, British games were transformed in such a way as to contribute to the development of unique sporting cultures. Elsewhere, and most notably in nationalist Ireland, a wholly alternative set of games were promoted, albeit in ways that continued to reveal the influence of the British approach to sport. In other situations, particularly within the empire, indigenous peoples took up the British games but sought to give them a distinctive flavor and, thereby, link them to broader anti-imperialist struggles. Good examples are provided by the enthusiasm for cricket in the Caribbean and the adoption of rugby union as a "national" game by South Africa's Afrikaaners. Ironically, association football (soccer), which originated in its modern form in Britain but has become the truly universal game, has arguably spread more rapidly and with greater success in countries which were not part of the British Empire than in those that were.

Overall, the picture that emerges, and which shall be given more light and shade in the chapters that follow, is a confused one. Despite both Britain's historic role in the creation of modern sport and also the considerable political, economic, and cultural power of British imperialism, the introduction of British sports to the rest of the world was by no means a smooth and irresistible process. Rather, there a emerged the pattern of cultural flows that are highlighted by more sophisticated applications of globalization theory, with distinctive identities flourishing within the overall context of global processes as opposed to being destroyed in a stampede toward global sporting homogeneity. Thus, we are witnessing something other than straightforward British cultural imperialism.

The question for contemporary sports sociologists, however, focuses on the degree to which more recent global trends can be legitimately described as Americanization, with the cultural influence travelling only in one direction. In fact, few have been able to claim with any degree of conviction that American culture has played a similar role in the world of sport to that which it might have played in the fields of popular music and cinema (or even food if one is inclined toward an acceptance of the

McDonaldization and Cocacolonization theses). Indeed, as Donnelly (1996) observes, "Americanisation is denied by pointing to the truly international basis of sports such as tennis, golf, cycling, soccer, and track and field; to the international sport spectacles such as the Olympics, Pan-American and Commonwealth Games, and World Championships; and to sports such as rugby, cricket, Australian Rules football, sumo wrestling, and the like that have little (if any) American participation while still being shown on ESPN and ABC's *Wide World of Sports*" (245). Moreover, it is evident that the export of American games to other parts of the world has been only partially successful, with basketball and volleyball doing particularly well throughout the world but baseball only truly establishing itself on certain Caribbean islands as well as in some of the countries of the Pacific Rim. American football has a worldwide following, thanks to the efforts of the global media, but attempts to introduce it as a professional sport in countries where soccer already has a strong hold on the sporting imagination have enjoyed only limited success. Of the other major North American team games, hockey is popular in a number of European countries—Sweden, Finland, the Czech Republic, Russia, and so on—but this has more to do with the game's suitability in the first instance to native conditions than with the potency of American cultural imperialism. In any case, Canadians would be quick to point out that hockey is their game and not that of the United States and there is no one yet who has sought to equate the processes known as globalization with something called Canadianization. There is little evidence, therefore, that the Americans have gone anywhere near to achieving the success of the British in terms of the actual export of games. Indeed, one major obstacle they have faced in this regard is the fact that most countries had already established a sporting culture, which owed much to British influence, long before the United States became a dominant world power.

On the other hand, it can be argued that American ideas have impacted upon the organization and packaging of sports throughout the world regardless of whether or not the sports themselves have any significant American input. Rule changes often bear the stamp of American practices. Squad numbers and the addition of players' names mean that the shirts of Premiership soccer players in England increasingly resemble those worn in the National Hockey League (NHL), the National Football League (NFL), and the National Basketball Association (NBA). Rugby League clubs, initially in Australia and New Zealand but thereafter in England, were given names resembling those of American franchises—Sharks, Warriors, etc. Stadia throughout the world begin to look more and more like those that play host to top American sports teams. The graphics on scoreboards look increasingly American as does media coverage of non-American as well as American games in other parts of the world. For some, all of these developments might be regarded as evidence of the Americanization of sport, more subtle but no less powerful than would be signified by the successful transplantation of specific sports. It is doubtful, however, that this reflects the existence of a process called Americanization as opposed to the evolution of capitalism and its implications for the entire leisure industry.

It is perhaps not surprising, therefore, that most sports sociologists have been reluctant to endorse the Americanization thesis and even those who have chosen this general approach have tended to modify it to suit particular needs (Donnelly 1996). Some, for example, have chosen to refer to the Europeanization of sport. Thus, Standeven (1994) considers the possibility that "physical education, of which games are an important element within a fully developed education for leisure in the new Europe, may achieve again the influence it had a century ago within the public schools and colonial cultures of Britain" (241). Yet, even in this appraisal, there is a confidence that sport will continue to "ennoble cultural differences." This does not mean, however, that globalization, even in its more sophisticated form, must be discarded. In fact, if we take the concept to imply a process of cultural exchange that includes both "diminishing contrasts" and "increasing varieties," then sport is revealed as being global in much the same way as cuisine. Thus, we package our own games in American ways. Meanwhile, the Americans play our games whether these be martial arts imported from Japan (and given an American twist) or soccer, played originally in the United States by first-generation European immigrants but now one of the fastest growing American pastimes among people whose family links with the world's major soccer playing nations are increasingly distant.

It is pointless to deny the reality of time-space compression. The world has become a smaller place and cultural forms increasingly reflect this. Young people from New York to Tokyo and from Reykyavik to Cape Town listen to the same music. They drink the same soft drinks. They dress the same way in clothes derived from the world of sport, created by the major manufacturers of sportswear and often bearing the name of a internationally renowned athlete, most notably Michael Jordan. The products themselves originate in multinational corporations, most of which are based in the United States, but are manufactured in different parts of the world. Thus, in many respects, these youngsters are proof that there is such a phenomenon as globalization. But it would be meaningless to seek to equate totally the life of a young American with that of a Japanese contemporary or the experiences of a teenager in South Africa with those of an Icelandic youngster. To understand the world of each of these young people, it is necessary to take into account the local conditions under which they live as opposed to merely drawing conclusions from what is ultimately superficial. Huge differences persist in the ways in which people live their lives and one of the major sources of these differences is national identity.

NATIONALISM: RESISTANCE TO GLOBALIZATION AND SPORT

According to Smith (1995), "Politics and cultures have characteristics and patterns of their own, which are quite different from those of economic systems" (28). "Nowhere," he continues, " is this more evident than in the sphere of nations and nationalisms" (28). Arguably Smith's comments are primarily relevant only to relatively unsophisticated interpretations of globalization. Maguire's notion of "diminishing contrasts" and "increasing varieties," for example, is not necessarily contradicted by the prevalence of ethnic and nationalist rivalry. But Smith is surely correct to make the point that, however nationalism emerged, it actually means something to large numbers of people. Perhaps it is more artificial than natural. Certainly it relies to a considerable degree on myths. This is Anderson's "imagined community." But it touches people's hearts and minds in ways that cosmopolitanism does not and may never be able to, regardless of the development of global economics, power structures, and cultural forms. As Smith (1995) expresses it, "A timeless global culture answers to no living needs and conjures no memories" (24). The nation-state may well be in crisis (Dunn 1994), yet it remains the globally recognized structure of political organization: hence the United *Nations* not the Assembly of the Planet Earth's Population. In any case, if it is facing a crisis, the nation-state is threatened at least as much, if not more, by alternative expressions of nationalism as by globalization. Ultimately, as Smith (1995) suggests, "National identity, as opposed to other kinds of collective identity, is preeminently functional for modernity, being suited to the needs of a wide variety of social groups and individuals in the modern epoch" (155). Indeed, even the nation-state as opposed to nationalism in general is better prepared to resist the pressures of global transformation than some commentators would have us believe (Holton 1998). All in all, then, nationalism's death, like that of Mark Twain, has been greatly exaggerated. As Kamenka (1993) notes, "For at least one hundred years now, the death of nationalism has been predicted by good people confidently—and erroneously" (78). In the face of a variety of theses, nationalisms flourish. Furthermore, national identities, at their best, make the world a more interesting and joyous place.

As Miller (1995) observes, "National identities can remain unarticulated, yet still exercise a pervasive influence on people's behaviour" (27). For example, sports fans may dress in national costumes and paint their faces in national colors without being remotely attracted to nationalist politics. In such ways, however, sport does provide us with an important arena in which to celebrate national identities. It also forces us at times to consider the precise nature of our own national identity. It provides opportunities for representatives of different nations to engage with each other in honest competition and for their fans to enter into the world of carnival. It is also disfigured at times by the darker side of nationalism. Competitors cheat and are often officially encouraged to do so in order to promote the athletic prowess of the nation. Fans riot in some strange attempt to conduct war by other means. Benign or aggressive, the relationship between sport and nationalism is, nevertheless, inescapable. Indeed, as Kellas (1991) asserts, "The most popular form of nationalist behaviour in many countries is in sport, where masses of people become highly emotional in support of their national team" (21).

Except in times of war, seldom is the communion between members of the nation, who might otherwise be classed as total strangers, as strongly felt as during major international events. There is nothing great or glorious about writing one's nationality in a hotel register. Moreover, the action itself is essentially solitary and thus fails to bring one together with one's compatriots except in an abstract sense. But sporting events unite members of the nation in highly emotional circumstances. As Jarvie (1993) expresses it, "It is as if the imagined community or nation becomes more real on the terraces or the athletics tracks" (75). As the athletes compete and their compatriots support their efforts, there exists a bond that can often only be understood with reference to the concept of nationality. "Sport," writes Jarvie, "often provides a uniquely effective medium for inculcating national feelings; it provides a form of symbolic action which states the case for the nation itself" (74). Sport can also help to ensure the persistence of multiple national identities within the same political formation. In South Africa, for example, it has long been possible to differentiate between white and urban black sporting identities, which have fed into rival constructions of what it has meant to be South African. Furthermore, these are two among many identities that have contributed to the slow emergence of a sportive nationalism appropriate to the new "rainbow nation" (Nauright 1997). But what does all of this actually tell us about national identity or sport or even the interplay between the two? Is it possible even at this early stage of our investigation to speak of a phenomenon called sporting nationalism?

SPORTING NATIONALISM

According to Hoberman (1993), "Sportive nationalism is not a single generic phenomenon; on the contrary, it is a complicated sociopolitical response to challenges and events, both sportive and non-sportive, that must be understood in terms of the varying national contexts in which it appears" (18). Hoberman himself tends to focus on the nationalism that is associated with "the high performance ideal and any techniques that might serve it" (315). Essentially, this means what political theorists would describe as "official nationalism" (Kellas 1991, 4). Existing nation-states have frequently been shown to use sport for a variety of purposes, including enhancing prestige, securing legitimacy, compensating for other aspects of life within their boundaries, and pursuing international rivalries by peaceful means (Hargreaves 1992).

This type of sporting nationalism has received considerable attention (Hill 1992; Houlihan 1994; Illmarinen 1982), but the resultant debate has tended to ignore the question of national identity and its complex relationship with official nationalisms. Thus, it has little to say, for example, about ethnic nationalism which is as likely to pose a threat to the existing political order as to provide the basis for its maintenance. This study does not deny the useful role played by sport in aiding and abetting state sponsored nationalism. But, sport also has the capacity to help to undermine official nationalism by linking itself to sub-nation-state national identities and providing a vehicle for the expression of alternative visions of the nation (Cronin and Mayall 1998; MacClancy 1996; Mangan 1996). For example, as Kidd (1992) observes about Canada, one of the countries that is examined in this book, "the Canadian unity celebrated by the triumph of Team Canada in international ice hockey helps reinforce the hegemony of English-speaking, central Canadian patriarchy, and the legitimacy of high performance as the ultimate measure of cultural validity in sport" (153). On other occasions, however, "the ideology of dominant meanings is contested as such" and "while cultural struggle has occurred at every Olympic Games, it was particularly acute at the time of the Montreal Games [1976], when the very definition of the host nation and the purpose of sports—both of which frame the staging and interpretation of an Olympics—were openly and fiercely debated" (153). Seldom is the linkage of sport and national identity straightforward and it is only by looking at particular nationalities that its nuances are revealed. In addition, by examining the complexities of this issue, it becomes possible to establish a more accurate theoretical conceptualization of the relationship between sport and national identity. One approach to these issues, for example, is to try to understand what is meant when people refer to their "national" sport.

It is true that sports fans of any nation will delight in the sporting success of their compatriots. But sporting nationalism is also linked to the sport in which that success has been obtained. Thus, the depth of celebration may still vary from one sport to another and the sport (or sports) that attracts most widespread attention will commonly be linked to the idea of a national sport. One criterion of a national sport might be that the sport in question was actually invented in a particular nation. It may have remained exclusive to its place of origin although it is more likely that it is played in other countries but retains its cultural link to the parent nation. However, a national sport may also be one with which a particular nation and its people identify strongly even though it is played in many other parts of the world, including countries that have been seen as enemies and may still be conceived of in this way. The sport may also be regarded as national inasmuch as the people of a particular nation have influenced its development in a certain fashion or play in a unique way. The question of what constitutes a national sport will be addressed in the chapters that follow. But this is only a part of the overall objective of this study.

Ultimately, the book explores two related themes—the extent to which sport has been implicated in the development of particular national identities and the ways in which sporting nationalisms have responded to the forces of globalization. The nations or nationalities that have been chosen for examination were not selected on any scientific basis but largely because of their own intrinsic interest together with the author's knowledge of them. That said, they do offer a range of different nationalist experiences out of which, it is hoped, some valuable theoretical conclusions can be drawn. Despite their differences, however, all of the nationalisms that are examined in the book are located in Western societies either in Europe or North America. It is there that the modern idea of nationalism first emerged. In addition, given the supposed relationship between material progress and globalization, it is in these developed societies of the West that one might expect to see the clearest evidence of cultural convergence. As a result, they are good places in which to conduct a study not only of links beween sport and national identity but also the impact of global change.

Some of the discussion that follows deals with the idea of official nationalism. More often, however, what is revealed is the degree to which below the superficial veneer, in most social formations the relationship between sport and nationality remains contested terrain. In some cases, this refers to the existence of more than one national identity within the same nation-state. Or it could be a matter of a specific national identity being shared between two different political entities. Then again, it may simply mean that there are divisions concerning how the nation is understood and presented—in this particular instance, by way of sport. For many people, none of this really matters. They remain oblivious to the excitement of sport or disinterested in the idea of the nation. For more

extreme cases, equally hostile to sport and nationhood. But for at least as large a group, in every corner of the world, both sport and nationality matter as, indeed, does the relationship between the two. It is the precise nature of that relationship that forms the main subject matter of this study.

chapter two

British Nationalism or Ulster Nationalism?

SPORT AND THE PROTESTANTS OF NORTHERN IRELAND

POLITICS AND SOCIETY IN NORTHERN IRELAND

It is evident that many of the world's most deep-seated conflicts involve questions of national identity. In an era in which globalization is thought by some to be flattening out the differences between the various peoples of the world, the violence that has followed the breakup of the former Yugoslavia provides compelling evidence of the degree to which ethnic and nationalist rivalries are still able to transcend superficial moves in the direction of homogenization. Another example of the enduring nature of struggles centered around national identity is offered by the conflict in Ireland. While there are those who for reasons of convenience talk about the rivalry as being between Catholics and Protestants, it is obvious that what has always been at issue is the very real difficulty of constructing a political entity that is compatible with the presence of two different expressions of national identity—one Irish, the other British, and neither of them, as we shall see, being themselves watertight concepts.

Although the current conflict in Northern Ireland, which began in the late 1960s, has provoked a plethora of academic responses and analyses almost since its inception, the role of sport in reflecting and perhaps even contributing to sectarian division and concomitant violence was ignored until the author and a former colleague in the University of Ulster at Jordanstown, John Sugden, started to publish a series of studies on the subject. The reasons why sport in Northern Ireland was neglected by academia are, for the most part, similar to those that have been responsible for the traditional lack of serious analysis of sport in numerous other social formations. The tendency to either ignore totally the place of sport in the development of modern society or at the very least to seriously underestimate its importance resulted, as Allison (1986) suggests, from two competing and equally erroneous assumptions, namely, "that sport was both 'above' and 'below' the political dimensions of social life" (5). According to the first misconception—that sport is "above" politics—the world of sport is presented as an autonomous realm that is capable of transcending social and political divisions; as for the notion that sport is "below" politics, the misconception lies in the belief that sport is a trivial element of human society and, thus, unworthy of serious academic attention. Fortunately for students of sport, both of these erroneous views have been successfully challenged in recent years. In divided societies such as Northern Ireland, however, obstacles are still in place. Since the benign view of sport suggests that it can play a transcendent role, it is almost regarded as bad form to address the divisive potentialities of sport. This is particularly true in Northern Ireland where the sporting culture is so strong and those who speak on behalf of sport in general or even individual sports are regarded as pillars of society. By pointing out sport's darker side, one is not necessarily questioning the integrity of those people who are most involved in promoting sport. Yet that is often how such critical analysis is regarded. As this chapter (and chapter 4) reveal, sport does offer a window through which to look at the conflict in Northern Ireland and, as one looks, one sees plenty of evidence of the political significance of many elements of the Northern Irish sporting culture. The role of sport in the construction and reproduction of national identity is but one such example.

The partition of Ireland, which created a newly independent Irish Free State and left six counties, thereafter known as Northern Ireland, within the United Kingdom, has remained a bone of contention for Irish nationalists and republicans. For Ulster unionists, on the other hand, the continued union of the Great Britain and Northern Ireland represents the only way in which their British identity can be secured. The clash between these two mutually exclusive ambitions lies at the heart of what have become euphemistically known as the Northern Irish "troubles." Naturally neither community is monolithic, and there remains room for political debate. Before examining the relationship between sport and the protestants of Northern Ireland, therefore, it is worth spending a little time discussing the ideology of Ulster unionism, particularly as it relates to matters of national identity.

Ulster Unionism

Coulter (1994) rightly argues that there has been a general failure to understand the diversity of Ulster unionism.

> The preoccupation with the radical periphery of unionist politics—coupled as it is with the unreasonable assumption that the intemperate voices raised therein may be taken as representative of the unionist community as a whole—has inevitably ensured that many existing interpretations have failed to acknowledge or accommodate the sheer diversity of unionist sentiment and experience. (2)

With regard to the politics of nationalism, there is a school of thought that suggests that Ulster Protestants have never developed a fully fledged national identity (Nairn 1981). Others have sought to argue that there is an Ulster nation that is as deserving of national self-determination as the Irish one. According to Coulter (1994), one of the major problems with these rival views is their shared assumption that there is something intrinsically progressive about nationalism. For Coulter, this is self-evidently untrue and "viewed in this particular context . . . the ambiguity of unionists' national identity begins to appear less problematic than has frequently been assumed" (11–12). What is not denied, however, is the ambiguous character of the relationship of Ulster unionists to the idea of the nation. Moreover, in terms of the politics of identity, some unionists appear to be in no doubt as to who they are and what they stand for, as a 1998 statement from the Grand Orange Lodge of Ireland makes clear.

> Orangemen and Orangewomen are "Queen's men and women" and they are 100 per cent British in their identity. Like all decent law-abiding people they want normal cordial relationships with the republic to the south but not at the expense of their British heritage or identity. (*Orange Standard*, September, info@goli.demon.co.uk)

Yet, in general, analysis of Ulster unionist ideology has tended to ignore the question of national identity or to make certain untested assumptions about the nationality of this community. Indeed, according to Aughey (1989), one of the most important commentators on Ulster unionist politics, to properly understand unionism, or at least certain strands of unionism, it is necessary to go beyond the concept of nationalism and turn instead to that of citizenship. For Aughey (1989), "The idea of the Union is properly one which transcends such outdated concepts as nationalism" (202). The problem is that, despite Aughey's seductive argument, nationalism remains one of the key elements in identity formation in the contemporary world or is, at the very least, viewed as such by nationalists of varying hues who are themselves important political actors. The nation, as we have seen, is still regarded as the main basis for political organization in the world. Thus, the question—What is the nationality of Ulster unionists?—is a reasonable one. But, it is one that has been largely ignored by the more serious analysts of unionist political culture.

In an influential article, Todd (1987) identifies two traditions in unionist political culture. On one hand, there is Ulster loyalism, which is defined by a primary, imagined community of Northern Irish Protestants and a secondary, conditional loyalty to the British state. According to Todd (1987), "The ideological structure of Ulster loyalism is such that loyalists see dominance as the only means of preserving their identity" (10). Thus, they define themselves in opposition to the Other—Irish Catholicism. In this instance, "religious affiliation is established as the primary demarcator of the 'collective other'" (Bairner and Shirlow 1998, 167). On the other hand, there is an Ulster British ideology, which is defined by a primary loyalty to the imagined community of Greater Britain and a secondary, regional patriotism for Northern Ireland. The "collective other," in this example, is "the 'Menace' which can come from a range of social groups or agencies but which is particularly constructed in terms of the Republican-Nationalist communities of Ireland" (Bairner and Shirlow 1998, 167). According to Todd (1987), "Ulster British ideology . . . is not a closed ideological system" (21). But one is entitled to assume that it is at least closed to certain representations of Irishness. However, what Todd fails to assess in sufficient detail are the national identities, if any, that may be involved in these ideological positions. What is Britishness? How do unionists specifically relate to Irish national identity?

There is also no discussion in Todd's analysis of the curious weakening of British nationalist identity, particularly since the end of World War II, in the other component parts of the United Kingdom. The Orange Order (1998) makes reference to the "massive Orange population" in Scotland. But as regards national identity, most modern Scots describe themselves as Scottish first and British only second if at all. So to what extent is it possible for Ulster unionists, Orangemen included, to define themselves as both British and Irish? Todd (1987) refers to membership of British institutions, civil as well as political, as an important element in the construction of Ulster British ideology and, as an example, she cites trade unions. What she fails to mention is that most trade unions that operate within the six counties of Northern Ireland are affiliated to the Irish Congress of Trade Unions and therefore contribute to a cross-border and potentially Irish national civil society while simultaneously maintaining a British connection. Todd (1987) notes that, even among the Ulster British, let alone the Ulster loyalists, "there is no understanding of the value of preserving the Irish language and little interest in historical traditions or

Gaelic games" (19). But as we shall see, members of this Ulster British tradition represent Ireland in sports such as rugby union, field hockey, and cricket, which suggests that at some level of their consciousness at least there is an awareness of an Irish as opposed to a British or narrowly Ulster identity. The Ulster British, according to Todd (1987), "may move from a primary imagined community of Greater Britain to placing as much importance on an Irish imagined community as on a British imagined community—from Ulster British to British Irish" (22). Arguably, however, many members of this community, as sporting examples reveal, may always have possessed a multiplicity of national identities with political expediency and everyday pragmatism obliging them from time to time to highlight one of these at the expense of the other. Certainly, as Ruane and Todd (1996) argue, "A British identity is usually seen as an addition to rather than a replacement of more specific Northern Irish, Ulster or Irish Protestant identities" (59). This point should be kept in mind when the construction of Ulster unionist identity through sport is under discussion.

GLOBALIZATION IN NORTHERN IRELAND

Supporters of the hard globalization thesis would argue that all of this debate has been rendered irrelevant for the simple reason that the penetration of consumer culture has deepened in Northern Ireland as elsewhere despite almost thirty years of civil disorder and armed conflict. McDonalds has played its part in the regeneration of blighted urban landscapes. The youngsters, regardless of their religious and ethnic identities, drink the same soft drinks, listen to the same music, and wear Nike and Adidas trainers. What is impressive and even frightening, however, is the extent to which, even in an era of Coca-Cola and McDonalds, members of the rival communities in Northern Ireland live separate lives. The author recalls hearing a republican prisoner being criticized for wearing the soccer shirt of an English team, watching English soap operas on television, and reading an English tabloid newspaper. His accuser asked him how he actually differed from a soldier in the British army. His answer was succinct and deeply meaningful. "The difference is," he said, "I'm in the IRA."

The young people may do many of the same things but they are most likely to do them in the company of their co-religionists in places that are exclusive to their community. It is arguable that the rave culture has succeeded in transcending intercommunity division to a greater extent than any other global cultural phenomenon. In general, however, political division impacts upon most social activities in Northern Ireland and one of the most pervasive of these is sport. Globalization has had an impact on the sporting culture of Northern Ireland and, indeed, of the island of

Ireland as a whole. What is more, this is not simply a matter of superficial manifestations of the process in the form of clothing and training shoes. But before there is any discussion of this, what is required is a detailed examination of what makes the sports culture of Northern Ireland and specifically that of Ulster unionists different.

BRITAIN AND THE ORIGINS OF SPORT IN MODERN IRELAND

Although games and, thus embryonic sports, have existed since primitive times throughout the world, there is no denying the pivotal role played by Britain, and more specifically England, in laying the foundations during the eighteenth and nineteenth centuries of the modern sports culture. Above all, it was in the English public schools that many games were first regulated. It was also in England that the notion of national sporting administrative bodies first emerged. In no way, however, can this be said to have remained a parochial matter. The British approach to playing and organizing sport was rapidly exported to the various parts of the expanding British Empire along with Christianity and the English language. Of these it can be argued that the role of sport was of equal worth and some might feel that, in the long term, the sporting legacy was to prove even more durable than those other "gifts" of imperialism.

As Stoddart claims (1988), "Through sport were transformed dominant British beliefs as to social behaviour, standards, relations, and conformity, all of which persisted beyond the end of the formal empire, and with considerable consequences for the post colonial order" (651). This viewpoint is supported by Perkin (1986) who writes that "in the case of Britain and its Empire in the last hundred years or so, sport played a part both in holding the Empire together and, paradoxically, in emancipating the subject nations from tutelage" (3).

Given Britain's pioneering role in the modern development of sport, it is scarcely surprising that this came to assume such a high profile in the British Empire. Nevertheless, the sheer scale of sport's importance to imperial policy is difficult to take in. According to Mangan (1987), "The formation of character was the essential purpose of Victorian elitist education—at home and overseas," and, for the export of character, it was deemed necessary to have "trainers of character, mostly from public school and ancient university, who used the games field as the medium of moral indoctrination" (139–40).

In the light of the short distance between Britain and Ireland and the extent and strength of family and kinship ties between the two countries, it is scarcely surprising that the missionary aspect of the English sporting revolution had an early and significant impact on the neighboring island. As the author has previously written about the sporting ties between

Britain and Ireland, "Because of the geographical proximity of the two and the close links between their respective upper classes, it is more difficult than in other imperial contexts to draw a clear distinction between the imperial elite and the indigenous elite" (Bairner 1996a, 60). Indeed, Jeffery (1996) has pointed out the the difficulties involved in accurately depicting Ireland's status vis à vis British imperialism, cultural or otherwise. For Irish nationalists, of course, it has been customary to present Ireland as an oppressed constituent of the Empire. Yet, as Jeffery (1996) reveals, "Ireland, as part of the metropolitan core of the Empire, supplied many of its soldiers, settlers and administrators" (1). Similarly, the sporting missionary work done in Ireland in the nineteenth century was at least as likely to be the work of Irish-born enthusiasts as of British colonizers. Between them, these two categories of people had an enormous impact on the development of a modern sporting culture in Ireland. Indeed, before discussing in detail the nature of Ulster's sporting traditions and the manner in which they evolved, it is worthwhile devoting a little space at this stage to mapping out the history and broad contours of the general sporting culture in Ireland as a whole without dealing at any length for the time being with what may be regarded as indigenous pursuits.

In the first instance, in Ireland as elsewhere, the British games were played by members of the military garrison and by civil servants entrusted with the task of administering colonial rule. As also happened elsewhere, however, games such as cricket, rugby, and field hockey were quickly taken up by members of the indigenous elite, which, in Ireland, was already more closely bound to Britain than was the case in other parts of the empire. Moreover, this linkage was put on a more institutionalized footing by the establishment of educational institutions in Ireland that closely resembled those schools and universities in England in which the modern sporting revolution had its roots. Thus, the pioneers of British games in Ireland were most likely to be British themselves or to have been educated either in Britain or in institutions in Ireland that had followed the English example in terms of education, sport, and the interrelationship between the two. Moreover, since Dublin was the administrative capital of British rule in Ireland, it was hardly surprising that it was there that most of the emergent ruling bodies were established. These included the Irish Rugby Football Union, formed in 1879 through the amalgamation of the Irish Football Union (1874) and the Northern Football Union (1875), the Irish Lawn Tennis Association (1877), the Golfing Union of Ireland (1891), and the Irish Hockey Union (1893). One notable exception was the Irish Football Association, established in 1880 in Belfast, to govern soccer throughout Ireland and still responsible for the game in what is now Northern Ireland.

Despite its origins in the English public (private) schools, soccer rapidly became the favorite sport of industrial working-class men throughout Britain. Significantly, one area in which the people's game quickly established secure roots was the west of Scotland. Many of the Protestants who lived in the northeast corner of Ireland and were to constitute the bulk of the unionist population in the years ahead had strong ancestral links with Scotland. Furthermore, the cities of Glasgow and Belfast had close economic ties. Thus, it was no coincidence that interest in soccer quickly crossed the Irish Sea and established a place in the affections of the Protestant working class of Belfast and its immediate hinterland. From Ulster the game spread to other parts of Ireland, reversing the direction that had taken the British games north from Leinster, the most anglophile area of what is now the Irish Republic. The subsequent development of soccer throughout Ireland in general and in the north in particular has had major, albeit at times contradictory, effects on the relationship between sport and national identity. The political implications of soccer in the Irish Republic and for Irish nationalism in general will be discussed in due course. This chapter, however, offers a detailed consideration of how the game has impacted upon the thinking of Ulster unionists. It is important in this respect to recognize that soccer belongs to a different category of sport than games such as rugby union and cricket.

Sport in Modern Ireland

In recent writings on sport in Ireland, it has been useful to make a tripartite distinction between British, universal, and Gaelic games (Sugden and Bairner 1986; Sugden and Bairner 1993a; Sugden and Bairner 1993b). British games have been construed as those that arrived in Ireland largely as a result of political and cultural links between Britain and Ireland and which are still associated with Britain not least because they continue to be played most enthusiastically in those countries that have historic links to Britain and the British Empire. The category of British games includes rugby (which, with the exception of France, is played at the highest level in former British colonies) and cricket, so associated in popular imagination with Englishness that the phrase "it's not cricket" has come to symbolize a form of non-British behavior. The arrival of all of these games in Ireland testifies to the permeation of British and, thus, for Irish nationalists, unacceptable political and cultural influence. Particularly influential in this respect were the army and the education system (Bairner 1996a). For example, to begin with at least, as Bergin and Scott (1980) observe, "Whatever cricket was played in Ireland was confined to the military, the gentry and members of the viceregal or Chief Secretary's staff and household" (508). Indeed, the first recorded cricket match in Ireland took place in Dublin's Phoenix Park in 1792 between an

"All-Ireland" selection and a team representing the military garrison (Hone 1956). Golf too, although it has long since ceased to be regarded as a British game, is relevant in this respect since Ireland's second-oldest club was founded at the Curragh in 1883 by soldiers of the Highland Light Infantry (71st Regiment) (Gibson 1988). There are even some claims that the game was actually invented in Ireland but firmer evidence indicates that it arrived on the island, in embryonic form at least, during the Hamilton and Montgomery Plantation of Ulster, which began in 1606 (Gibson 1988). Field hockey was another popular regimental sport not only in Ireland but throughout the British Empire (Dagg 1944). But by no means all British sports owed their initial success in Ireland to the military presence.

From the outset, the development of rugby union in Ireland was rooted in educational institutions rather than in army garrisons. A rugby club was established at Trinity College Dublin in 1854, making it the second oldest club still in existence anywhere in the world (Van Esbeck 1973). Indeed, according to West (1991), "The 1854 foundation date gives Trinity a substantial claim to be the oldest club in existence," since "Guy's Hospital FC, which was founded in London in 1843 and played its football initially on Kennington Oval, is certainly older, but went into abeyance for some years in the nineteenth century" (25). Many of the club's founding members had received their schooling in England and the first Honorary Secretary and Treasurer, Robert Henry Scott, although Dublin-born, had attended Rugby School, the cradle of rugby, at least according to the game's foundational myth. In the north of Ireland, cricket clubs too were often set up by the products of English public schools and they became instrumental in the growth of rugby in the north. For example, the North of Ireland Cricket Club, established in 1859, inspired the foundation of the North of Ireland Football Club, many of the founding members of which had been educated at English public [private] schools. Significantly all of these British games were played increasingly by Irish nationalists as well as by supporters of the union and in Catholic schools as well as in other educational institutions.

Universal games include basketball and soccer as well as more individual activities such as golf, boxing, tennis, track and field, and swimming. Given the impact of the sporting revolution in nineteenth-century England, most of these sports are British in origin but have long since ceased to be confined to countries that formed part of the British Empire. For example, golf, as we have seen, probably arrived in Ireland by way of the plantation and was firmly established by members of the military garrison. Today, however, Irish professional golfers, from whatever background, are members of a global circus that travels the world in search of tour victories and enormous winnings. Basketball, on the other hand, was an import from North America, an example perhaps of the process in which globalization and Americanization have become synonymous, although the accuracy of this equation is challenged in this particular study of the relationship between sport and national identity. What is certain is that, regardless of their point of origin, universal games can be played by Irish people whatever their political affinities, unlike British games, which, in Northern Ireland at least, are most likely to be played by those members of the population who believe that the constitutional link between their part of Ireland and Great Britain should be maintained. The third and final category of sports in Ireland consists of Gaelic games. Although played by members of the Irish diaspora (and others) in various parts of the world, these are primarily Irish-based activities. In Northern Ireland, in particular, this means that they are participated in almost exclusively by Catholic nationalists. The historic and contemporary role of Gaelic games in the construction and reproduction of Irish national identity will mainly be discussed in chapter 4. This chapter examines the part played by sport in the development of a national identity for those people who, outside of Britain itself, most enthusiastically embraced the products of the English sporting revolution—namely, the Ulster unionists.

SPORT AND ULSTER UNIONISM

As has been shown, whether or not it is appropriate to describe the ideology (or ideologies) of Ulster unionism as nationalist can be debated. For some, including many unionists themselves, unionist politics can best be understood as a response to the aggressive nationalism of the other (i.e., Irish) nationalism. Certainly it is true that divisions exist within unionism as regards the idea of national identity. Are the Protestants of Northern Ireland British or Irish or Ulster people and need these definitions be mutually exclusive? Whatever the answer, however, there has emerged an overarching conception of (British) nationality, defined at the general level as being non-Irish, which transcends the various other nuanced constructions of identity. As a consequence it is possible to speak of a unionist sporting culture that in significant ways is national in character.

Arguably the Ulster unionists possess a sporting culture that is closer than anyone else's to that of the English. There are, of course, differences of emphasis. For example, there is a greater per capita interest among Northern Ireland's Protestants than among the English in motor sports and, in particular, motorcycling. The place of cricket in the construction of Englishness far outweighs its importance to Ulster unionists except in certain areas. Overall, however, it is reasonable to state that the English and the Ulster Protestants play the same games and neither group is in possession of sports that are unknown to the other. In this respect, as in so many others, therefore, the civil society of Ulster unionism differs markedly from that of Irish nationalism. It is ironic then that the most popular team sport both in England and in Protestant Ulster is also highly valued by Irish nationalists. Indeed, such is the level of interest in soccer among the people of the north of Ireland, nationalist and unionist, that one frequently encounters the strange phenomenon of members of the two communities united in their support for prominent English teams such as Liverpool and Manchester United.

More generally and somewhat confusingly the development of soccer in Northern Ireland reveals evidence both of integration between the two main rival traditions and also a very clear strengthening of a distinct unionist identity. Unlike the British games, which, largely because they were so closely linked to middle-class unionism, never captured the imagination of northern nationalists as they did their southern counterparts, for whom participation in rugby or cricket was not regarded as evidence of nostalgia for the union, soccer was soon adopted by working-class nationalist males in Ulster, particularly in the conurbations of Belfast and Derry. Moreover, despite the rival attractions of Gaelic games and, indeed, a campaign by the proponents of the latter to portray soccer as a British game and, therefore, one that was inappropriate for nationalists to play, this has remained largely the case up to the present. The result has been that soccer is the one major team game that is played in Northern Ireland by members of both communities. Indeed, all the senior clubs in the Irish League employ Catholics and Protestants and representative sides are equally mixed. At the same time, soccer is also unique inasmuch as it was the only major sport that, in terms of its organization, followed the contours established by partition. Thus, the island of Ireland possesses two separate ruling associations, two leagues and, consequently, two national sides. In the north, the governing body, the Irish Football Association (IFA), has tended to be dominated by Protestants. Their national selections, on the other hand, have reflected the fact that both traditions have provided their share of top class players. All the senior clubs, including Belfast-based Linfield, which for many years had an unstated but implicit policy of employing only Protestants, include players from both traditions. Only three of these clubs (Cliftonville, Newry Town, and Omagh Town), however, derive a substantial amount of their support from the nationalist community. In addition, most Irish league grounds are situated in what could be described as Protestant spaces and the atmosphere surrounding the majority of games is unionist and loyalist in terms of imagery, symbolism, and rhetoric (Bairner 1997; Bairner 1999; Bairner and Shirlow 1998). More significantly as regards issues of national identity, the same holds true for home international matches involving the Northern Ireland team.

Although fans around the world would no doubt recognize George Best as Northern Ireland's greatest-ever soccer player, not far behind Best in any all-time list would come Pat Jennings, the most-capped internationalist and regarded at the peak of his career as the best goalkeeper in the world. Jennings is a Catholic. Despite this, he was loved by the mainly Protestant fans of the national team. At the same time, however, and again in spite of Jennings's religion these fervent admirers would congregate behind his goal to sing loyalist and, by implication, anti-Catholic songs. Can one conceive of American track and field fans celebrating the achievements of an African American athlete by singing racist songs? It is hard to imagine. Yet this is precisely what has confronted Catholic players, even the most successful ones, who have represented Northern Ireland in recent years. When their team scores a goal, the fans frequently celebrate by singing a song that begins with the words, "Hello, hello, we are the Billy Boys," and goes on to speak of being "up to our knees in Fenian blood." In such circumstances it is easy to understand why few Catholics now wish to attend Northern Ireland games regardless of the fact that the team itself may include a relatively high number of their co-religionists. There are, of course, other reasons why they do not support their "national" team and these shall be explored in chapter 4. Equally, there are compelling reasons why Ulster unionists (and loyalists) and specifically Protestant working-class men are so attached to the Northern Ireland team despite the presence within it of Catholic, Irish nationalists.

When the Northern Ireland state was set up in 1921 after the partition of Ireland, no less a person than the first Prime Minister referred to the devolved parliament at Stormont on the outskirts of Belfast as "a Protestant parliament for a Protestant people." That assembly was prorogued and direct rule from the Westminster parliament in London introduced in 1972. For many unionists this meant that Ulstermen had lost administrative control over their own affairs and the reality of Northern Ireland as a distinct political entity was under threat as a consequence of both British disinterest and the territorial ambitions of the nationalist "enemy within." It is scarcely surprising, therefore, that those bodies that retained a recognizable Northern Irish identity, the Ulster Defence Regiment, for example, or the Royal Ulster Constabulary (RUC), came to be particularly cherished by unionists. In the world of sport, however, even among those sports that are dominated by Protestants, such institutionalized symbolism was hard to find. Most sports bodies were organized on an all-Ireland basis. Thus, soccer, the one major sport that was not, assumed greater politico-cultural importance than ever before.

At the level of club soccer, similar observations can be made. The reasons why most Irish League teams are situated in areas where there is a

Protestant majority are, in the first instance, historical. T
in which industrialization, a major catalyst for the de'
worldwide, was most advanced. In addition, the tie
workers and their Scottish counterparts were well developed. ..
surprising, therefore, that soccer clubs were established in the Protesta..
districts of Belfast and in towns with a majority Protestant population such
as Portadown and Ballymena. But this does not tell the whole story.

Given soccer's almost universal appeal it would have been curious
had it made no impact on an emerging Catholic working class in cities
such as Belfast and Derry and, indeed, with the emergence of Belfast
Celtic and Derry City, nationalists acquired a strong interest in Irish
League football. Yet, these clubs did not survive difficulties linked to
ethno-sectarian conflict. Their departures from the league, which shall be
discussed at greater length in chapter 4, reduced considerably the level of
involvement by nationalists, at least as fans, and this has never been
recaptured. Moreover, in towns such as Lurgan, with a significant nationalist population, the character of support for the local team, Glenavon,
has been so symbolically Protestant and loyalist as to dissuade all but the
most thick-skinned nationalist to follow his or her local club. Attempts
have been made in the 1990s to rekindle Catholic interest in domestic soccer with Omagh Town, located in a predominantly nationalist town,
being admitted to the Irish League, and substantial sums of money being
invested in Newry Town which is situated on the border between
Northern Ireland and the Irish Republic and has a potentially large
nationalist following. Cliftonville has provided Belfast nationalists (as
well as a few nationalists from other parts of the six counties) with a team
to support, but there is no senior club in west Belfast, which is home to
the biggest nationalist community in the north of Ireland. Indeed,
attempts by Donegal Celtic to bring senior soccer to the area have been
consistently frustrated by a combination of forces including the IFA, the
RUC, and Sinn Fein. As a consequence of all of this (and it is difficult to
believe that the situation has unfolded accidentally without conscious
sectarian decisions having played their part) senior soccer in Northern
Ireland is symbolically Protestant, unionist, loyalist.

Soccer in Northern Ireland is characterized by the same patterns of
male working-class culture as elsewhere in the United Kingdom—heavy
drinking, sexism, and profanity (Bairner 1997; Bairner 1999). The additional feature, however, is sectarianism, which afflicts some games in
Britain, specifically in Scotland, but is scarcely a major issue when crowd
trouble in England is being discussed. There are muted warnings both
from the ruling bodies and from club officials about the behavior of certain fans at Irish League and international matches, but the widespread

.ging of anti-Catholic sectarian songs continues and a huge swath of .ne population who love the game of soccer are consequently, to all intents and purposes, excluded from the world game, at least at the local level. The Irish League, like the Northern Ireland national team, is essentially a Protestant affair in which some Catholics take part but not in such a way as to threaten the local game's hegemonic unionist identity.

In the past, the author has considered this situation in terms of its potentially harmful political and social impact (Bairner 1997; Bairner 1999). It has never been suggested that those Protestants who attend soccer games and sing sectarian songs, are directly associated with violence directed at Catholics. It can be argued, however, that sectarian songs are at one end of a spectrum of antisocial activities, at the opposite end of which stands sectarian violence. "Whilst very few of the Protestants who attend football [soccer] matches in Northern Ireland are or have been involved in violence, most of those who have acted violently towards Catholics have also taken part in the sort of celebration of working-class Protestant identity witnessed at football matches" (Bairner 1997, 112). It is worth stressing that the identity that is constructed around Irish League soccer and support for the national team is predominantly working class and male as well as Protestant. The masculine element is not surprising given the patriarchal power relations that affect sport throughout the world. But it is also important to recognize the extent to which class provides an additional source of division both in the production of sporting identities and also, specifically, in terms of the construction of an Ulster unionist national identity.

As the working-class game soccer has engaged the attention of members of some of Northern Ireland's most deprived areas, both nationalist and unionist. In addition to dealing with the consequences of unemployment and poverty, these neighborhoods have also been most regularly and directly exposed to the violence associated with sectarian conflict. Thus, soccer thrives among many of those people who have the most entrenched sense of their own identity. For example, as far as working-class Protestants are concerned, the author has previously argued that "unemployment, coupled with a perceived threat to the political identity of Protestants in general, has certainly been an important factor in determining the character of hegemonic masculinity in Protestant working-class areas, which then finds expression in the sectarian chants of soccer fans or the violence of paramilitaries" (Bairner 1999, 299). As a universal game of such immense global appeal, however, soccer's attraction is as strong in the nationalist community. Almost inevitably, therefore, it has frequently offered a focus for crowd trouble and for bitter exchanges as regards identity issues. British games, on the other hand, have encountered no such problems within Northern Ireland. This is not to suggest, however, that their role has been essentially integrative.

Arguably, the major sporting achievement for Northern Ireland in 1999 was the victory of the Ulster rugby team in the European Cup Final played at Lansdowne Road in Dublin on 31 January. Not only was their victory celebrated by local rugby enthusiasts, the Ulster players were also identified as having brought the people of the north of Ireland closer together. Writing in the *Guardian* on the eve of the final against the French club side, Colomiers, Frank Keating (1999) suggested that the occasion would give "a unifying shot in the arm to the Good Friday peace agreement." According to Keating, "Rugby, unlike football [soccer] and other sports, cuts across the political and sectarian divide." In fact, although a considerable number of Catholics did go to Dublin to support the Ulster team and many more did so from the comfort of their own homes, the overwhelming majority of the "home" crowd at Lansdowne Road and of the rugby fraternity in Ulster as a whole belong to the unionist tradition. Catholic involvement in rugby has undoubtedly increased in recent years. There are two main reasons for this. First, as professionalism has impacted on the game in Ireland as elsewhere, leading Ulster clubs such as Dungannon and Ballymena have recognized the need to recruit players from as wide a range of sources as possible. Inevitably this has meant recruiting Catholics, many of them with a previous sporting background in Gaelic football. Second, one of the most discernible developments in the course of the troubles, and one that some might regard as the result of a political response to the troubles, has been the growth of a Catholic middle class in the north of Ireland. Given that rugby has tended to be associated with a middle-class lifestyle and provides key element in the social network of the middle classes in Ireland, as in many other places, it is scarcely surprising that sections of the emergent Catholic middle class in Ulster have been attracted to the game. It was they who showed most interest in the fortunes of the Ulster rugby team and created the impression of a people united by a shared sporting enterprise. Many working-class nationalists in the north, however, found little cause to cheer on "the Ulster boys" and, for that reason, it is safe to say that Frank Keating's remarks were considerably wide of the mark.

Despite recent developments in the world of Ulster rugby, the principal nurseries in Northern Ireland for games such as rugby, cricket, and men's field hockey are the state (Protestant) schools. Although these do not formally bar Catholics from entry, in practice they are virtually exclusive to the unionist community, given the existence of an alternative Catholic education sector. In addition, the institutions that nurture the British games players of the future are mainly the grammar schools, in a system which divides children at the age of twelve on the basis of perceived academic ability. The result is that not only are the overwhelming majority of players of British games Protestant, they are also middle class

and, as such, more likely to have grown up in areas less affected by political violence and the more extreme ideologies that have flourished in
more deprived areas and helped to prolong the conflict. This is not to
suggest that the people involved are apolitical or that they successfully
eschew sectarian attitudes in their entirety. It is arguable, however, that,
in most cases, they are more able than working-class soccer fans to keep
their sporting and political interests separate. The sports they play,
administer, and watch are organized on an all-Ireland basis and
"national" teams represent the whole of Ireland. This explains why
northern unionists finish up representing an entity they would not wish
to see being given constitutional legitimacy. Their background and
upbringing explain why this is not a problem for most of them and also
why their unionism remains unaffected by their sporting allegiance just
as the latter is revealed despite their political views. If the only way to
play international rugby or cricket is to play for an all-Ireland team, then
so be it. But sporting expediency need not be taken as evidence of political uncertainty. In any case, as was suggested earlier, there is a kind of
unionism that takes on board the Irishness of Ulster Protestants but
which nevertheless stops short of supporting moves toward the establishment of a thirty-two-county Irish Republic. This is the unionism of
those who are British in political terms but are willing to admit to an Irish
dimension to their lives. This joint identity is perfectly consistent with
playing rugby for Ireland and defending the union between Great Britain
and Northern Ireland. It is ironic that British sports are part of the process
through which a limited degree of dual identity has been maintained
within the unionist population. One might have expected that this would
be a more appropriate role for universal games, which are played by
members of both major traditions, but this is only partially true.

Sports such as golf and tennis are organized on an all-Ireland basis
and attract participants from both the unionist and nationalist communities. It would be reasonable to assume that most of those who are
involved in these universal games belong to the middle classes and, thus,
have much in common with the rugby fraternity. In addition, individual
sports tend to be less contentious in terms of identity formation that team
games, particularly those that attract fans as well as players. There is
some anecdotal evidence of sectarian attitudes in golf clubs although less
than that which would indicate gender discrimination. Membership of
such clubs, moreover, will clearly be heavily influenced by their location.
In general, however, these primarily middle-class, individual sports
either fail completely to get involved in the politics of identity or are such
as to encourage unionists to identify with their Irishness, albeit not at the
expense of being British. For example, most Protestant golf enthusiasts
are supportive of most if not all Irish professionals on the European tour

although they might be particularly enthusiastic about an Ulster player and even more so if that player is himself a Protestant. The fact that such calculations are made may suggest that in fact golf is linked to identity politics. But there is a strong case to be made for simply saying that people tend to identify most with those things with which they are familiar and that this does not necessarily have any serious implications for issues of national identity. But what happens when the universal games have a more working-class constituency?

Two sports are of particular interest in this regard—soccer, which has already been discussed at some length, and boxing. Both were transformed into modern sports in Britain. Undeniably, however, they came to acquire a universal appeal, particularly among poor people in many parts of the world. In Ireland, north and south, they are played by both Protestants and Catholics, unionists and nationalist, and although they attract middle-class interest, their strength still lies in working-class and particularly urban communities. In terms of their contribution to cross-community relations in the north and to the construction of identities, however, their impact is clearly rather different.

Boxers are able to represent both Ireland as a whole and, if they are from the north, Northern Ireland, in the Commonwealth Games for example. Northern boxers can also represent the United Kingdom of Great Britain and Northern Ireland in events such as the Olympic Games. Thus, boxing is tied to a multiplicity of identities. Indeed, this may help to explain some of the controversies to which the sport has given rise. In particular, there is the case of Wayne McCullough, a Protestant from a loyalist area of Belfast, who carried the Irish tricolor at the opening ceremony of the 1988 Olympic Games. Two years later, he won a gold medal for Northern Ireland at the Commonwealth Games, his achievement being recognized with the playing of the Londonderry Air ("Danny Boy") at the award ceremony. In 1992, representing Ireland once again, McCullough won a silver medal. For some loyalists, his willingness to represent Ireland as well as Northern Ireland meant that McCullough stood condemned for political and cultural treachery. In general, however, there was an acceptance that the decisions he had taken were principally located in a reasonable desire to do well in his chosen sport and, indeed, regardless of the shirt he was wearing, his triumphs were still those of a northern Protestant (Bryson and McCartney 1994). McCullough and his family, however, raised some additional controversy in the wake of the 1992 Olympics. Having been saluted at a public reception in Dublin along with his gold medal–winning teammate, Michael Carruth, McCullough was then invited to Belfast's City Hall by the unionist-led council. He and his father demanded to know why Carruth had not been invited. The answer, of course, was as predictable as it was inherently logical. Not only was Carruth not from the city of Belfast, he actually came from a foreign state—and one that, worse still, continued to lay claim to Northern Irish territory. McCullough's father put Carruth's name at an empty place setting during the celebration meal, which itself did little to lessen the disquiet felt by some loyalists about his son's representation of Ireland.

Loyalist prisoners in the Maze Prison have frequently expressed the view to the author that McCullough, a young man when he first represented Ireland, had been consistently manipulated during this period of his boxing career. He had mistakenly put sport ahead of political loyalty, something that he, along with certain unionist rugby players for example, has subsequently regretted. The fact of the matter is, however, that McCullough has progressed to a successful professional boxing career in which the concept of representing one's country becomes virtually meaningless. That said, there are many in Northern Ireland, and one suspects that a disproportionately large percentage of them are unionists, who have continued to follow his career with interest and support rather than skepticism about his loyalty to the crown or, indeed, the shamrock. In any case, by choosing to live and work in the United States, McCullough has managed to put some distance between himself and the politics of mistrust that have tended to dominate Northern Ireland since its formation.

In McCullough's story there are echoes of what happened a few years earlier to Barry McGuigan, who was born in Clones, Co. Monaghan, and went on to become flyweight champion of the world. Having represented Ireland at amateur level, McGuigan turned professional under the managerial guidance of Northern Ireland turf accountant, B. J. (Barney) Eastwood, and fought for British titles in preparation for a highly successful career. McGuigan chose to enter the ring under the flag of the United Nations rather than the tricolour, the union flag or the flag of Northern Ireland. As a prelude to his fights, however, "Danny Boy," the "anthem" used by the Northern Ireland Commonwealth games team was played or, more often, sung by his father. His refusal to identify fully with his roots in the twenty-six counties led some northern nationalists to regard him as a traitor, and, despite claims that he managed to transcend sectarian division and gain support from fight fans in both communities, some loyalists continued to view him with suspicion. It is undeniable, however, that when McGuigan took part in some of his most important bouts in Belfast's King's Hall, he enjoyed considerable cross-community support in Northern Ireland. Certainly, in their different ways, both McCullough and McGuigan were able to some extent to usurp traditional sporting identities. That they were able to do so in the sport of boxing is not wholly coincidental.

Despite the role of people such as the Marquis of Queensberry in the modern evolution of boxing, organized hand-to-hand combat has been a feature of human societies from time immemorial (Sugden 1996). Thus, in Northern Ireland, as Sugden (1996) notes, "Boxing has been able to develop as a genuinely universal sport, which is not intrinsically bound up with a particular nationalist or post-colonial tradition" (127). But the same could be said of soccer and, yet, we have already noted the divisive nature of that particular universal game in the Northern Irish context. Boxing, however, possesses its own peculiar properties. It is more of an individual sport than one involving team spirit and identification. Moreover, as Sugden (1996) reveals, "The central core of boxing is physical aggression, but its existence as a sport is dependent on the strict delineation and control of the boundary between aggression and violence" (129). Thus, "The boundless violence which seems to be endemic within the modern inner city, whether it be random, gang warfare or politically motivated, has no place within the subculture of the boxer, and this is as true in Belfast as it is in Chicago, Detroit and Mexico City" (130). As Sugden (1996) concludes, "The gatekeepers of Holy Family and other boxing clubs in Belfast are well aware of this and they carefully police their boundaries to ensure that the malevolence, wildness and disrespect often associated with street youth culture are not allowed to contaminate the atmosphere of their sport" (130). They also make strenuous efforts to keep out sectarian attitudes that are clearly linked to violence, both political and criminal, in Northern Ireland. As a consequence, boxers from rival communities are given safe passage as they travel to and train and compete in clubs which otherwise would be hostile territory for them. To that extent, boxing represents something of a success story in terms of cross-community relations through sport. As Sugden (1996) has warned, however, it would be dangerous to draw excessively benign conclusions from the specific experience of boxing. When the young boxers leave the ring and become soccer fans, for example, it is doubtful that there will be any manifest change in their national, cultural, and political identification.

Apart from international soccer competitions, the Commonwealth Games, held every four years, provide Northern Irish sports people with the best opportunity to represent their "nation." In 1998, however, the poor performance of the Northern Ireland team in Kuala Lumpur was followed a series of recriminatory statements, many of which raised the issue of nationality. There appeared to have been a hemorrhage of talent from Northern Ireland to the Irish Republic with two runners, James McIlroy and Dermot Donnelly, both opting to represent the latter and, therefore, not take places in the former's Commonwealth Games team despite actually coming from the north. "The net result," as Des Fahy reported in the *Irish Times* (29 September 1998), "has been to bring, blinking into the spotlight, a by-product of sporting life here [in Ireland] that most officials and administrators would prefer to ignore—the issue of dual nationality for Northern Ireland–born competitors." In part, this is a matter of political principle and relates to the bigger question concerning the political legitimacy or otherwise of Northern Ireland. But it is also an issue that involves both sporting pragmatism and an advanced level of self-interest among everyone concerned.

Sports people, as we have seen, frequently make decisions on the basis of what will enhance their own career prospects as opposed to what can best complement their sense of political identity. Sports associations, for their part, are at times less than scrupulous about selecting people whose national identity is indisputable. The IFA, for example, has increasingly widened its net, following the example of their southern counterparts, it must be added, and have chosen players whose links to the six counties are tenuous to say the least. Sports administrators, however, are not only concerned with putting out the best available representative teams. They are also concerned to ensure the future of their own particular bodies and, by implication, their own jobs. The choices made by McIlroy and Donnelly, for example, raise questions about the national affiliation of Irish athletes and, in the long run and on the back of cross-border initiatives linked to the peace process, may serve to undermine Northern Ireland as a separate sporting, or, at least, athletics, nation. Such a development, just like the emergence of an all-Ireland soccer team, would have serious implications for sports officials. As Fahy (*Irish Times*, 29 September 1998) suggests, for example, "If Northern Ireland's athletics autonomy disappears, so too do all the little perks that international competition brings."

According to Fahy, "The equation is a straightforward one—no more Northern Ireland teams, no more all-expenses paid foreign junkets." With reference to soccer, one can add that if the two separate associations became one, not only the lives of the game's administrators would be affected. Half the number of Irish clubs would be allowed to play in European competitions. Fifty percent fewer Irish referees and referees' assistants would have the opportunity to officiate at European and world levels. Only one national team would represent Ireland in international competitions. In purely self-interested terms, there would be an awful lot at stake. There remains, in addition, the small matter of political principle. Many Ulster unionists, for example, if faced with the threat of losing Northern Irish national teams would prefer to see a merger with British teams rather than ones representing the Irish Republic (Sugden and Bairner 1993a).

It is no surprise, for example, that Protestant soccer fans have been heard to cheer the news that the Irish rugby team has lost to one of the other "home" nations. This practice is particularly widespread when

Ireland's opponents are Scotland. Others have gone further and argued that sports, in addition to soccer, should encourage the idea of Northern Irish national representation. Loyalist prisoners, for example, have suggested to the author that the Ulster rugby authorities should follow soccer's example and enter a Northern Ireland team in international competitions. Whilst the team would be potentially weaker than that which represents the whole of Ireland, given the fact that selection would be made from a considerably smaller pool of players, it is argued that the team spirit engendered by a greater sense of shared identity would more than compensate. There is little likelihood that such a development will occur, not least because the present national squads in the northern hemisphere already appear very weak in comparison with their major southern hemisphere opponents. In addition, the people who run rugby in the north of Ireland tend to belong to that section of the Protestant community that is able to square playing for Ireland with being politically unionist. But the fact that the idea is even canvassed reveals the degree to which some Ulster Protestants believe that sport can play a crucial role in the construction of a distinctive national identity especially if that identity is related to a feeling of being from Ulster rather than from the United Kingdom in general. It is likely, however, that this sentiment is more strongly felt amongst the loyalist working class whose favored game is soccer. Indeed, it may well be that the idea of an independent Ulster has been strengthened by the existence of a separate national soccer team. Thus, rather than claim that political attitudes determine sporting identities, we may be forced to conclude that, in this instance at least, sporting attitudes play a vital role in influencing political opinions.

ULSTER UNIONISM, NATIONAL IDENTITY, AND CONSTITUTIONAL CHANGE?

A major reason why there has been growing concern within the unionist community about matters of identity relates to constitutional change in other parts of the United Kingdom as well as in Northern Ireland itself. Growing pressure from Scotland and Wales for self-government has resulted in the setting up of assemblies in Edinburgh and Cardiff respectively. In Northern Ireland too, an assembly has also been instituted as a consequence of talks aimed at bringing about a political resolution to the bitter political conflict, which, in its most recent manifestation, has lasted for almost thirty years. The impact of these developments on unionist and loyalist thinking about the very idea of the United Kingdom has been considerable. On one hand, there is a sense that the union is under threat and that devolved government is merely a stepping stone toward independence for Scotland and Wales. In addition, at least partly in response to these developments although arguably also as a reaction to the impact of certain aspects of globalization, many English people have also embarked on a quest to identify their true national identity. No longer satisfied to equate Englishness with Britishness, they have begun to assert the distinctive nature of the former. It should come as no surprise that this development has manifested itself most directly at sporting occasions, with England soccer fans increasingly favoring the English cross of St. George rather than the Union flag and their rugby counterparts acquiring their own anthem—"Swing Low Sweet Chariot." All of this raises questions about what it now means to be British and what it would it mean to be an Ulster unionist in the event of the breakup of the union. Furthermore, in the case of Northern Ireland itself, the restoration of a devolved assembly is something for which many, although by no means all Ulster unionists, have yearned for many years. The fact is, however, that this has only been established on the basis of the introduction of power-sharing mechanisms, involving nationalist opponents, together with closer administrative links between Northern Ireland and the Irish Republic. The new set of arrangements even allow for Irish republicans to become involved in government. It is scarcely surprising that, in such circumstances, many unionists feel more threatened than ever before and that they cling all the more tenaciously to those elements of life that confirm their distinctiveness. It is often the case that "reactive forms of cultural opposition are tied to notions of cultural dissipation, beseigement and disintegration" (Bairner and Shirlow 1998, 167). In such circumstances, the symbolic importance of the Northern Ireland soccer team or soccer clubs that are more imbued than others with an attachment to the unionist tradition assume an almost devotional status. Furthermore, the places where they play become quasi-religious meeting points at which Protestant Ulster, both real and imagined, can be celebrated (Bairner and Shirlow 1998). Ironically, one such holy place is not even in the north of Ireland. Ibrox Stadium in Glasgow, home of Rangers Football Club, has been a place of pilgrimage for generations of Ulster Protestants who have regarded the team and its fans as upholders of a Protestant tradition the central values of which they share. The links between the Ulster unionists and Scotland, however, extend far beyond Ibrox and, indeed, soccer.

According to the historian A. T. Q. Stewart (1977), "At the core of the Ulster problem is the problem of the Scots . . ." (34). Walker (1995) agrees, writing that "'the problem of the Scots' is indeed central to any analysis of Ulster or Irish history" (1). The relationship can be traced back to the pattern of Scottish settlement in Ulster during the seventeenth century. Subsequently it has involved strong personal, linguistic, theological, and cultural ties to the extent that, for many Ulster unionists, the union has meant in particular a link with Scotland. This is not to deny the importance of loyalty to the British crown and, indeed, to a sense of Britishness, however that has been understood. In emotional and cultural terms, however, many unionists have felt their closest affinity to be with Scotland and the Scots. Those loyalists who support, from a distance for reasons of social class, the Scottish rugby team against the Irish are not simply making a sectarian statement. They may also genuinely feel that they are supporting the country of their forebears, and many of them will possess the Scottish surnames to underline the point. In the world of sport, this link between the Scots and the Northern Irish was particularly encouraged by the part played by Scots in promoting soccer in the north of Ireland. The debt has been repaid many times over by generations of Ulster fans who have followed the fortunes of two of Scotland's major clubs, Celtic and Rangers. But we should be careful about taking from this a feeling that the relationship between sport and national identity is the same for Scots as it is for Ulster unionists.

The links between Scotland and Northern Ireland are perceived very differently in the two places. In the latter, the relationship has a significance far in excess of any feelings it invokes in Scotland. At a very basic level, it is instructive to note how many young people leave the north of Ireland each year to study at Scottish universities. This pattern is not replicated in the opposite direction. In addition, although the relationship has been invested with particular significance by unionists, the links between nationalist Ireland and Scotland (continuing labor migration from the west of Ireland to Glasgow and its surrounding region, the origins and traditions of Celtic Football Club, and so on) are equally strong but do nothing to diminish enthusiasm for the dissolution of the union.

As regards sport, Scotland, as we shall see, possesses elements of a distinctive sporting culture that differ markedly from those in Northern Ireland. In addition, in part because of the way in which they perceive their Britishness, far more Ulster unionists than Scots would support English representative teams as well as those of their own country. This is linked to the fact that they are also more inclined to follow English League soccer teams, sometimes along with Rangers but often at the expense of any significant interest in Scottish soccer. In examining the relationship between sport and national identity in Scotland, therefore, we will hear echoes from Northern Ireland but we will also be looking at a separate sporting culture and a separate national identity.

chapter three

"We Are the England Haters!"

SPORT AND NATIONAL IDENTITY IN SCOTLAND

SCOTLAND, SPORT, AND NATIONHOOD

In May 1999, a Scottish parliament met for the first time since 1707. It is too early to say whether this event in itself will assuage the national thirst for greater control over Scottish affairs or if, as some unionists in Northern Ireland and elsewhere fear, it will merely hasten the breakup of Britain. What is certain is that sport has played its part in maintaining a distinctive sense of national identity without which the demand for a devolved government for Scotland would have been voiced only by a handful of eccentrics. That said, however, sport also reflects divisions in Scotland that may well become more politically sensitive in the context of new constitutional arrangements than was the case in the former, more centralized United Kingdom system of government. This chapter explores the dual role of sport in both constructing a sense of Scottishness and at the same time revealing significant fault lines along which the Scots have been and remain divided.

Like the Ulster Protestants, the Scots share a sporting culture with the English, but there is one major substantive difference in the shape of a distinctive Highland Scottish tradition, which stands comparison with that of Irish nationalists on both sides of the border, and also significant differences of emphasis (Jarvie 1991). For example, cricket is even less popular in Scotland than in Northern Ireland and this despite the fact that a Scot, Mike Denness, captained the English test side as recently as

1975 and that two other England captains, Douglas Jardine and Tony Greig, each had a strong Scottish connection. Any analysis of Scottish sport and its relationship to national identity should be prefaced by two simple observations. First, there exists a separate Scottish approach to sport but only to a limited extent and, second, being Scottish, however that is to be defined, does not mean sharing or having access to a common sporting experience. Despite these words of caution, however, there is no shortage of commentators ready and willing to present the cause for a close and unproblematic relationship between sport and Scottishness. A central element of this chapter is a critique of the simplistic nature of their arguments, which lead inevitably to equally naive assumptions concerning Scottish national identity.

As Walker (1994) observes, "Sport and nationalist feeling in relation to Scotland have been linked promiscuously by commentators both lay and scholarly." Yet, although some sort of linkage certainly exists, "it is seldom made clear precisely what the nature of the nationalism expressed through the medium of sport is" (142). This is not to suggest that sport might be better ignored in discussions about Scottish nationality. As Walker and co-author Jarvie (1994) argue, "No dialogue on Scotland or Scottish civil society is complete without acknowledging the social space occupied by sport" (8). Conversely, one might add, no analysis of sport in Scotland would be complete without some reference to Scottish society and politics in general and specifically to the question of national identity. The problem is that this can often lead to large, unsubstantiated claims concerning sport and Scottish nationality which do little to deepen our understanding of either of these phenomena.

According to sportswriter Roddy Forsyth (1992), "Sport can claim not only to have been the most popular manifestation of Scottishness within Scotland, but actually to have been its distinct assertion of nationality" (334). There is certainly no denying sport's popularity in Scotland, particularly with Scottish men. Golf can claim 260,000 active participants, while the two biggest team sports, soccer and rugby union, have 134,000 and 15,000 adult players respectively. Even larger numbers of Scots are involved in sport as administrators, coaches, and, above all, as spectators. We can assume, moreover, that the involvement of these Scots in sport is bound to impact, to some degree, on their understanding of what it means to be Scottish. But, as Jarvie and Walker (1994) point out, "While Scottish sport has both contributed to a sense of nation, class and even community it is important to ask the question whose nation? whose community? and during what time period?" (3). However, in much of the writing on Scottish sport, and particularly on the symbolic importance of soccer, such considerations are simply ignored.

According to Forsyth (1990), "No other people has such a sporting obsession, such an extraordinary fixation with a single game, as the Scots with football (soccer)" (13). One's thoughts turn at once to the Brazilians, the Italians, and even to most of sub-Saharan Africa but Forsyth is by no means alone in making grandiose claims concerning the relationship between the Scots and the game which they know as "fitba'." Not only is soccer's popularity emphasized but also its general impact on Scottish society, culture, and politics. Above all, frequent reference is made to the role the game has played in maintaining a sense of Scottish national identity in the absence of political structures that would otherwise have secured it. So, in the words of Henry Drucker, an American-born academic and sometime Edinburgh resident, "Football in Scottish life is much more than a sport. It's really an arena in which Scotland and Scots can assert themselves and play a role in international affairs" (cited in Forsyth 1990, 178). Even a more cynical observer, Stuart Cosgrove (1991), suggests that "Scotland has spent a century and more craving for football to relieve the dilemma of nationalism" (143). This suggestion is endorsed by historian Richard Holt (1994) who argues, indeed, that soccer became "too culturally important to the Scots" (65). Not surprisingly, therefore, the performances of the national soccer team have often been regarded as having a significant effect on the self-confidence of the Scottish people. Thus, as Blain and Boyle (1994) recall, "It was commonplace in Scottish political circles at the end of the 1970s that success, instead of embarrassing failure, as for Scotland in the 1978 Argentina football World Cup, could have transformed the nature and result of the 1979 referendum on devolution or even that year's General Election" (139). Far from revealing a straightforward relationship between sport and nationality, however, such speculation has led some to the view that sport may actually have had an adverse effect on attempts to forge a political national identity in Scotland.

As journalist Kevin McCarra (1993) suggests, "For nationalists Scotland's intense emotional investment in sport can be a source of frustration" (279). This frustration was given most strident voice by Jim Sillars, a former Scottish National Party Member of Parliament who had just lost his seat in the House of Commons at the 1992 General Election. Sillars accused his fellow Scots of being "ninety-minute patriots," referring to the duration of a soccer match, although no doubt he would have been equally happy to describe them as "eighty-minute patriots" (rugby union) or "eighteen-hole patriots" (golf). The implication would be the same. Although Scots support their sporting representatives as if their lives depended on a successful outcome to a particular contest, they had consistently proved themselves unwilling to take the steps needed to secure political independence for the nation, which, by their fanaticism at sporting occasions, they profess to love. According to Jarvie and Walker (1994), Sillars's outburst was "a classic expression of the view that sport has functioned as a substitute for political nationalism in modern Scotland" (1). They admit, moreover, that "there are many who share Sillars' exasperation and even more who regard the matter in a resigned way as proof that Scotland lacks the will to control its own destiny" (Jarvie and Walker 1994, 1–2). But they offer the opinion that "the 'substitute thesis' is at once too static and too one-dimensional to help us explain the way sport has reflected Scottish life in its different political, social, and cultural manifestations" (Jarvie and Walker 1994, 2).

In part, this chapter seeks to ascertain the nature of sport's impact on Scottish national identity and political attitudes. In addition, however, it reveals the extent to which sport reflects deep divisions in Scottish society and, in so doing, challenges the false premise that there exists a single, uniform Scottish identity that is influenced by sport and that, in turn, operates through sport either to promote nationalist demands or, as Sillars and others would have it, to weaken the support for political independence. As Harvie (1994) puts it, sport in Scotland has become "a constitutive part of national identity—but of a peculiarly fractured sort" (1994, 45). To understand fully the complexity of the relationship between sport and national identity in Scotland, therefore, it is necessary first to map the contours of the wider debate on Scottish national identity.

SCOTLAND THE NATION!

There is little doubt that Scotland can be described as a nation or that some sense of Scottish identity has existed for centuries. Lynch (1992) suggests that a notion of the kingdom of Scotland can be traced back to the twelfth century. Elsewhere, Lynch (1993) admits that "Within the geographical entity which by the eleventh century had come to be known as Scotland, locality, different *nationes* and an inchoate but potent sense of nationhood competed." By the fourteenth century, however, "This hybrid society was held together by an overweening loyalty, both to a 'king of Scots' and a compelling sense of nationality" (Lynch 1993, 37). Significantly in the light of what is to follow in this analysis, the national identity that had emerged was strengthened in the course of a series of wars with Scotland's English neighbors.

Although unquestionably a nation, however, Scotland does not possess the full trappings of a modern nation state (McCrone 1992). Specifically, it can be described as a stateless nation, Scottish parliamentarians having yielded Scotland's right to exist as a distinct political entity in 1707 when the Act of Union united their country with England and thereby established Great Britain (Marr 1992). As Paterson (1994) has shown, however, Scotland has enjoyed a considerable measure of autonomy during the three centuries that have almost elapsed since political nationhood was surrendered. According to Paterson, "In effect, if not in constitutional theory or political rhetoric, Scotland has been autonomous for most of the three centuries since the Union—not a fully independent state, of course, but far more than a mere province" (4). This relative autonomy from England, and indeed from the United Kingdom more generally, was partly assured by the favorable terms of the Union itself, which allowed for the continued existence of a number of institutions (religious, legal, educational, and political) that were peculiar to and characteristic of Scotland as a separate nation. The implications for Scottish national identity of this unusual, although by no means unique, set of arrangements has provoked considerable comment over a number of years.

Most commentators arrived at the conclusion that the Scottish national psyche had been split in two as a result of the Union. Scots were able to function within the United Kingdom by being Scottish and British simultaneously. Thus, as Kiernan (1993) observes, "It may be arguable whether on the whole Scottish nationality was overlaid and smothered by the Union, or in the long run could develop best within its framework" (26). Nationalists are in no doubt as to the disastrous effects of the Union on Scottish identity. According to Scott (1993), "Scotland had become an invisible country internationally, and the culture of invisible countries is also invisible" (10). Yet, a sense of Scottishness continued to exist. As Scott himself admits, "The fact that a distinctive Scottish culture has not merely survived, but is in many ways in robust health, is a proof of its inherent strength" (12). It is proof also, one might suggest, that at no time did Scotland's more powerful partners seek to eradicate it in its entirety. Furthermore, this may well have represented a clever political strategy inasmuch as the resilience of a separate Scottish culture became a crucial factor in dissuading a majority of Scots from seeking that political independence which, according to nationalists at least, would be the appropriate accompaniment to a distinctive national identity.

A 1991 opinion poll, published in the *Scotsman* newspaper, indicated that many Scots are now getting to grips with the dilemma of dual nationality. Forty percent of those questioned claimed that they were Scottish and *not* British. Another 29 percent claimed to be more Scottish than British whereas only 21 percent professed to being equally Scottish and British. Only 10 percent emphasized their Britishness or some other national identity (McCrone 1992). One reading of these figures would lead to the conclusion that an overwhelming majority of Scots are not only Scottish but presumably have a clear understanding of what that involves. A more disturbing assessment, however, is that 50 percent of the Scottish people remain confused, to varying degrees, about their national

identity and that 10 percent of those currently domiciled in Scotland do
not regard themselves as Scottish at all. According to these figures, cultural schizophrenia would appear to be alive and well. But, arguably,
dualism is not the only, nor even the most important, problem facing
those who wish to construct a unified sense of Scottish identity. Indeed,
Nairn (1991) argues that "Scottish intellectuals are not just tiresomely but
wilfully obsessed with duality" (9). He goes on, "The complaint normally
implies that we can't act because we have a divided, sickly or two headed
'identity', because nature or . . . a very ancient history, has made us the
tragic world leaders in communal schizophrenia, as well as in heart dis-
ease and lung cancer" (10). Indeed, "communal schizophrenia" may be
the least of the identity crises faced by modern Scots.

Scottish National Identity

As devolved government, if not full political independence, has become a
reality, the question, "Who are the Scots?" might appear to have been
resolved. Yet there is considerable concern at the barbarism associated
with numerous contemporary nationalist movements and, in the specific
case of Scotland, at the growing level of violence directed at perceived
non-Scots—in particular Asians and, above all, English residents in the
country (*Observer*, 8 November 1998). In seeking to preempt such un-
healthy manifestations of national sentiment, journalist Joyce MacMillan
expressed the view that "a Scot is someone living in Scotland, no less, no
more." Although sensitive to her fears, however, MacMillan's fellow
columnist Neal Ascherson responded with a very different opinion.

> I wish things were so easy, and so innocent. But the dimensions of cul-
> tural difference, of language and outlook, cannot be overlooked when
> a new political society is trying to emerge. To say that is not racialist or
> hate-laden, but to state a fact about nationalism. (*Independent on Sunday*,
> 11 August, 1991)

"Scottishness . . .," according to Ascherson, "isn't just postal." Ascherson
is surely correct, not least because so many people living away from
Scotland continue to regard themselves as Scots. The problem with
Ascherson's analysis, however, is that it assumes that all of those who
describe themselves as Scottish share a common identity, thereby implying that the only people who might feel threatened in an independent
Scotland would be immigrants, particularly from England, bringing with
them and seeking to cling to an alien national identity. No doubt these
non-Scots could well have problems but so too presumably might those
Scots who were not sufficiently enthralled by the dominant interpretation
of what being Scottish actually means. Thus, it is important to discern

what unites those people who say they are Scots and, perhaps more importantly, what may divide them, either today or at some point in the future. Scottishness, as we shall see, consists of a multiplicity of identities, any one of which may on occasion threaten to undermine the claims of a unifying and transcendent national identity.

Paterson (1993) writes that "the core of the problem is that debate about Scottish culture has little room for the idea that there might be several and deeply contradictory cultures coexisting, all of them with an equally valid claim to being truly Scottish" (1). Most commentators, however, while recognizing what Paterson calls "the multifariousness of Scottish cultures," have argued that this does not negate the possibility of a transcendent national identity. Smout (1994), for example, recognizes that "there are, of course, those who would deny there is any common identity possible in Scotland, a small country of quite exceptional regional and cultural diversity" but that, he claims, is "to misunderstand the point, and to assume that we have but one identity (102). In a similar vein, McCrone (1992) accepts that "if Scotland is a 'society' insofar as it provides a set of meaningful frameworks through which to judge social experiences, we need not deny that there are other levels of association—being a Gael, a Shetlander, a Glaswegian, for example" (26). We could add to this list the levels of association involved in being a man or a woman, a Christian, of whatever denomination, or a Muslim, a factory worker or a lawyer, and so on. McCrone's response, however, is that "none of these necessarily negate, are at odds with being 'Scottish.'" Perhaps not, but there is surely a possibility that some of the identities that are formed at non-national levels of association in Scotland may be sufficiently strong to offer substantial challenges to a transcendent sense of Scottishness, unless the latter is formulated in a particular way. As O'Hagan (1994) puts it, "Behind many an apparent Scottish unity, within each togetherness I can think of, runs a bickering stream of segregationist delight."

The evidence provided by an analysis of sport in Scotland supports O'Hagan's view. As we shall see, it is frequently only to the extent that sport can be recruited to the traditional anti-English cause that it truly unites the Scottish people, or, to be more precise, the overwhelming majority of those who live in Scotland together with numerous exiles who would continue to describe themselves as Scottish. More commonly, however, Scottish sport highlights the differences between Scots and provides an important vehicle for the perpetuation of these differences even in a world in which globalization is thought by some to threaten to engulf all sorts of particularism. The irony is that any superficial account of Scottish sport would lead inevitably to the conclusion that its main political achievement has been to contribute massively to the autonomy or quasi-autonomy of Scotland within the context of political union and contingent statelessness.

SCOTLAND: THE SPORTING NATION

As Jarvie (1993) points out, "Aspects of Scottish sport are strongly nationalist."

> There is a separate Scottish Football Association and Scottish Football League; football loyalties centre around Scottish teams, and football internationals, particularly against England, arouse a fierce partisanship. Other sports are also organised on a Scottish rather than a British basis while the important place of sport within Scottish popular culture is also reflected in the effect that it has on other aspects of Scottish culture such as the composition of the newspapers and the time devoted to sport on Scottish television. (58–59)

But not always is Scotland's sporting, and hence national, distinctiveness recognized. As McCarra (1993) recalls, Scottish cricketers were refused Associate Membership of the International Cricket Conference in July 1993, partly on the grounds that Scotland is not a separate country. According to McCarra, "It is a conclusion which would bewilder the average Scotsman, who has tended to believe that our independent sporting life was itself a touchstone of nationhood" (279). Yet, Scottish sport is not always pursued autonomously and this fact has tended to be accepted by the majority of Scots over many years.

At successive Olympic Games, although not for the Commonwealth Games to which Scotland enters a separate team, Scots have traditionally taken their places in a team representing Great Britain and Northern Ireland. In doing so, they have accepted that if they were to win a medal it would be the Union Flag that would fly in their honor and if that medal was gold the achievement would be saluted by the playing of "God Save the Queen." Yet this would not mean that the athlete in question was less than patriotically Scottish. Indeed, although the current relationship between sport and national identity in Scotland is usually expounded upon in relation to the emergence of a separatist nationalist ideology, this was not always the case.

Paterson (1994) refers to the close connections between unionism and nationalism in nineteenth-century Scotland. "To be a true unionist," he writes, "it was necessary to be a nationalist, because otherwise Scotland would not be a partner in a Union but become dependent on England" (60). Conversely, to be a true nationalist it was felt essential by many to promote Scottish interests within a Great British context. This attitude was to be encountered in sport as much as in other spheres. Commenting on the relationship between nationalism and sport, therefore, Walker (1994) makes the important point that "it is often forgotten that in the Scottish context at least it (sport) functioned for a time largely as a means of emphasising Scotland's identity within the wider British nation state" (142).

Today, however, it is in the quest for a separatist national identity that Scottish sport appears to play its most important political role. But does it? Certainly the existence of separate Scottish national teams and of individual athletes competing as Scots helps to maintain the idea of Scotland as a distinct political, or quasi-political, entity. In addition, sport, as shall be shown, is implicated in the perpetuation of some of the myths that have contributed greatly to the idea of a distinctive Scottish identity. But the extent to which sport has played a key role in the construction of a cohesive national identity, capable of acting as an ideological catalyst in the struggle for political independence, remains questionable. How far, indeed, have Scots even been able to construct a truly distinctive sports culture, as opposed to one that is shared with other people, albeit with a degree of self-government?

According to Daiches (1952), there are two ways in which a people, placed in the situation Scots have experienced since 1707, can respond in cultural terms to the loss of statehood. On one hand, "it can attempt to rediscover its own national traditions and by reviving and developing them find a satisfaction that will compensate for its political impotence." Alternatively, by "accepting the dominance of the culture of the country which has achieved political ascendancy over it, it can endeavour to beat that country at its own game and achieve distinction by any standard the dominant culture may evolve" (8). In terms of sport, it can be argued that both of these options were taken by Scots, sometimes seeking a fusion of the two, but the latter of them was clearly the more decisive. It is for that reason that, for the most part, in spite of different emphases, Scots today share a sporting culture with their English neighbors. Within that culture, however, it may still be possible to identify a national game or national games. To assess whether this possibility has become a reality, one must examine a group of sports—soccer, shinty, golf, and rugby union—each of which, for very different reasons, could be considered for the title of Scotland's "national game." Most of this discussion will focus on soccer, first played in the public schools of England and, thus, indicative of the choice made by many Scots to beat the English at their own game while at the same time seeking to give that game a peculiarly Scottish dimension.

SOCCER AND THE SCOTS

Forsyth (1990) is in no doubt concerning soccer's status as Scotland's national sport.

> A team without glory, a country without Parliament, a nation without nationality, Scotland exists on the international stage only through sport, and mainly through football. (14)

According to Holt (1994), "Football has been the dominant sport in Scotland and its great players are folk heroes" (58). It is not just that Scots enjoy playing and watching soccer. The game has also provided them with access to a high international profile, for example when the national team qualifies for the World Cup Finals, and an opportunity to exert some influence on the wider world. As Murray (1994) expresses it, "The role of Scotland in the establishing, but more particularly in the promotion, of association football was paramount" (19). According to Forsyth (1990), indeed, Scotland's influence on the early development of the game was "so profound that it transformed the winter pastime of English public schoolboys into the most popular sport in the world" (14). Of the many examples of Scottish influence on soccer's early history, perhaps the most important and certainly the most ironic is the fact that a Scot, William McGregor, was instrumental in the formation of the first-ever national soccer league, namely the Football League founded in 1889 *in England*. In addition, Scottish players have made a substantial contribution to the game in England ever since (Forsyth 1990; Moorhouse 1986).

There is much for Scots to feel proud about in their promotion of a game that has reached out so expansively to the international community. It is scarcely surprising, therefore, that, at home, soccer is often treated with something close to religious reverence, for example by the Scottish media. As Blain and Boyle (1994) observe, "It is football whose coverage in the media makes it carry the national-symbolic weight" (128). It should be recognized, however, that sexism permeates the world of Scottish soccer and this is one of the factors that arguably undermines the game's claim to be truly national in its appeal. That said, soccer cannot be ignored in attempts to understand Scottish identity.

Criticizing those who have explored the concept of Scottishness without making reference to the game, Holt (1994) suggests that for them "a whole dimension of the Scottish male community is closed off" (72). But again the implication is of a masculine Scottishness. Moreover, the gender issue is by no means alone in weakening the case for seeing soccer as a national game capable of transcending divisions and differences in Scottish society. Five major sources of division are worthy of attention (Bairner 1994a). They are sectarianism, gender, class, localism, and ethnicity.

Some of these sources of division are clearly more significant than others and their impact on different sports varies considerably. But they are all illustrative of problems in contemporary Scottish society. In relation to soccer, the problem that has the highest profile is religious sectarianism, not least because the best-known rivalry in the domestic game can be defined almost totally in sectarian terms, with Catholics from all over Scotland giving their support to Celtic and Protestants from throughout the country supporting Rangers. Furthermore, the sectarian affiliations of these two clubs, which constitute what is known as "The Old Firm," have been instrumental in helping to make them the richest and most successful teams in the country.

The history of the Old Firm is woven into the very fabric of the story of Scottish soccer (Murray 1984). The fact that this rivalry is rooted in sectarian tensions between Scottish Protestants and Catholic immigrants from Ireland is undeniable. Contemporary debate, however, has centered around the question of whether or not the sectarianism that formerly fuelled the rivalry is now on the wane with all that remains being a sporting engagement, albeit one that is surrounded by sectarian trappings as one group of fans celebrate the deeds of the IRA and the other celebrates their loyalty to orangeism and to the British Crown.

According to Moorhouse (1991), some commentators have overemphasized the role played by sectarianism in modern Scotland.

> Of course, "identities" are situationally relevant, and people can move through levels speedily in certain eventualities, but talking of Glasgow as "a divided city" with "simmering hostilities" and so on has been pretty dubious for at least twenty years and now Rangers have suddenly exploded a lot of the old verities about this matter in relation to Scottish football. (205)

To explode these verities, Rangers had recently signed a Scottish internationalist, Maurice Johnston, who had been brought up as a Catholic. The furor that surrounded this signing, however, suggested that there was still considerable scope for change. How different it was when Rangers' Argentinian striker, Gabriel Amato, could make the sign of the cross as he went out on 11 August 1998, to play in a qualifying tie for the European Champions' League without causing any adverse comment from the fans (*Daily Record*, 13 August 1998). Despite such a dramatic development and the fact that by the late 1990s, there were numerous Catholics on Rangers' payroll, however, and contrary to Moorhouse's optimistic analysis, the fact is that Rangers remains a club that is firmly identified with a particular strand of Scottish Protestantism. It is significant, for example, that the Catholics brought to the club have customarily been continental Europeans rather than Scottish or Irish. Walker (1990) argues that in the past Rangers were part of "a celebration of Scottishness which was underpinned by a strong unionism or loyalism" (146). In recent years, however, particularly as conflict in Northern Ireland intensified, many Scottish Protestants have felt increasingly uneasy about a sports club with an essentially exclusivist ideology. This is not to suggest that they felt comfortable with the other half of the Old Firm. Although less exclusive in terms of the recruitment of players and coaches, Celtic has also continued to reach out for support from a particular community in Scotland.

The role of Celtic in helping to maintain a distinctive identity in Scotland cannot be exaggerated. As Bradley (1995) points out, "The importance of the Celtic club as a focus for the Irish identity should not be underestimated." "Throughout its history," according to Bradley, "the club has been perceived as a safe and appropriate environment for the singing of Irish nationalist songs." As a result, the club's ground has become "an arena for the promotion of a nationalist sub-culture" (167). While hoping for an upsurge of interest in gaelic games among the "Irish" in Scotland, Bradley (1998) is only too aware of the role played by Celtic in the creation of a specific identity for many Catholics living in Scotland.

In one sense, of course, the adoption of soccer by the Irish immigrant community represented a degree of integration into Scottish society and cultural life. As Finn (1994) suggests, "The foundation of Irish-Scottish football clubs mainly indicated a willingness to participate in Scottish life, to meet with other Scots and to demonstrate their competence to the disdainful majority community" (91). This helps to explain why soccer rather than traditional Irish games was chosen by the descendants of Irish immigrants to celebrate their identity. Paradoxically, however, by identifying so closely with Celtic and, to a lesser extent, with other "Irish" clubs such as Hibernian (in Edinburgh) and Dundee Harp, the immigrant community drew attention to itself and attracted the disapproval of the more sectarian sections of that "disdainful majority."

Almost inevitably, obvious attitudinal differences can be detected between the supporters of Celtic and those of other Scottish clubs, most notably Rangers, and even between followers of both Old Firm teams and fans of other Scottish clubs (Bradley 1995). This is particularly evident in attitudes toward the Scottish national team. The followers of most Scottish clubs would appear to be unequivocal in their support for the national team. Celtic supporters, on the other hand, are frequently lukewarm in their response and, in some cases, positively hostile, preferring instead to follow the Irish Republic's team rather than that of their "native" country (Bradley 1995). The position of Rangers fans is somewhat ambivalent. They certainly support the national team although arguably to a lesser extent in per capita terms than do followers of Scotland's smaller clubs. More significantly, however, as regards the issue of Scottish national identity, the club and its supporters seek strenuously to underline their Britishness. Union Flags are waved at matches and songs such as "God Save the Queen" and "Rule Britannia" are sung, along with a variety of battle hymns borrowed from Ulster Loyalism.

From time to time, Rangers and, to a lesser extent, Celtic threaten to leave Scottish domestic competition for British or European league. The result might be fatal damage to Scotland's separate sporting identity. But, for many supporters of the Old Firm, that would be a price worth paying in exchange for the elevation of their respective clubs to even greater international status.

Moorhouse (1994) argues that the study of Scottish soccer and society "would benefit if academics and journalists would put a moratorium on the use of a whole bundle of terms like 'sectarianism,' 'sectarian hatred,' 'bigotry,' 'tribalism' . . . protestant/catholic/Irish 'community,' 'religious tensions,' and the like . . ." (192). As Purdie (1991) indicates, however, for generations sectarianism "has been part of the culture of some of the most heavily industrialised and densely populated areas of Scotland" (78). Certainly it was not gloomy academics who created the hate-ridden atmosphere at Celtic Park on 2 May 1999 when Rangers defeated Celtic and thereby won the Scottish Premier League or who fought in the streets of Glasgow into the early hours of the following morning. The fact that Celtic and Rangers are by far the best-supported clubs in Scotland is not solely attributable to their longstanding supremacy in the Scottish game. Indeed, the latter owes much to the clubs' financial strength, which is based in turn on the size of the support each receives from fans who continue to celebrate deep-seated sectarian differences within the context of Scottish soccer. Thus, as Bradley (1995) puts it, "Football is a crucial element of religious identity in Scotland" (178). Furthermore, rival religious identities have manifest implications for the construction of a Scottish national identity as long as Celtic fans prefer to celebrate the Irishness of their forebears and Rangers supporters proclaim a conception of Britishness that is virtually unknown in the remainder of the United Kingdom with the exception of Loyalist areas of Northern Ireland. One can look to the supporters of other Scottish clubs to find a definite correlation between soccer enthusiasm and Scottish national identity. But as one casts one's eye more widely over the Scottish scene other sources of division begin to emerge.

As Forsyth (1992) admits, "Not everyone likes sport and it is often said that more people visit museums in Scotland annually than attend Scottish league matches" (337). Among those Scots who dislike soccer or are, at best, apathetic towards it are large numbers of Scottish women. Time and again, the masculinity of Scotland's soccer culture is mentioned. For many women, the main significance of the televised results service on a Saturday night is to allow them to anticipate the mood of a returning husband, father, son, or brother. Bradley (1995) is, of course, correct to point out that "although women are less involved in football than men, they often retain a passive attachment to the club supported by the male members of their families" (178). In addition, there are certainly more women attending matches today than was the case even twenty years ago. But soccer, like most sports in Scotland, remains dominated by men, just as it was in the nineteenth century when the modern sporting culture first emerged (Tranter 1994). As Tranter (1994) sensibly points out, this may well have had as much to do with choices made by women as with conscious efforts on the part of men to keep sport to themselves (39). The fact remains, however, that soccer, of necessity, is a less important activity for women than for men and plays a concomitantly smaller part in the construction of a female sense of Scottishness. In addition to sectarianism and gender moreover, there are other sources of division that impinge on the world of Scottish soccer and which, although intrinsically less significant, weaken the game's capacity to form the basis of a unifying national identity.

Just as the masculinity of Scotland's soccer culture is self-evident, so too is its working-class character. This may be less apparent than in the past as a result of changes in occupational patterns and in the very nature of work itself. But the bulk of the Scottish population, and thus the majority of those who play and watch soccer, are concentrated in the region known as the Central Belt, once heavily industrialized and now a classic example of deindustrialized society. It is scarcely surprising therefore that a majority of those who follow Scotland's senior soccer clubs are either working class themselves or just one generation removed from the traditional working class. Thus, any contribution soccer can make to the construction of a national identity inevitably assumes a class dimension. Many middle- or upper-class Scots would find it difficult to partake of an identity constructed in part on the basis of a game that thrives in a culture so alien from their own.

The fact that so many of Scotland's leading soccer clubs play in the Central Belt also serves to highlight the ways in which regional differences are manifested in soccer support with resultant negative implications for the construction of a unifying national identity. Local loyalties remain strong in most parts of Scotland regardless of the globalizing pressures that have resulted in every small town's High Street looking almost identical to each other. This is manifested in the support received by clubs that can never expect to compete on equal terms with Rangers or Celtic. Localism is encouraged, however, not only within the structure of Scottish League soccer but more importantly as a result of the League's relatively exclusive character. Despite recent developments, indeed, the very concept of *Scottish* League soccer remains flawed. Not until the beginning of the 1994–1995 season did teams from the Scottish Highlands, Ross County and Inverness Caledonian Thistle, take their places in the Scottish League. Other teams from the region continue to compete in their own separate Highland League. Moreover, the applications for Scottish League membership made by Ross County and Caley Thistle succeeded at the expense of hopeful applicants from the Border region of the country, which still remains woefully underrepresented in national League competition. Overall, the Scottish League continues to be rooted in central Scotland, although soccer is played and watched throughout the country and on the occasion of Scottish international matches the support from the Highlands and the Borders is likely to be no less passionate and arguably even more so than in those parts of the Central Belt where sectarian rivalries have a stronger pull on many soccer fans than do the fortunes of the national team.

Localism, of course, can be transcended and even incorporated into the idea of the nation. Commenting on popular pastimes in nineteenth-century Scotland, Telfer (1994) writes, "The point that needs to be made here is that it is not necessary to see recreational customs or sporting traditions at the local level as not contributing to any sense of community or nation" (119). The fact that someone supports Dunfermline Athletic and someone else supports Raith Rovers need be no barrier to their sharing a national identity. However, to the extent that these soccer allegiances are linked to strong local attachments, a potential for more serious divisions, concerning political decisions, for example, or the allocation of scarce resources, clearly exists. While the claim is made that Scottishness can transcend other identities, one cannot discount the possibility that even local or regional identities may possess the power to transcend Scottishness. In terms of answering the question, "Who are the Scots?," however, more serious problems arguably emerge as a result of ethnic rather than local differences.

As regards the relationship between ethnic groups in Scotland and the game of soccer, it can be stated at once that only the Irish and to a lesser extent the Italians have contributed significantly to the game's development. Asians and Jews have found it far more difficult to integrate into Scottish society by way of involvement in soccer. In part this has been the result of overt racism in the world of Scottish soccer (Dimeo and Finn 1998; Horne 1994; Spiers 1994). Often, however, it has been due simply to a feeling of not fully belonging to the society in general and specifically to a sports culture in which soccer plays such a dominant role. This feeling is heightened by the prominence of Christian religious sectarianism within the Scottish game. Arnold Brown's witty but at the same time deeply serious recollection of growing up Jewish in Glasgow and having to respond to the Celtic-Rangers rivalry illustrates the difficulties faced by some ethnic minority groups.

It was no picnic being Jewish in Glasgow without a team to call your own. Eventually most of the Jewish supporters decided they would follow Third Lanark. Unfortunately, Third Lanark turned out to be the only Scottish club to go out of business since the war and I often thought retrospectively that God punished Third Lanark because Saturday is the Jewish Sabbath and we should have been at the synagogue instead of Cathkin Park. (Cited in Forsyth 1990, 124)

Sectarianism, gender, class, localism, and ethnicity are all important sources of division in Scottish society and all are not only reflected in the soccer culture but may even be exacerbated as a result of the emphasis so many Scots, especially Scottish men, place on the game. Far from uniting the Scottish people behind a common purpose, soccer often appears to have more potential to divide or at the very least to strengthen existing divisions. As Holt (1994) observes, even approaches to playing the game reveal "different kinds of Scottishness" (66). Or, as Wagg (1995) puts it, "In football, as in other cultural realms, Scottishness, like all other national identities, is contested terrain" (16). The national team's travelling support, the so-called Tartan Army, might appear to testify to the existence of some transcendent national identity. But the Scottishness the Tartan Army promotes is akin to a music-hall parody in which wearing tartan is taken to be sufficient evidence of a national identity. Their behavior in foreign countries has been described as carnivalesque (Giulianotti 1995). Yet far from detaching themselves from a quasi-mythical parental culture, the Tartan Army's members drape themselves in tartan and perform their self-assigned roles as the most visible representatives of what Paterson (1981) has memorably described as "a community of pawky inadequates" (70). In conclusion, therefore, soccer's right to the title of Scotland's national sport must remain, to borrow a term from the Scottish legal system, not proven. But what are the alternatives?

The adoption of soccer by the Scots is a classic illustration of a people seeking to beat a more powerful neighbor at its own game.Thereafter maybe it was the game's own popularity that inevitably made it a repository for the divisions within Scottish society. However, there are also problems in seeking to construct a national identity on the basis of more uniquely Scottish sports and pastimes with a relatively small level of support.

SHINTY: THE NATIONAL GAME?

Rather than seek to beat the English at their own games, an alternative for Scots, faced with lost statehood, would have been to reinvigorate national pastimes, in the way in which hurling, for example, was harnessed to the nationalist cause in Ireland. Had this option been taken, the obvious sport to be used would have been shinty, which can best be described as a cross between the Irish sport of hurling and field hockey and which, it is said, has been played in Scotland for 1,500 years (McCarra 1993). Shinty's potential to become a national game, however, was seriously weakened by the fact that it was played primarily in Scotland's western highlands and islands. During the nineteenth century, as Burnett (1995) reports, "It was wiped out in the Lowlands because the police stopped it being played in its usual venue, the streets, thinking it was dangerous" (56). Inasmuch as it has returned to the densely populated Central Belt at all, it has done so only in Glasgow, which has traditionally become home for generations of Highland immigrants. Thus, it was always unlikely that shinty could find a place in the hearts of most Scottish people in the way that hurling and Gaelic football, as we shall see, were embraced by Irish Catholics (Jarvie 1993). Shinty has certainly contributed to a sense of Highland identity (Telfer 1994), but there was never the political impulse that existed in Ireland to turn this indigenous sport into a vehicle for the promotion of political nationalism (Harvie 1994). For a time, moreover, it seemed as if the future existence of the game was in doubt. As recently as 1990 and 1992, however, there were new winners of the game's major trophy, the Camanachd Cup, in the shape of Skye and Fort William respectively, suggesting that shinty is capable, for the time being at least, of resisting national and global pressures that demand its marginalization. Even with its future secured, however, shinty is unlikely to provide a sporting basis for a unifying national identity.

The evidence is that the leaders of shinty in the Camanachd Association will continue to be obdurate in the face of attempts by nationalists to politicize their game (Hutchinson 1989). This is not to deny that the game of shinty can be used by nationalists to underline Scotland's distinctiveness. Highland Games, although of considerably shorter lineage and far more contrived in their relationship to Scottishness, can also serve this purpose (Jarvie 1991). As Jarvie (1993) argues, "Highland Games and shinty may arguably represent various visions of Gaelic culture, visions and identities which are often drawn upon to fuel the oxygen tanks of Scottish nationalism" (66). This indeed is part of a broader process whereby the Highlands and the history of the Highland people have been subsumed within a general history of Scotland that disregards inconvenient facts about the ways in which lowland Scots joined forces with the English to undermine the religion, language, and customs of their Highland compatriots. As Webb (1978) remarks, "The cultural schizophrenia of Scotland has only been resolved in modern times with the popular acceptance of a mythical Celtic version of Scottish history" (29). According to Nairn, writing in *Scotland on Sunday* (11 November 1990), furthermore, "to 'borrow' the geist of Gaeldom in this way was, inevitably, to travesty it; the penalty of such ethnic misuse and overstretching was nationalised kitsch." The image projected by soccer's Tartan Army is a good example. In sum, therefore, the attitudes toward shinty offer important insights into the complex ways in which attempts to construct a Scottish identity have been made. But there is no reason to think of shinty as Scotland's national game in any meaningful sense.

GOLF: SCOTLAND'S GIFT TO THE WORLD?

The idea that there are only two cultural options to offer to people faced with the responsibility of responding to lost statehood is slightly misleading. It is also possible to find comfort in a pastime that unites the national and the universal. In Scottish sport, the game of golf provides such an option. However, any analysis of Scottish golf must arrive at the conclusion that the game reveals more about the myths involved in the search for a national identity than about the likelihood that such a transcendent identity can be found. According to McCarra (1993), "Of the world's major games it is only golf which might be termed a Scottish invention" (286). Although its precise origins are actually uncertain, golf was certainly established in Scotland by the fifteenth century. In addition, as home to the game's traditional ruling body, the Royal and Ancient club of St. Andrews, Scotland has continued to play a prominent role in the game's development.

But golf has also been implicated in one of the most potent myths about Scottish society, namely the widespread belief that the country is intrinsically democratic and egalitarian. Whereas in most other countries, golf is the preserve of the relatively affluent, in Scotland, it is believed, anyone can play. According to McCarra (1993), "Individual clubs may be bastions of privilege but the pastime itself remains unusually democratic in Scotland" (286). Rather more cautiously, Forsyth (1992) supports McCarra's central proposition arguing that "while it is a myth that golf in Scotland is a classless occupation accessibility is a feature of Scottish golf, which can be said to be more the sport of the common person than it is elsewhere" (342). Yet, as Forsyth himself reveals, male golfers outnumber female players in Scotland by a ratio of 5:1 and far less access to golf courses is available if one happens to live in Glasgow than is the case in other parts of the country. In general, it can be argued that many golf clubs retain the character, if not the precise form, of their exclusive origins when, in the words of Burnett (1995), "Members were obliged to dine, required to wear uniforms, and were initiated into secret societies, and women were rigorously excluded" (23). Ironically, however, the myth of Scottish golf's egalitarianism is believed even by many of those Scots who are unlikely ever to play the game. National myths, of course, need not necessarily be dangerous (Archard 1995). As McCrone (1995) and his fellow researchers point out, "Using the term 'myth' might seem to imply a value judgement, as if the whole thing was a fraud, but myths provide guides to the interpretation of social reality . . ." (52). On the other hand, it is doubtful whether the myths that surround Scottish golf can provide the basis for a national identity centered around sport. Nor do they permit golf to be accurately described as Scotland's national sport. In a particularly acute analysis of the relationship between golf and Scottishness, Lowerson (1994) argues that "Scotland may not have invented golf, but it has refined it and encouraged its development along lines which have exploited ascribed national identity to such an extent that it has distorted much of what really happens in the homeland." "In so doing," Lowerson claims, "it reflects an ambivalence in Scottish society as to what Scotland and its people really are" (89). Golf makes an input into the idea of Scottishness but that conception, as a consequence, ignores the realities of Scottish society and the various divisions it contains. The identity that results cannot, therefore, serve to unify the Scottish people.

RUGBY AND THE FLOWER OF SCOTLAND

Rugby union has seldom been proposed as Scotland's national game. But more than any other sport in recent years, it appears to have tapped into patriotic sentiment and as a result to have won support from every section of Scottish society. Certainly by agreeing to the use of the modern nationalist song "Flower of Scotland" as an anthem for the national team, the Scottish Rugby Union (SRU) succeeded in appealing to the sentimentality that is a feature of most national identities. According to Forsyth (1992), "At the 1990 Grand Slam match with England the emotional rendering of 'Flower of Scotland' suggested that the traditionally conservative rugby constituency had shifted its ground" (353). But were people who had traditionally supported the Union now revealing an enthusiasm for Scottish independence? This would hardly explain why the Princess Royal, in her capacity as Patron of the SRU, was willing to sing the song so lustily. Rather, as Jarvie and Walker (1994) suggest, "the adoption by such a conservative Scottish institution as the Scottish Rugby Union of the populist national anthem 'Flower of Scotland' at one level might seem insignificant and yet at another level it was a profound gesture of sentimentality which in part encapsulated for a brief instant the mood of many Scots" (4). What it did not suggest was that rugby had the capacity to become the national game and either heal or transcend divisions in Scottish society. Instead, the character of Scottish rugby is such as to highlight all the same divisions as afflict soccer, albeit to differing degrees.

It can be argued that rugby is even more of a male preserve than soccer, in spite of the contribution of women to the social life of clubs and the slow emergence of women's teams. In terms of class, rugby is also divisive, reflecting even more clearly than soccer the stark social divisions in modern Scotland. Whereas middle-class Scots are involved with soccer at a variety of levels, few working-class people participate in rugby although it is unfortunate that critics of rugby's apparent exclusiveness choose to ignore the ones who do. Rugby also reflects the continuing importance of local and regional identities in Scotland, with the Borders being the only region of the country in which rugby can be regarded as the main team sport (Drysdale 1995a). Very little rugby by contrast is played in the Central Belt, with the notable exceptions of the cities of Edinburgh and, to a much lesser extent, Glasgow (Drysdale 1994).

Rugby has also had difficulties in attracting the support of ethnic and religious minorities. Again to select an example from the experiences of Scotland's Jewish community, David Daiches (1987) remembers the problem of not being able to participate in the game at the Edinburgh school he attended, where playing rugby was an important mechanism for establishing oneself.

> [T]hat way was completely closed to me, not because I was naturally incompetent at sport . . . but because games were played on Saturday, the Jewish Sabbath, and my playing them was quite out of the question. (46)

Impressionistic evidence would also suggest that few Asians have been attracted to rugby and arguably more significantly in terms of the relatively greater size of Scotland's Catholic population the sectarian divisions that blight Scottish soccer also impact on the world of Scottish rugby. This does not mean that there is a rugby equivalent of the Celtic-Rangers rivalry. But far from implying integration through rugby, the absence of such a rivalry is in large part attributable to the fact that until quite recently few Catholics learned the game in their schools (Drysdale, 1995b; Drysdale, 1995c).

SPORT AND SCOTTISH NATIONAL IDENTITY

For a variety of reasons, therefore, none of the sports that have been examined meet the criteria that would be required of a truly national game. They do offer clear insights, however, into the divisions in Scottish society which themselves make the construction of a unifying national identity such a difficult enterprise. Yet, it is undeniable that most Scots celebrate sporting victories achieved by their compatriots, regardless of the game being played. Thus, although their everyday sporting experiences are more likely to divide than to unite, there is still some impression of sporting unity. It can be argued, however, that this unity is most securely rooted when negative rather than positive aspects of Scottishness are to the fore. Specifically, Scottish sporting nationalism is most cohesive when it is most clearly characterized by anti-English sentiment.

One of the main reasons why rugby union has acquired greater significance in terms of Scottish sporting nationalism in recent years is the fact that, whereas the national soccer team has not had an annual fixture with England since 1989, the rugby side plays England each year in the Six Nations Championship and the two teams have also met in the rugby World Cup. The idea that anti-Englishness is the key element of what passes for a unifying Scottish national identity has been played down by some commentators. Writing in the *Guardian*, Andrew O'Hagan, for example, suggests that "Scotland's dislike of England, for the most part, is just a sort of Hogmanay blether." "England," he argues, "for all that's said, is not really a target of everyday Scottish venom" (*Guardian*, 23 July 1994). In sport, however, nothing is more guaranteed to heighten Scottish emotions than a contest involving England, even, most significantly, when Scotland does not provide the opposition. Of that, at least one English journalist, Edward Pearce, was in no doubt.

> To take up Mr Tebbit's cricketing test, the Scots, according to all sorts of good authorities, now reflexively support any opponents of England in any sports fixture, rooting spitefully for Pakistan, Cameroon or Czechoslovakia in preference to a neighbour they seem to hate. (*Guardian*, 29 January 1992)

Although some Rangers supporters may be exceptional in this regard, the general point is well made. Describing Denis Law's sense of national identity, Holt (1994) writes, "For him anti-Englishness at a crude cultural level, the fierce commitment to beat England at football, was the proof of true Scottishness" (60). Time and again Scottish sports fans have gathered to watch their national representatives play English opponents with banners bearing the legend "Remember Bannockburn" or "Remember 1314." As Forsyth (1990) puts it, in colorful although not very politically correct terms, "It is as if the Sioux Indians were allowed to enter the world archery championships" (14). Certainly, when the annual Scotland-England soccer international was part of the sporting calendar, it was given far greater significance by Scots than by the English. As Murray (1994) observes, "Unlike England, where the Cup Final became the main event of the year, in Scotland national attention focused on the annual encounter with England" (18–19). Beating the dominant partner at its own game, it would appear, has continued to be an important mechanism by which Scots can respond to lost statehood.

In recent years, much has been made of the improved behavior of Scottish soccer fans. Yet even that can be seen as part of an attempt to outdo the English who had acquired a reputation for having a major hooligan problem (Bairner 1994a). Giulianotti (1995) refers to the Tartan Army's "joking uniformity of anti-Englishness" (202). He also comments on the antiracism and internationalism exhibited by Scottish fans abroad (203, 212). But he reveals too that these characteristics are manifested in a context in which one objective (arguably the sole objective) is to show up the chauvinistic English hooligans. As a result another myth about the Scots is enhanced. The extent to which Scots can justifiably be described as internationalist, however, is necessarily brought into question by the realization that expressions of international solidarity may well have been prompted by deep-seated animosity toward Scotland's closest neighbors. According to Finn and Giulianotti (1998), "Euro 96 was but one of many tests of Scotland and Scottishness, but there was little evidence of real progress towards a less anti-English, more positive Scottish social identity" (200). On the other hand, in terms of constructing a national identity, anti-Englishness has the merit of being able to transcend those divisions that otherwise set one Scot against another.

Having reviewed the relationship between sport and national identity in Scotland, therefore, one is forced to conclude that Scotland has no truly national game, that this conclusion in itself is a reflection of the divisions that beset Scottish society in general and the world of Scottish sport no less so, and, finally, that not only do major sports individually reflect differences and divisions, they may even reinforce them. As a result, it is difficult to see sport as a potential source for the emergence of a cohesive Scottish identity. As Jarvie and Walker (1994) themselves conclude, "Sport may at times contribute to a notion of Scottishness and yet within each of the amorphous identities and expressions of nationhood which make up Scotland it is almost impossible to distinguish what exact identity is being reflected, symbolised, reproduced or even imagined" (8). Perhaps the divisions encountered while analyzing Scottish sport do not all have major political importance, particularly since anti-Englishness may well possess sufficient strength to form the basis of some common purpose. But sexism, sectarianism, and racism are certainly serious matters in modern Scotland and sport has played a part in their perpetuation. One last issue, however, remains to be considered. Is it likely that the divisions in Scottish society, transcendent anti-Englishness, and even the very idea of searching for a cohesive national identity might all be rendered redundant as a result of the impact of globalization on Scottish sport?

GLOBALIZATION AND SCOTTISH SPORT

Scotland was affected by global trends long before the concept of globalization ever emerged. As Lynch (1993) expresses it, "Native continuity and tradition have been continually exposed to cross-examination by foreign or cosmopolitan connections, and new patterns have resulted" (38). Indeed, in terms of sport, the Scots themselves have figured prominently as globalizers, since there is no denying their role in the international dissemination of soccer and golf (McCarra 1993; Murray 1994). It is ironic, therefore, that globalizing tendencies have in turn made these games less distinctively Scottish than once was the case. For example, the packaging of soccer, at least at the highest levels, is identical to that of other major soccer nations. The "home of golf" now plays host to Japanese and American club-making companies happy to be associated with Scotland's historic relationship to the game but so massive as to have all but decimated the indigenous club-making industry. Away from soccer and golf, changes in the structure of world rugby will mean that national bodies such as the SRU will have far less influence on the international stage and countries such as Scotland will lose a vital part of their international sporting profile.

While all of these developments are taking place, numerous imported sports—hockey, martial arts, basketball, rugby league, and so on—occupy the attention of small but growing numbers of Scots. All have the potential to be far more successful than more traditional pastimes at transcending the divisions within Scottish society. None of them, however, has secured a sufficiently high profile to make any major impact on the reproduction of national identity.

So far, the most audacious attempt to promote an imported sport at an international level has been the formation of an American football team, participating in the World Football League and playing its home matches at the SRU's Murrayfield Stadium in Edinburgh (Karowski 1995). In their 1995 debut season, however, the football team failed to attract a substantial following. Indeed, at present the most interesting point to emerge from the football experiment as conducted in Scotland was the choice of a name for the Edinburgh-based team. In a classic case of glocalization, these American footballers became the Scottish Claymores, a claymore being a broad sword used in the past by Scots in battles with the old enemy, England. Even more evidence of nationalist resistance to suffocating global trends could be found in the heightened interest shown in the Claymores when they played matches against the London Monarchs, the only English-based team in the WFL. In terms of its players' origins, neither team has much connection with the country in which it is based. But Scots, nevertheless, wanted victory against England's representatives regardless of the fact that their "own side" could scarcely be described as

Scottish. Thus, globalization joins forces with the negative element in Scottish national identity.

Something similar happened in 1998–1999 with the appearance of a Scottish team, the Edinburgh Rocks, in basketball's British Budweiser League. Coach and former NBA player, Jim Brandon, was shocked to discover on his arrival in Scotland that a major sports store in the capital did not even stock basketball shoes (*Scotland on Sunday*, 13 September 1998). He expressed his fears that much work needed to be done if local people were to be persuaded to get behind the new team. These fears were justified but glocal elements have clearly been invoked to meet the challenge. The very name "Edinburgh Rocks" makes reference to a well-loved, locally produced type of candy. In addition, the fact that the Rocks would be taking on the best basketball teams in England would be sufficient reason for most Scots to give at least tacit support. The fact that most of the leading players were not Scots was a pity but, as in the case of the Claymores, not an insurmountable obstacle.

It can legitimately be argued that anti-Englishness remains Scotland's best defense against the forces of globalization. When Scottish soccer fans sing, "We are the England haters," their words may carry more significance than they themselves realize. Whether in a spirit of self-parodying humor or of genuine antagonism, hating the English is the main ingredient of Scotland's sporting national identity. More sinisterly, hating the English might also be the main element in a national identity which could act as an ideological weapon in the struggle for an independent Scotland. According to Jean Rafferty, writing in the *Sunday Times Magazine* (3 October 1998), "Hostility to the English is there at all levels of Scottish society, from the classroom to the boardroom." Perhaps hating the English at the level of sport is a typical example of what N. T. Phillipson referred to as Scotland's "noisy inaction" (Phillipson 1969, 186), or, as Sillars would have it, "ninety-minute patriotism." What can safely be said, however, is that up until now globalization has been unable to weaken the distinctive features of Scotland's sporting culture. It is a bitter irony, however, that this distinctiveness contributes more to divisions within Scotland than to the construction of a common national identity.

Unlike its Scottish counterpart, Irish nationalism has traditionally done more than engage in noisy inaction, primarily because of a very different political context. Sport has been deeply implicated in the Irish nationalist struggle. But its involvement has taken different forms, not least because it has been forced to take into account the relationship of Ulster unionism to sport, which was discussed earlier, as well as changes in Ireland's relationship to the United Kingdom and the latter's evolving constitution. The next chapter examines the changing role of sport in the construction of Irish national identity or, to be more exact, Irish national identities.

chapter four

National Identity and International Recognition

SPORT AND THE DEVELOPMENT OF IRISH NATIONALISM

Whereas the relationship between Ulster unionism and the concepts of nationalism and nationality may be problematic, there are no such difficulties in stating that both Irish nationalism and Irish nationality, like Scottish nationalism and nationality, actually exist. How they came into existence and are currently constituted, however, are matters for debate. According to Garvin (1981), "[A]n Irish nationalist consciousness of some sort is possibly primordial, and certainly dates back to the seventeenth century" (14). Thus, modern Irish nationalism reveals clear traces of a premodern ancestry. Garvin admits, however, that "Irish separatist nationalism as a popular political creed originated in the towns in the late eighteenth century and it penetrated the popular consciousness rather slowly during the nineteenth century" (14). It was mainly centered around Catholicism although the contribution made, in the early years of its modern development, by Anglican parliamentary nationalists and also by radical Presbyterians should not be forgotten. An important element in the growth of the Irish nationalist movement in the nineteenth century was the setting up of quasi-political cultural organizations, including the Gaelic League, which sought to defend the Irish language in the face of widespread anglicization, and the Gaelic Athletic Association, which aimed to protect and promote traditional Irish games and pastimes.

Ireland's Gaelic Athletic Association (Cumann Lúthchleas Gael) (GAA) is frequently offered as the best example of a sporting organization formed for the precise purpose of producing and reproducing a sense of national identity. Houlihan (1994), for example, refers to the GAA's success in terms of cultural resistance as "impressive" (191). Mandle (1987), moreover, leaves us in little doubt as to the contribution of the GAA to the development of Irish nationalist politics.

However, the fact that this book contains two chapters dealing with the way in which sport is organized and played on the island of Ireland is a clear indication that the relationship between Irish sport and national identities in Ireland is by no means straightforward. The relationship between Ulster unionists and sport has already been explored and it would be convenient, of course, if it were possible to state simply at this point that the experience of Irish nationalists in this regard is diametrically opposite, thereby confirming a polarized situation in which unionists play British games and nationalists Irish ones. In addition, one might easily assume that the relationship between Irish nationalism and sport is also rendered relatively easy to understand by virtue of the fact that Irish nationalism itself is a more coherent and less fragmented doctrine than Ulster unionism. As this chapter reveals, however, Irish nationalism is not without its own internal contradictions, which, in turn, are reflected in and perpetuated by the attitudes of the Irish to sport. Indeed, the fact that much of this chapter concentrates on sport in the Republic of Ireland rather than on the island of Ireland as a whole is an indication of the sort of theoretical issues to be discussed. Although nationalists in Northern Ireland (or what they would refer to as the north of Ireland or even the Six Counties) would argue that this ignores the territorial integrity of the Irish nation, there are those in the Irish Republic who clearly express a twenty-six-county nationalism for which sport, and particularly the achievements of the "national" soccer team, has provided a significant rallying point. As one young man from Galway told me, it was only when celebrating the successes of the Irish soccer team that he felt that he could wave the Irish tricolor without being mistaken for a fervent supporter of the idea of a thirty-two-county unitary state. Ironically, northern nationalists were simultaneously waving the same flag to celebrate the same sporting victories but with wholly different political aspirations in mind. So much for any notion that the links between sport and Irish nationalism are simple. In addition, the chapter also assesses the extent to which sport has allowed Irish nationalism, whatever form is takes, to resist global forces. This too raises some interesting issues as regards the general relationship between sport and Irish nationalism. To begin the analysis of these two separate but related themes, it is necessary first to trace the history of Irish sport in Ireland.

SPORT, EMPIRE, AND IRELAND

Before looking at the origins and subsequent development of Gaelic games, however, it must be reiterated that the creation of a modern sporting culture in Ireland owed almost everything to the British. Given Britain's pioneering role in this area, it is scarcely surprising that sport came to assume a high profile throughout the British Empire. Nevertheless, the extent to which it became an instrument of imperial policy is astounding. According to Mangan (1987), "The formation of character was the essential purpose of Victorian *elitist* education—at home and overseas," and, for the export of character, it was necessary to have "trainers of character, mostly from public school and ancient university, who used the games field as the medium of moral indoctrination" (139–140). Generation after generation of imperial administrators took British sports to every far-flung outpost of the Empire, first to amuse themselves, then to help cement relationships with the indigenous elites, and, finally, to introduce entire native populations not only to these sports but also to the idea that the British way of life was superior to their own and, thus, demanded their respect. As a result, as Stoddart (1988) observes, "At the height of the empire . . . sport as a cultural bond had considerable force, conveying through its many forms a moral and behavioural code that bonded the imperial power with many if not most of the influential colonial quarters" (666). However, not everywhere was affected in exactly the same way by the introduction of British sports as an element in the broader colonial project. In this respect, as in many others, Ireland reveals a more complex picture than that projected by certain other parts of the British Empire. With specific reference to sport, the relationship between Britain and Ireland is problematic for three main reasons.

First, because of the geographical proximity of the two and the close familial and personal links between their respective upper classes, it is more difficult than in other imperial contexts to draw a clear distinction between the imperial and the indigenous elite. For example, members of both were traditionally educated at the same types of school and university and, in many instances, in precisely the same schools and universities. As a result, they shared a common grounding in British games. Second, as has been discussed in chapter 2, there exists in the northeast corner of the island of Ireland a substantial Protestant and unionist community, which has important ethnic links with Britain as well as a longstanding loyalty to British traditions, including those in the realm of sport and leisure. This community cannot readily be compared with native populations in other parts of the British Empire but neither can it be wholly equated to a conventional colonial elite. The adoption of British sport has consistently been seen by Ulster unionists as part of a rightful cultural inheritance rather than the result of the imperialist imposition of an alien culture. Finally, however, and of particular significance to the subsequent linkage that was to be established between sport and Irish nationalism, in Ireland, unlike most other parts of the empire, there existed a flourishing system of organized or at least semi-organized sports, such as football and hurling, long before the British sporting revolution and this was to provide a significant vehicle for the expression of resistance to British rule. In other countries, it was enough to beat the British at their own games. The Irish nationalists, however, were to go one step further and engage in sporting activities that were exclusive to them and, thus, helped them to maintain their sense of having a separate and unique identity. The extent to which such activities can continue to be successful in this respect, not least given the pressures of globalization, shall be examined toward the end of the chapter.

British games are played enthusiastically throughout Ireland, primarily by unionists in the north and by a wide variety of people elsewhere, most of them claiming an attachment to some rendition of Irish nationalism. Games such as rugby union and cricket are organized on an all-Ireland basis and when representative teams take the field they do so on behalf of the entire thirty-two counties of Ireland. While this has led to the strange consequence of northern unionists standing to attention for the national anthem (*Amhran na bhFiann*—The Soldier's Song) of a foreign (and what some of them might regard as a hostile) state, it also means that Irish sports people are celebrating their national identity, albeit by playing sports that do not have their origins in Ireland. Indeed, rugby has given the Irish a particularly valuable vehicle for the promotion of sporting nationalism since it provides annual opportunities to play (and hopefully to beat) the English at one of their own games. Gaelic games, on the other hand, provide no such opportunities. Rather, as the author has suggested to generations of unamused students, these basically allow the Irish to play with themselves. Yet playing Gaelic games is still regarded in some nationalist circles as the ultimate means of expressing Irish sporting nationalism.

SPORTING NATIONALISM AND THE GAELIC ATHLETIC ASSOCIATION

As was shown in chapter 2, British games spread rapidly in Ireland from the eighteenth century onward, and by the last quarter of the nineteenth century, British sporting hegemony in Ireland had become a very real threat in the eyes of nationalists. It was feared that this development both paralleled and complemented similar trends in other areas of activity, resulting in a diminished sense of distinctive Irish identity and a weakened desire for political independence (Bairner 1996b). Despite his florid language, Archbishop Croke spoke for many when he condemned England's "mashier habits and other effeminate follies" (cited in Puirseal 1982, 50). Croke, like many of his fellow nationalists, was concerned by what he regarded as British cultural imperialism, carried out with the support of the ruling Anglo-Irish elite and, increasingly, of the Protestant working-class community in the province of Ulster whose love of the imported game of soccer was to become, as we have seen, a crucial element of their support for the continuation of the political union of Britain and Ireland. It is against this backdrop that the emergence of the GAA must be understood (Mandle 1987). By the 1880s, as Healey (1998) reports, "Native games were clearly in desperate need of a guiding hand, not to mention round-the-clock medical services" (14). Furthermore, this was a politically turbulent time in Ireland's history, with the Irish Republican Brotherhood (IRB or Fenians) involved in a bitter and armed struggle against the British for Irish independence. Michael Cusack was the man identified by the IRB as being most capable of revitalizing Irish games and harnessing them to the wider cause of Irish nationalist politics. Although Cusack himself had taken the Fenian oath, it would be true to say that his interests had long been more sporting than political. He had played British games as well as hurling and had organized his own Sports Academy in Dublin's Phoenix Park with a view to making track and field events more accessible to the working man. His great love, however, was hurling, and Dublin and Metropolitan Hurling clubs became the foundations upon which the GAA was constructed.

The GAA was established at Hayes Hotel in Thurles, Co. Tipperary. The meeting was chaired by Maurice Davin who was to become the association's first president but most of the talking was done by Cusack. From the outset, the stated purpose of the GAA was the cultivation of Irish pastimes. In the first instance, however, more attention was paid to athletics, more popular than Gaelic games at the time but under British as opposed to Irish control and, thus, part of the imperial cultural hegemonic project. Increasingly, however, the status of both hurling and football was enhanced and, in sporting terms at least, the future shape of the GAA began to develop. The political character of the association, on the other hand, has been decidedly more complex and has assumed a variety of forms in response to the ebb and flow of Irish history. The inaugural gathering, for example, included Protestants, which was in keeping with the spirit of an age in which the Gaelic language had also been invigorated to no small degree by the activism of Protestant supporters. In addition, the GAA also contained within its initial membership representatives of all the main elements of nationalist Ireland.

Although Cusack himself was a Fenian as was Michael Davitt, one of the GAA's original patrons, other patrons were Archbishop Croke representing the powerful Catholic church and Charles Stewart Parnell, leader of the Irish Home Rule Party and, therefore, of constitutional nationalism in Ireland. Thus, the key elements of Irish nationalism—the church, the physical force movement, and constitutionalism—were brought together in the establishment and early activity of the GAA. Moreover, the association's first president, Maurice Davin, is arguably better remembered as a superb athlete than as an exponent of any political ideology (Ó Riain 1994). Despite its primary concern with sporting activity, however, as the GAA grew, "like a prairie fire" to use Cusack's own words (Healey 1998, 19), perhaps inevitably, as we shall see, a battle for its soul between the various shades of Irish nationalist opinion unfolded and, it can be argued, remains influential to the present day.

The specifically Gaelic games that are played in Ireland and further afield today are hurling, Gaelic football, handball, and camogie. Of these, hurling has the purest lineage although there are two distinct traditions of the game (Maolfabhail 1973). One of these, the northern version, *iomaín,* survives today in Scotland and is known in English as shinty. The other, southern version, *camanácht,* has become the modern game of hurling (West 1991). Stick and ball games, such as shinty and hurling, have been played by different peoples since primitive times and, despite claims that there is something typically Gaelic and, therefore, typically Celtic about hurling, according to Maolfabhail, "There exists no evidence to show that hurling in any form ever belonged particularly, or at all, to the ancient continental Celts" (Maolfabhail 1973, 2). In fact, a similar game was known in Britain in ancient times, which militates against any suggestion that hurling might possess some ethnically pure character. Nevertheless, according to one historian, a game resembling hurling has been played in Ireland for more than two thousand years (Mandle 1987). The first recorded reference traces hurling to a battle fought at Moytura in County Mayo between the native Fir Bolg and the invading Tuatha Dé Danaan who engaged in a hurling contest while preparing for the conflict (King 1998). Whether this is an accurate account of the true origins of the modern game is open to question. However, it is suggested that evidence exists that embryonic forms of hurling were certainly being played in Ireland from around 1600 A.D. onward, which clearly indicates a sporting tradition with well-established roots (Maolfabhail 1973). Certainly the Brehon Laws, Ireland's first legal system, declared that there should be compensation in cases where people died as a result of hurling accidents. Moreover, hurling is accorded a prominent place in Irish folklore and legend where it is depicted as an aristocratic or even a royal game. Indeed, many of the main legendary heroes, including King Labhraidh Loinsech, Diarmuid, Cahir the Great, Cuchulain, and Fionn Mac Cumhaill, are associated with hurling exploits. These legends of hurling, as Mandle

(1987) points out, have played a crucial role in surrounding the game with nationalist mystique.

Hurling's popularity grew markedly during the Middle Ages to the extent that it was proscribed by the authorities in the Statutes of Kilkenny (1366) and the Galway Statutes (1527) (Dagg 1944). The seventeenth and eighteenth centuries witnessed another marked upsurge in interest with members of the gentry and landowners fielding teams consisting of tenants (King 1998; Mandle 1987). Games began to attract large audiences and significant amounts of wagering occurred. However, from the beginning of the nineteenth century this expansion was arrested temporarily. In part, this was due to the fact that the Irish nobility, like their European counterparts, ended their patronage of popular culture (King 1998). Social and political developments were also influential. According to Mandle (1987), "As with English cricket the Napoleonic wars and, in the case of Ireland, the consequences of the 1798 rising, caused a noticeable lull in the development of hurling in the early years of the nineteenth century" (16). In addition, the Famine and emigration each had a detrimental effect not only on hurling but also on numerous other games and pastimes. So serious was this situation that some actually began to lament the passing of hurling (Mandle 1987).

Ironically, in the ensuing period it was kept alive above all by the efforts of students at Trinity College, Dublin, albeit in the northern form, which was to be transformed into the modern game of shinty and in spite of the fact that Trinity was a key center for the promotion of the British games tradition. As West (1991) observes, "Trinity had made a major contribution to Gaelic games by keeping a form of hurling alive when it was virtually extinct in the rest of the country" (57). As the hurlers of Trinity grew closer to their English (and Irish) hockey-playing counterparts, however, it was to be left to Michael Cusack to build upon their efforts and on the traditions of Irish hurling to revitalize the "national" game, first in the Dublin (later Metropolitan) Hurling Club, which he set up in 1882 and, thereafter, under the auspices of the GAA, formed in 1884.

Since the formation of the GAA, hurling has remained a popular sport throughout Ireland albeit with obvious strongholds, including Cork, Kilkenny, and Tipperary in the south and Antrim and Down in Northern Ireland. The future of the sport, however, is uncertain. It is generally agreed that there are fewer players, not least because the game has to compete with countless other forms of physical exercise. The influence in Irish education of the Christian Brothers, among the most passionate advocates of hurling, has waned (King 1998). In addition, Ireland itself has changed, becoming more urbanized, to such a degree that the rural communities in which hurling was traditionally most supported have become increasingly depopulated. There are also suggestions that the

GAA has done less in recent times to promote hurling not least because it is largely restricted to certain core areas (King 1998). Instead the emphasis has been on Gaelic football, more easily understood, more widely dispersed throughout Ireland, and arguably more modern in style.

Early forms of football played in Ireland were never accorded the same legendary status as hurling. Their pedigree, however, was almost as long, the oldest recorded form, *caid,* having first been played at least one thousand years ago (Sugden and Bairner 1993a). There are historical references to a form of Irish or Gaelic football being played as early as the fourteenth century (Healey 1998). The original game resembled the rough and tumble exchanges that were currently being played throughout Europe and no doubt farther afield as well. Indeed it closely resembled football played in England and had tended to become established primarily in the area of the medieval English settlement in north Dublin (Garvin 1981). In areas where it was popular, moreover, it posed a threat to the more traditionally Irish game of hurling. Rough and tumble football persisted in Ireland up to the nineteenth century. As Healey (1998) records, "As recently as the mid-1880s a typical game of football in Ireland involved hundreds of people playing across miles of open countryside, with the obligatory frequent pauses for bouts of wrestling and fist-fighting" (11). However, as with hurling, more organized versions of the game had begun to grow in popularity during the eighteenth century, and, although frowned upon by the aristocracy, football was played regularly at College Park by students of Trinity College. As in Britain, it gradually assumed the rival forms of association football (soccer) and rugby football and, with the direction of the GAA, an additional form, Gaelic football. What is apparent, however, is that when the GAA came into existence, the two major team games for which it would have responsibility were in a disorganized condition. As Healey (1998) comments, "With violence rampant and organization virtually non-existent as recently as one hundred and fifty years ago, all that could be said for Ireland's native games was that they were being handed on from generation to generation—surviving, despite their coarseness, because they offered the people brief prospects of happiness, and a respite from everyday problems" (13). Under the aegis of the GAA, however, they were quickly to become major elements in the movement to promote Irish national identity as part of the struggle to overthrow British rule in Ireland. Other games, although less visible, were also brought under the control of the GAA. These included activities that were by no means exclusive to Ireland, such as track and field and cycling, but also camogie, a form of hurling played by women, and handball.

Camogie was invented and formally established in 1904, some twenty years after the formation of the GAA, and is now administered by an independent organization, *Cumann Camógaíochta na nGael,* albeit as part of the GAA family (Healey 1998). Camogie teams consist of twelve players as opposed to the fifteen who make up both hurling and Gaelic football teams. Scoring is on the same basis as the other games, with a goal (worth three points) being awarded when the ball passes between the posts and under the crossbar and a point being scored when the ball passes over the bar but between the posts. Like hurling, the game is played with a stick but on a smaller pitch than the men's games. Camogie is played throughout Ireland although there are some fears that its popularity is on the wane, supplanted particularly by field hockey, once regarded as a foreign game, and the women's version of Gaelic football, which is a rapidly expanding sport in Ireland and beyond (Campbell 1997).

Unlike camogie, handball, described by McElligott (1984) as "an old game of uncertain age" (9), has been played for centuries in rural Ireland, and, as Healey (1998) observes, "Uniquely among Gaelic games, it has a thriving international dimension, being played in the United States, Canada, Australia, Mexico, Spain and other parts of Europe" (56). It resembles squash but is played with the hand rather than with a racket and although it has tended to be the poor relation among Gaelic games, at least in Ireland itself, it nevertheless continues to be honored as an element in the nation's distinctive sporting culture (McElligott 1984).

Initially, the strength of the GAA was confined to the southern half of the island—to Munster and south Leinster where secret societies and the factional tradition in Irish politics had long been influential and where, in addition, the ancient game of hurling had survived as a consequence of feudal and landlord encouragement since the time of the Norman settlement (Garvin 1981). Within a few years of its formation, the GAA had been taken over by members of the IRB who had defeated the Catholic clergy in the struggle to control the rapidly expanding Gaelic games movement. From that point onward, the GAA "was to become a central source of recruits to nationalist causes in Ireland in later years" (Garvin 1981, 65). The GAA, as Garvin (1981) observes, "by organising young men into football and hurling clubs, acted as a substitute for the old parish factions which had absorbed the energies of the young men in the pre-Famine period" (65). In time, indeed, the church began to recognize the benefits of the cultural *cordon sanitaire* provided by the GAA, and clergymen started to play a prominent role in the Association, one they have retained to the present day.

Indeed, despite the IRB's position in the early years of the GAA, constitutional nationalists continued to show an interest in the association and began to reassert their influence. The 1880s, however, were a difficult time for all nationalist organizations, the GAA included (Garvin 1981). Supporters of the great constitutional nationalist leader Charles Stewart

Parnell were prominent in the GAA during those years. Indeed, it is often argued that the association was to suffer for this in the wake of the O'Shea scandal in 1890, which ended Parnell's political career and severely damaged the work of his followers. In fact, according to Garvin (1981), the association was already in a period of temporary decline in any case. There is no denying, however, the GAA's support for Parnell. So highly was he regarded by members of the GAA that, when he died in 1891, six of them carried his coffin and thousands more, bearing black draped hurley sticks, marched with his cortege. However, during the last decade of the nineteenth century, it was the physical force nationalists as opposed to Parnell's successors in the constitutionalist tradition who assumed a growing role in the leadership of the GAA, and by the 1890s the IRB was still recruiting from its ranks (Garvin 1981).

However, despite the dominant position of IRB men within the GAA during the last years of the nineteenth century, the association continued to encompass all strands of Irish nationalist opinion. Indeed, according to Mandle (1987), "It is arguable that no organization had done more for Irish nationalism than the GAA" (69). As we shall see, the importance of the GAA to Irish nationalism is disputed in revisionist Irish historiography (Cronin 1996). But it was perhaps inevitable that when the Easter Rising of 1916 took place some Gaels would be intimately involved in the events as they unfolded while others would be just as taken aback as were most of their fellow citizens. Similarly in the Civil War that followed the rising and ended only with the signing of a treaty that brought twenty-six Irish counties under the authority of a newly established Irish Free State and left six of Ulster's nine counties under British jurisdiction, members of the GAA found themselves on both sides of the conflict.

The GAA had succeeded in uniting its membership around a shared love of Gaelic games and a general acceptance of what was involved in being an Irish nationalist. In order to do so, as we shall see, it had enforced fairly exclusivist rules, including a ban on playing and watching foreign games and a rule that stipulated that members of the crown (British) security forces could not join the GAA. Although these restrictions clearly had the effect of driving away most of the already small numbers of Protestant supporters of Gaelic games, they may well have helped to forge a sense of national affiliation that was able to transcend power struggles within the association and serious political schism beyond. However, the consequences of the treaty that had followed civil war presented new and far more formidable obstacles to the maintenance of this united front.

According to O'Halloran (1987), "Partition provided nationalist ideology with its greatest challenge" (xi). For many, it represented an attack on the Irish nationalist vision of Ireland. Somehow nationalists, both north and south, had to make sense of what had happened. In the newly established Irish Free State, this involved stereotyping the north and its inhabitants. As O'Halloran (1987) relates, "The depiction of Northern Ireland as a British colony of garrison enabled southern nationalists to respond in a traditional way to partition by diagnosing it as a problem of British origin, rather than the outcome of irreconcilable differences between the inhabitants of the island" (26) With this in mind, the new state's constitution asserted its territorial claim on the six counties of Northern Ireland and proclaimed an ongoing aspiration for a united and independent thirty-two county Irish republic. On the other hand, Northern Ireland, with its industrial and commercial infrastructure, was also seen as the antithesis of the nationalist vision of Ireland that was being projected by the Free State's president, Eamon de Valera. This contributed to the image of Northern Ireland as "a place apart" that, regardless of territorial claims and expressed nationalist aspirations, helped to secure the foundations of twenty-six-county nationalism. In turn, this inevitably impacted upon relations between northern and southern nationalists.

SPORTING NATIONALISM IN THE TWO IRELANDS

The partition of Ireland has had a huge impact on the relationship between the GAA and the reproduction of Irish nationalism. In the Free State (later the Irish Republic), the association and Gaelic games in general have played an important part in consolidating a sense of Irish national identity. While the latter has continued to include a vision of the unification of Ireland within a thirty-two-county republic, it has also helped to promote the existing political order and to celebrate the existence of the twenty-six county state as an independent political entity. For example, the early years during which the process of consolidating partition began witnessed the Tailteann Games, organized in part by the GAA. Thereafter, all-Ireland finals in both hurling and Gaelic football assumed a role similar to that played by major sporting occasions in England, with leading politicians in attendance and the contests themselves celebrated as national events. Ironically, from time to time these finals were contested by teams from the six counties of what had become known as Northern Ireland in which the meaning of the GAA and ambitions of many of its members remained very different.

According to Todd (1990), northern nationalism can be distinguished from Irish nationalism more generally. She writes, "Nationalism, for Northern nationalists, is not simply a romantic desire for a united Ireland" (32). It is also necessary to recognize both a sense of community (i.e., within the northern six counties) together with a desire for justice as constituent elements in their ideology. As Todd (1990) suggests, "The move from a sense of nationality to a desire for national unity and independence is by no means automatic" (33). Indeed, she argues, "Communalist identity and the desire for justice have always been important, and are especially so in the reconstituted forms of nationalism which emerged in the 1970s" (41). Despite having previously examined cleavages within Ulster unionism, Todd (1987) fails to address the divisions that exist within Irish nationalism in the north. For some nationalists, bolstered by a sense of communal identity, the pursuit of justice may appear to be able to stand alone. For others, it is necessarily contingent upon the struggle for national unification. Purer still is the nationalist vision that, in the short term at least, places the cause of Irish freedom above all other considerations. These divisions soon become apparent, as does the general distinction between northern and southern nationalism, when we come to consider further the role of the GAA in post-partition Ireland.

It is generally accepted that the attitudes of northern nationalists toward the Irish Republic are ambivalent to say the least. In general, there remains some sense that it is a kind of metaphorical "home" whereas the north, which is truly home, is tainted by unionism and is, therefore, at some level a hostile environment. On the other hand, with the declaration of an Irish Republic in 1945, it appeared to many northern nationalists that their southern compatriots had abandoned them, regardless of the retention of a constitutional claim on the six counties. This view has been strengthened over the years as increasing numbers of southerners lose interest in the ultimate nationalist vision of a united Ireland and content themselves instead with the twenty-six-county state. This affects some northern nationalists more than others. As O'Connor (1993) reports, "Northerners from the most troubled areas who have grown up with the Troubles are not disposed to make allowances for the South" (251). Developing the point, she quotes a woman from Ardoyne, in north Belfast, whose husband had been a republican prisoner.

> They can't get away from the fact that we are a part of this island—that I'm Irish and nobody's going to tell me anyway otherwise. We invested too much, I think, as a people, individually and collectively in this country, to be told that we're not part of the nation, not part of Ireland as a nation. (252)

It is a view that even a majority of moderate nationalists would share. Northern and southern Irish nationalisms have moved in different directions and inevitably their parting has profound implications for organizations such as the GAA which are central to Irish nationalism in general.

In the north of Ireland, the GAA has continued to play the same counterhegemonic role for which it first came into existence and northern Gaels have expressed little or no interest in the association's achievements as regards underlining the identity of the existing Irish Republic. Instead, they have seen Irish history and the role of Gaelic games in terms of unfinished business and have continued to regard the GAA as an embryonic form of the thirty-two-county national unity, which will be expressed politically only by way of unification. To a large extent, this interpretation of the GAA was forced upon many northern nationalists not only by the new of political arrangements but also as a result of the hostile attitudes of the unionist establishment in Northern Ireland (Bairner and Darby 1999). Although Gaelic games were not officially restricted, their significance was informally obscured. For example, the broadcasting of Gaelic results by the British Broadcasting Corporation in Northern Ireland was ended in 1934 in response to unionist complaints. Furthermore, throughout the period of the Stormont administration, there are reports of police and loyalist harassment of people participating in Gaelic games (Ruane and Todd 1996). During the conflict from 1969 onward the number of incidents of this sort increased. In addition, unionist-controlled local authorities obstructed the activities of the GAA. Members of the association were wounded and, in some cases, killed by loyalist paramilitaries and, on occasion, by members of the British security forces. GAA premises were attacked (Bairner and Darby 1999; Sugden and Bairner 1993).

It is undeniable that these events strengthened the sense of northern nationalist communalism together with the desire for justice. But they also fuelled the demand among many nationalists, GAA members included, for a united Ireland in a period when that aspiration was weakening considerably in the Irish Republic. The difference between these two outlooks became most apparent during the second half of the 1990s when the issue of the GAA's ban on membership by functionaries of the British security forces was brought under close scrutiny.

The original GAA bans, on foreign games and Royal Irish Constabulary membership, were enacted in 1885 and 1887 respectively and lifted soon afterward to be replaced in 1905 by a combined ban that threatened the suspension of GAA members found playing imported sports and prevented policemen and soldiers from taking part in Gaelic games. The comprehensive ban was finally removed in 1971 to be substituted with Rule 21, which is primarily concerned with the relationship between the GAA and members of the crown forces in Northern Ireland (Healey 1998).

The context within which discussions about Rule 21 took place was one of an improving political situation that had witnessed ceasefires by the main paramilitary organizations and talks involving most of Northern Ireland's political parties, and which was to result in an agreement that was put to the people of Ireland, north and south, was accepted by a majority of voters in each jurisdiction, and led to the establishment of a new Northern Ireland assembly together with cross-border institutions. Given the changed political climate, it was proposed in 1995 by members of the GAA, particularly in the Irish Republic but with some support from northern county boards, that the removal of Rule 21 would not only be possible to effect but could also be presented as the association's contribution to the peace process. But the proposal was rejected. Three years later, however, the GAA's new president, Joe McDonagh, believed that the political situation had moved on even farther and so initiated further debate on the ban in anticipation that it would finally be revoked.

As discussions progressed, however, it became increasingly obvious that there was likely to be considerable resistance to the removal of Rule 21 in the north. Two factors dominated the debate in Ulster. First, there was the feeling that despite signs of political progress, the Royal Ulster Constabulary (RUC) had not yet been disbanded or even undergone fundamental reform. In such circumstances, therefore, it could still be portrayed as precisely the same sectarian force it had always been and whose members had rightly been excluded from GAA membership. The same was said about the Royal Irish Regiment, a locally recruited regiment of the British Army and successor to the RUC's "B" Special Constabulary and the Ulster Defence Regiment. Second, in recent years, loyalist paramilitary organizations had intensified their campaign against GAA members and property. In a political context in which rumors and conspiracy theories abound, it is scarcely surprising that there were frequent suggestions in nationalist and republican circles that at least some of these attacks had taken place with security force collusion or, at the very least, nonintervention. With such arguments to the fore, it became obvious that many clubs in Ulster, especially in the six counties of Northern Ireland, would reject the bid to rescind Rule 21. The fact that only Ulster clubs would have to confront the practical implications of an ending of the ban meant that their reluctance carried considerable weight with certain southern representatives. The end result was that the GAA decided that, although it was its declared intention to remove Rule 21, this could not actually happen until policing reforms had been implemented in Northern Ireland.

This decision prompted extensive criticism throughout Ireland. Attacks by northern unionists were to be expected. But equally damning were comments by representatives of nationalism throughout the country. Passions were further inflamed in August 1998 when in the wake of the Omagh bomb that resulted in the deaths of twenty-nine people, some of whom even had strong GAA connections, the association refused to sanction the use of Healey Park in the town for a charity soccer match in aid of the victims. The informal ban on foreign games was invoked in the statement that only sports supported by the general council of the association could be permitted on GAA premises. It was interesting to note that such permission had been granted in the past to American football but soccer was clearly still perceived as an "English" game rather than simply a foreign one. Strong reactions to these GAA decisions could have been anticipated particularly given the optimism that surrounded the peace process and Good Friday agreement in certain quarters. But they are also given intellectual substance by revisionist interpretations of Irish history in general and the history of the GAA in particular.

Cronin (1996) identifies what he regards as "the GAA's self-perceived belief that it forms a central part of the force of Irish nationalism, and has operated both North and South of the border along these lines" (1). According to Cronin's revisionist analysis, it is a myth that, in the period 1884–1921, the association was central to the cause of Irish nationalism. Citing evidence from Rouse (1993), Cronin argues that the activities of the GAA in those formative years had more to do with ensuring its success as a sporting body than with the promotion of a particular political ideology. However, the belief in its own contribution to the nationalist cause "has meant that the GAA has been unable to move forward in the general spirit of the peace process" (Cronin 1996, 1). Instead, according to Cronin, "It has clung onto old dogmas and past history and has not attempted to create the new relationships needed to perpetuate peace" (1). Commenting specifically on developments in Northern Ireland generally and within the northern nationalist community in particular, Cronin asserts that "the GAA is existing in an historical backwater and is not prepared to deal with the current realities of the changing situation in Northern Ireland" (18). Specifically, "The nationalist community in the North, from which the GAA draws its members and its goodwill, no longer needs any advice about making the first move towards reconciliation" (18). Yet members of that northern nationalist community, not people who live outside that community on some republican fantasy island, have themselves instructed the GAA to retain Rule 21. While it may be unfortunate that they have chosen to do so, to claim that their decision was taken solely on the basis of some mythical reconstruction of the GAA's history is unhelpful.

Furthermore, to suggest that the GAA was relatively unimportant in the Irish nationalist struggle is to take a very narrow definition of the political. To offer as evidence the fact that only a minority of members were actively involved in politics is to miss the point. The GAA was (and is) important in terms of the politics of cultural resistance. Far from lessening its political importance, by becoming a successful sporting body, the GAA enhanced the counterhegemonic role it had been able to play in the past and that arguably it has continued to perform in Northern Ireland.

In fact, the reaction within nationalist circles, particularly in the south, to the GAA's refusal to remove Rule 21 immediately was indicative of a profound failure to understand fully the attitudes of northern nationalists, especially those who are most prominent in the GAA and who live in those areas of the six counties where Gaelic games play a significant part in community life. In those circles, there remains a profound suspicion, often bordering on hatred, of the British Army and the RUC. The fact that the security forces appear to harass GAA members on a regular basis and that in some instances, most notably in Crossmaglen in south Armagh, they had actually commandeered Gaelic grounds for their own purposes have done little to establish feelings of trust. Arguments that, by removing Rule 21 and making a generous gesture toward the security forces, the GAA could win a significant propaganda victory largely fell on deaf ears as regards the feelings of a majority of club members. The first gesture, they argued, should come from the security forces themselves. It has also been unhelpful to link Rule 21 with the informal ban on foreign games that persists in certain GAA circles. The refusal to allow GAA facilities to be used for a charity soccer match, or indeed any soccer match, is plainly nonsensical. Soccer's popularity in Ireland, even among the overwhelming majority of GAA members, is enormous. Rather than seek to compete with this universal game, the GAA must simply learn to live with it. Living with the RUC, however, is an altogether more daunting proposition.

In time, of course, Rule 21 will almost certainly be removed and the GAA will become even more like any other sporting organization with membership open to all, although by no means wholly inclusive in practice. In most societies, however, practical restrictions on membership are linked, for the most part, to gender and/or social class. Regarding the GAA, on the other hand, it is likely that, whatever the formal arrangements, membership in Northern Ireland will continue to be restricted to those with a particular view, even if it is held unconsciously, of the relationship between sport and Irish nationalism and, in the Irish Republic, to those from the communities and educational institutions in which an attachment to such a view remains influential. It is difficult to state categorically how the GAA will interact with Irish sporting nationalism in the years ahead. If hurling becomes less popular than ever then a symbolically important aspect of the association's contribution will be lost. Indeed, with this in mind, a leading historian of the game argues that the government should take action.

> Hurling is the oldest recorded field game. It is a link with our heroic
> past, part of our cultural heritage and part of what we are. It is still a
> strong and virile game, a game worth going a long way to see and one
> preserving. It is as much a part of our heritage as our language and our

music, and just as the Government considers itself duty bound to preserve them and to expend money in doing so, any help or subsidization
required for the preservation of hurling should be forthcoming from the
same source. (King 1998, 265)

It is clear, however, that Irish sporting nationalism of a sort could withstand the demise of hurling and even diminished interest in other games
that are administered by the GAA. Indeed, it is likely that playing games
and participating in other sporting activities will become even less mutually exclusive than is presently the case and that other ways of representing Irishness through sport will both complement and undermine the
Gaelic vision.

GAELIC GAMES GO GLOBAL?

In terms of the reproduction of sporting nationalism, Gaelic games suffer
from one serious deficiency. The fact that hurling, Gaelic football, and
camogie are virtually unique to Ireland and to the Irish diaspora means
that opportunities for international competition are severely restricted. In
one sense, this does nothing to weaken the importance of Gaelic games to
the definition of Irishness. Indeed, having national pastimes that are
unique is a privileged position to be in as regards consolidating a nation's
identity. But there is a problem. The national games of other peoples are
frequently assigned some mystical status precisely because they offer
opportunities to compete with other nations and to feel good about one's
own nation at moments of triumph or even glorious defeat. The national
games of the Irish, on the other hand, are insular affairs.

Largely in response to this failing on the part of games played under
their auspices, the GAA has sought to export Gaelic games and also to
foster links with nations that play similar games. As a consequence, compromise rules games have been staged between Irish hurlers and Scottish
shinty players and between Gaelic and Australian Rules footballers.
Contests involving the latter have taken place in 1984, 1986, 1987, 1990,
1998, and, most recently, in 2000. But whether these have successfully
provided Gaelic games with a secure international stage upon which to
perform remains highly debatable. For one thing, much of the publicity
the contests have received has owed more to on-field violence than to the
ability of the players or even the results. Moreover, a feeling has grown in
Australia that the rules are heavily biased in favor of the Gaelic players
and that the GAA needs these international contacts more than the Australian Football League (AFL). Aussie Rules fans have largely accepted
the fact that theirs is not an international game. As Ashley Browne wrote
in a Dublin paper, on the morning of the day when the 1998 series of
games began, "It never has been and never will be" (*Sunday Tribune*, 11

October 1998). So why are compromise rules games played? The explanation, according to Browne, lies in the fact that those who run the AFL, like their GAA counterparts, believe their game can be internationalized. Browne states that "what the AFL doesn't seem to understand is that the average football supporter doesn't care that it is not an international sport." Thus, there is no concern that a national sport must involve international competition. Browne is happy to see Australian Rules go it alone.

> We have a great game in Australia, one we think is the best in the world. It doesn't need an international compromise to make it any better, which is why the interest back here is lukewarm at best. (*Sunday Tribune*, 11 October 1998)

So why then does the GAA persevere with such contests when the very same arguments could be made in favor of Gaelic games? One reason is clearly financial. But there is obviously a feeling within the Gaelic fraternity that international links in some way enhance the status of Gaelic games and of Ireland more generally. It may be that this owes something to feelings of inadequacy when confronted with Britain's achievements in terms of the export of games and, through this, its establishment of sporting contact with the far corners of the globe. The GAA wishes to show that it has overseas friends too and does not simply occupy a small and parochial sporting space. But Irish sport does not need the GAA, any more than Australian sport needs the AFL, to provide opportunities for international sporting contacts. Indeed, it has long been apparent that to be Irish, in the world of sport, does not require participation in Gaelic games. What may be at issue, however, is the matter of what it means to be Irish.

IRISH NATIONALISM AND "FOREIGN" GAMES

With the exception of many, but by no means all, Ulster unionists, most of those who play universal and even British games in Ireland would regard themselves as patriotically Irish. Irish representative teams wear the emblems of the nation and stand to the Irish national anthem. Moreover unlike Gaelic players, they have the opportunity to represent their country regularly in international competition. From the standpoint of Gaelic sporting purism, Ireland's rugby, soccer, and field hockey players may have sold out, but in the real world in which most people, including most ordinary GAA members, live, they are recognized as being proud of their national identity and interested in promoting the interests of the nation by way of those sports in which they have a background and at which they have exhibited most prowess. They do not become English nor, indeed, fully cosmopolitan simply because they have turned their back on Gaelic games. In addition, they may well choose to compete at the highest level in a particular sport but that need not mean that they have no interest in watching or even playing other games. Throughout Ireland there are examples of people playing Gaelic games and soccer and there is even a well-established transfer between Gaelic and rugby, although not in the north, where the educational system and the resultant image of the game as belonging to the unionist tradition make it off limits to all but a handful of nationalists. In an area of the Irish Republic such as Limerick where rugby is the most popular team sport it would be nonsensical to regard the local population as being less Irish than those who live in the counties most associated with Gaelic games. Indeed, since rugby, like most other sports in Ireland, is organized on a thirty-two-county basis, regardless of its origins, it endorses what for most republicans can be described as Irish territorial integrity (something that, as has been seen, makes it contentious in the eyes of some Ulster unionists). More problematic is the role of soccer in the construction and reproduction of Irish national identity for the simple reason that here is a foreign game that has actually reflected, at organizational level, the partition of Ireland. This raises the question of how nationalists should view the two "national" soccer teams.

As was revealed earlier, the continued existence of a separate Northern Ireland team is of considerable symbolic importance to Ulster unionists. Here is one clear piece of evidence that Northern Ireland does, in fact, exist as a distinct entity rather than a community merely imagined by them. Given that this leads to the unionist and loyalist trappings that tend to surround the Northern Ireland team, it is hardly surprising that few nationalists in the north lend their support irrespective of how many Catholic players are actually in the national side. The fact that during the 1980s in particular the Republic of Ireland also had a more successful team was an added incentive for northern nationalists to withdraw their support from a team for which they had in the past shown greater enthusiasm. With a handful of exceptions, usually members of a slightly older generation or those such as the republican prisoner who told the author that he could support neither Northern Ireland nor the Republic as both teams were the product of partition, northern nationalists support the Irish Republic. In so doing they join forces with soccer fans from the south as well as from the Irish diaspora (Free 1998). What emerges is a far from monolithic approach to the relationship between football and Irish nationalism.

It has been suggested by Giulianotti (1996) that the essence of recent support for the Irish Republic's soccer team is carnivalesque and there are certainly numerous examples of Irish fans conforming to this description. Moreover, many of the supporters who have helped to add this element to Irish soccer fandom also involve themselves in virtually every major sporting occasion in which there is some Irish involvement, from the Cheltenham Festival to the All-Ireland hurling final. Giulianotti (1996) also expands on an argument made earlier by Holmes (1994) and Cronin (1994; 1996) that the success of the national side, especially under the leadership of Jack Charlton, was interwoven with social and cultural developments in contemporary Ireland. These include the emergence of pluralistic society, the development of a more mature attitude toward the British (and specifically the English) and, perhaps most pertinently, the growth of twenty-six-county Irish nationalism. Again, there is much truth in the argument. But there remains the additional factor of northern nationalist support which brings with it the sectarianized politics of the north and, consciously or unconsciously, transforms support for the Irish's soccer team into a proclamation of loyalty to an, as yet, unattained thirty-two-county republic. Thus, soccer's relationship with Irish sporting nationalism is multifaceted. How and why a particular fan supports the "national" team or even chooses to play the game of soccer depends to a considerable extent on the socioeconomic and political context in which that person finds himself or herself.

Soccer's links with urbanization and industrialization are as apparent in Ireland as in other parts of the world. It is also, of course, the sport of the working class in Ireland, as it is in Britain and in many other countries. It is manifestly the most popular team sport in the northern cities of Belfast and Derry and, in many urban areas of the Irish Republic where it is at least as highly regarded as Gaelic games. In Belfast, for example, it was a soccer team, Belfast Celtic, as opposed to Gaelic games, which did most to inspire a sense of sporting nationalism among Catholics during the first half of the twentieth century (Coyle 1999). Furthermore, soccer's appeal has been seen increasingly not only in the numbers of people who play and watch the game in these cities and towns themselves but also in the tens of thousands who follow the fortunes of teams in Scotland and England. As with a preference for British sports, however, an affinity with an English soccer club should not be taken as evidence of a growing threat to Irish sporting nationalism. Support for the Scottish Premier League club Celtic, for example, is bound up with Irish national identity. However, even support for an English club with no sectarian connotations need not signify a weakening of the fan's Irishness. Rather, it reveals the degree to which individuals possess multiple identities. Supporting Manchester United, the Republic of Ireland, and an Irish League or League of Ireland team are not mutually exclusive. Nor are supporting an English soccer team and playing hurling or Gaelic football.

SPORT, NATIONALITY, AND THE NEW IRELAND

It is apparent that sport has been deeply implicated in the construction of an Irish national identity or, to be more accurate, of Irish national identities. But to what extent is this linkage, and indeed that which contributes to the development of unionist identities as well, threatened by the process known as globalization? Alternatively, is there evidence that sporting identities in Ireland can succeed in resisting the forces of globalization? If one chooses the GAA as the central element in the latter, then there is some room for concern. Gaelic games, especially football, are still phenomenally popular. The perceived threat to hurling, however, is significant at least at the symbolic level. More important by far though is the increasing opposition to the GAA that has emanated from other sections of Irish national opinion. In the eyes of some, it stands condemned as an outdated organization which has little real relationship to the new Ireland that has emerged in recent years. From this perspective, it is essential that the Irish turn in even greater numbers to the more globally popular sporting pastimes and leave the past behind. The problem with such an analysis, however, is that it is rooted in a cosmopolitan, urban perspective that remains alien to the lives of many Irish people. The GAA may not have any meaning for the middle-class inhabitants of the more exclusive neighborhoods of south Dublin. But it remains, along with the Catholic church, as a major element in the social and cultural lives of a great many other Irish people on both sides of the border. The GAA does face serious challenges. Even if it fails to meet these, however, its loss of status would not signal the collapse of sporting nationalism in Ireland at the feet of the onward march of globalization.

With the exception of basketball, American sports have had a negligible impact in Ireland. American football is played by a handful of Irishmen and watched on television by rather more. Baseball has no presence although the use of baseball bats in paramilitary punishment beatings provides an interesting example of glocalization, not least because these "weapons" replaced hurling sticks in republican circles in response to claims that the use of the latter was detrimental to the image of Gaelic games. Hockey is now being played seriously at the Odyssey Arena in Belfast. All of the players are foreign, mainly Canadian. Their team, the Belfast Giants, plays in the British Super League. It is too early as yet to discern if the Giants will be successful either on the ice or in terms of attracting cross-community support.

It would be difficult even to argue that American influences have impacted upon Ireland's preferred sporting options. Certainly neither soccer nor rugby have undergone the kind of transformation that has occurred in England and, to a lesser extent, Scotland. Meanwhile, although Gaelic games, especially football, have moved in the direction of corporate sponsorship and greater professionalism, it is difficult to see this as the product of American sporting imperialism. The global force at work in this instance is capitalism rather than Americanization.

The case of basketball, however, is interesting although again primarily as an example of globalization rather than as testimony to the potency of American cultural imperialism. Whether one regards it as American or, by this stage in its development, universal, this imported game is popular with men and women throughout Ireland, being played widely in schools as well as in a national league structure. In the north, however, although played socially by both nationalists and unionists in schools, in terms of competitive matches and senior participation, basketball has come to be regarded as a nationalist game. In a society where perception counts for so much, this will be a difficult label to shed. Thus, a sport with no sectarian connotations arrives in Ireland and, instead of being able to transcend identity divisions, is soon linked to a particular tradition. The local and the global coincide and, arguably, in a charged political context, the local still takes precedence. In the Irish Republic, on the other hand, where the politics of identity are less concerned than in the past with nationality, basketball fits in with an increasingly inclusive sporting culture. Even there, however, it is doubtful whether those who play for representative teams are any less proud to be Irish than are the Gaelic footballers or the hurlers.

Overall, it is difficult to see how imported sports can develop given that the space they would need to occupy is already overcrowded by soccer, Gaelic football, and rugby union. In terms of participation and interest, far more successful than American sports in Ireland have been the martial arts and other physical activities imported originally from the Far East. It is possible that, like boxing, these have helped to channel violent impulses in more positive directions than those offered by political violence. The fact that the violence has continued, despite their presence, however, reveals the extent to which cultural resistance is deep rooted and frequently impervious to global forces. Moreover, this is as true of sport as it is of politics especially in contexts where the relationship between the two is particularly strong. Even at this stage, are we forced to conclude that only in the United States of America themselves has the Americanization of sport really taken place? The next chapter examines the role of sport in the construction and reproduction of an American national identity mindful of the possibility, however remote, that it may one day become a global identity.

chapter five

Isolation or Expansion?

NATIONALISM AND SPORT IN THE UNITED STATES

SPORT AND AMERICAN IDENTITY

At numerous gatherings of international scholars involved in the academic study of sport, the author has consistently been struck by the lack of interest shown by American colleagues in the relationship between sport and nationalism. In sessions devoted to this issue, the Europeans are there, as are the Canadians, the Australians, and the South Americans. But the Americans are usually absent, off to talk about sport and race, sport and gender, the political economy of sport, and so on. Why? According to one school of thought, to which many Americans themselves subscribe, it is because nationality is less of an issue for Americans than it is for most other people. The United States has its own national sports culture, albeit partly shared, as we shall see, with Canada. This might in itself be regarded as clear evidence of a link between sport and national identity that demands academic assessment. But there is a problem inasmuch as American sports do not easily lend themselves to international competition. At the highest level of spectator sport, city plays against city. Or rather, corporate franchise takes on corporate franchise. It is the foreigners with their commitment to universal sports such as soccer who are consumed by issues surrounding nationality and national identity. But this is to take a rather narrow view of the links between sport and nationalism. In fact, the reasons why this relationship concerns so many people, academic and otherwise, relate only to a very limited degree to the existence of international competition. What really interests most commentators is the extent to which sport is implicated in the construction of certain national identities and how effectively it is able to unite people around a sense of common purpose. In this respect, the United States is by no means exceptional since, as we shall see, sport has played a vital role in the construction and reproduction of a national identity or national identities despite, or arguably because of, the paucity of international competition. As Wilcox (1994) observes, "The United States is a nation barely emerging from infancy wherein its identity is weak and veiled in a shroud of uncertainty" but "patriotism remains an all powerful element throughout American sport" (75).

International competition is necessarily a part of the process whereby sport and the construction of national identities are related and, despite America's unique sporting culture, Americans themselves are by no means immune to the sensations that surround international sporting rivalries. The actions of golfer Dottie Pepper during the 1998 Solheim Cup were a clear indication of how passionate Americans can be about playing for their nation. In the words of one British journalist, David Davies, her "obnoxious behaviour" on the golf course "would see her banned from any golf club with even half an eye on etiquette" (*Guardian*, 22 September 1998). On the other hand, the fact that America's victory in the Solheim Cup meant very little to most Americans also tells us something about the relationship between sport and national identity in the United States. Similar intense emotions were made public during the 1999 Ryder Cup. But, for the most part, Americans are more concerned with the domestic rivalries that are fought out in their unique sporting environment than they are with international competition. What is evident in both forms of sporting contest, however, is the fact that sport matters to Americans. Precisely how it matters tells us a great deal about the United States as a nation and about how Americans regard themselves.

To that extent sport is intimately bound up with what it means to be American, with what unites the nation, if indeed we can even speak of an American nation as opposed to a nation-state, but also, and more often, what divides it. For that reason, the lack of interest in this issue, shown for example by American sports sociologists, is not only unfortunate but is reflective of the very real problems Americans in general have when dealing with questions of national identity. Whether one believes in the inevitability of Americanization or not, one cannot ignore the extent to which the American way of doing certain things has been exported to other parts of the world. This can be described as a process of national expansionism or, to be more ideological, cultural imperialism. Yet Americans, as we shall see, are also pleased to celebrate their own national sporting identities domestically. Thus, the course of American sport history has been characterized by a tension between expansionism and isolationism.

According to Mrozek (1995), the American people have a deep and special relationship with the physical experience of their fellow citizens. This is connected to a search for heroes, a belief in rugged individualism, and an espousal of the strenuous life (Crepeau 1980; Gorn and Goldstein 1993). Seldom has the linkage of sport, courage, and the national interest been more vividly demonstrated than in 1898 when the future president, Theodore Roosevelt, led his Rough Riders up San Juan Hill in Cuba in an imperialist, military adventure. Alongside him, as Gorn and Goldstein (1993) report, rode not only cowboys and frontiersmen but also "a Yale quarterback, Princeton's tennis champion, a renowned polo player and athletes from Boston's Somerset Club and New York's Knickerbocker Club" (149). From the time of the Spanish-American war onward, the links between American sport and the military have been extensive and profound (Wakefield 1997). But there have been numerous other connections between sport and Americanism that owe little to the armed forces but are nevertheless important.

Like Ireland, the United States of America succeeded in constructing its own sporting culture despite colonial links with Britain. Unlike Ireland, however, the Americans have been far more successful in marginalizing those sports that have remained British at least at the symbolic level if not in terms of where they are now actually played. The explanations for this achievement are relatively obvious. The colonists fought to end British rule in their country and were consequently keen to develop a culture that had broken with British paternalism. Second, these events took place well before the nineteenth-century modern sporting revolution had taken place. This meant that British sporting hegemony was not as serious a threat in the United States as it was to become in Ireland. Third, successive waves of immigrants, most of them no longer from Britain and with, at that stage, no particular interest in the British sports culture, embraced American sports quite readily. Finally, the United States were quickly to be transformed into such a large and diverse nation that sporting competition between one locality and another came to assume major significance. Although amusing at one level, the idea that the climax to the major league baseball season can be called the "World" Series is not wholly nonsensical. To call the All-Ireland hurling final the "world" championship. however, would be to stretch credulity too far.

SPORT IN EARLY AMERICA

Sports and games were being played in what is now known as the United States of America long before the actual foundation of the state. The First Nation peoples possessed a games culture that included embryonic forms of the modern sport of lacrosse. More relevant, however, in terms of the subsequent development of the American nation, were the sporting activities of the colonists. These were largely inherited from England and included hunting, horse racing, and cock fighting. The seventeenth-century puritans sought to discourage certain activities, but outside of New England and in the southern colonies, in particular, a lively and extensive sporting culture emerged. As Rader (1996) records, "Central to Southern sporting life was the growth of the powerful landed gentry" (10). It was they who played an especially vital role in laying the foundations of America's sports culture, and not only in the South. According to Gorn and Goldstein (1993), "By the eve of the Revolution . . . wealthy gentry men—Northern and Southern, rural and urban, mercantile and agricultural—had helped foster sporting traditions on American soil" (42). In the nineteenth century these elite groups continued to be the main proponents of a sporting culture. For Mrozek (1983), "Sport's rise to prominence hinged on its attainment of respectability among the middle and upper classes, whose support did not dictate what character sport must have but whose opposition could have frustrated and slowed the emergence of sport while pressuring it into different forms" (xiii).

For many of these gentlemen, engaging in sporting contests had originally represented an affirmation of their "Englishness" as opposed to the construction of a distinctive American identity (Gorn and Goldstein 1993). With independence, however, together with the massive transformation of American society during the nineteenth century, a new identity (or new identities) began to emerge. This period between 1825 and 1870 witnessed "the transformation of harness racing from a pre-modern to a modern sport" (Adelman 1988, 129). More generally, this was a period during which communication and transport improved and urbanization increased. These factors alone made the construction of a national sporting culture more possible to achieve. At least as significantly, however, the reconstruction of American society after the Civil War coincided with the era in which the modern sports culture established itself, first in Britain and then elsewhere. As Oriard (1982) claims, "Only after the Civil War did sport for the masses truly emerge, with an impetus from many sources" (3). One of the most important of these was the emergence of an American national consciousness (Mrozek 1983). Therefore, the popularization of sport in America no longer involved the promotion of British games to any significant degree. According to Mrozek (1983), "After the Civil War, America became a unitary political entity; and many leaders sought a unitary culture to ensure its continuity" (xvi). Inevitably the development of American sport interacted with this development of American society as a whole. The search was on, as Mrozek (1983) observes, for sports that "were national in scope and 'Americanizing' in effect" (xvi).

By the end of the nineteenth century, according to Gorn and Goldstein (1993), "athletics were enlisted in the cause of the new social alignments and ideologies" (99). One of the most significant of these was nationalism. According to Mrozek (1983), "The instinct toward nationalism—which showed itself in America in such varied forms as the movement toward immigration restriction, overseas imperialism, and the standardization of a domestic culture—created a kind of constituency of sentiment favoring sports supposed to foster an identifiably American character" (161). Rader (1988) reports that "the history of nineteenth century sport clubs reflected the process of acculturation by distinctive ethnic groups" (141). As the twentieth century approached many immigrant groups had adopted the indigenous sporting culture as concurrently the need for ethnic community subsided. The demise of the German Turnvereins and also of Caledonian clubs can be linked to their image as both premodern and un-American (Mrozek 1983). Sport had become intimately involved in the construction and reproduction of an American national identity in particular by assisting the transcendence of ethnic, racial, and linguistic differences.

The 1860s and 1870s witnessed a rapid expansion of sport as standardization came about on a national basis and commercial backing grew. In the period 1876–1926, a national sporting culture firmly established itself in the United States (Pope 1997). This was aided considerably by developments in the media which, in turn, assisted the formation of an American sporting audience. Sport had become a form of social glue (Pope 1997). During this period, many of the nation's main sporting bodies were founded, including baseball's National League in 1876 and American League six years later. Sports such as golf and tennis experienced a rapid growth in their popularity during the 1880s while American football and track and field were also properly formalized as widely popular activities.

In the process, there emerged a distinct American sporting culture in which considerable emphasis was placed on the team sports of baseball, American football, basketball, and hockey (although the latter, as shall be argued in the next chapter, has remained more closely linked to a separate Canadian national identity). Indeed, it has been shown that the emphasis on team sports as opposed to individual activities is itself a peculiarly American characteristic. Of these American games, arguably the most significant, in terms of representations of what it means to be American, is baseball.

Baseball: The National Pastime

As early as the mid-1850s, according to Rader (1996), "the baseball fraternity began to promote their sport as 'the national game'" (51). By the

1880s, Story (1995) reports, "baseball became what can only be described as a mass cultural movement, a large-scale, passionate American affair on the scale and intensity of other mass movements such as revivalism or temperance, and capable, therefore, of creating a bedrock of players and 'cranks' on which promoters and sponsors would build" (121). Certainly at this stage the level of public interest shown in professional baseball was unprecedented (Rader 1996). Certain factors involved in the growth of baseball have been identified—specific working-class occupations, Irish ethnicity, masculinity, the development of a railroad-based entertainment industry, and increased sponsorship (Story 1995). But the question remains: Why baseball? The answer, according to Story (1995), is obvious. Men loved it for the simple reason that it satisfied their need for comradeship, recognition, and order.

There is a legend that the rules of modern baseball were first set out in Cooperstown in 1839 by Abner Doubleday, a student at a military school and later to become a general in the Civil War. According to Pope (1997), "The myth about baseball's U.S. birth began to materialize in 1889 at New York's Delmonico's Restaurant, where a celebrity crowd gathered to honor a group of baseball players who had just returned from a well-publicized world tour . . ." (69). Since then, the Doubleday myth concerning baseball's origins has remained a key feature of the game's attraction. It provides baseball with purely American origins. The suggestion that it was merely a development of the English game, rounders, was unacceptable both in terms of establishing the credentials of a distinctive American sports culture and also, more generally, as regards the broader issue of what it meant to be an American. As Pope (1997) expresses it, "While true, the idea that baseball had evolved from a wide variety of British stick-and-ball games, did not suit the mythology of a phenomenon that had become so quintessentially American" (71). The Doubleday myth, on the other hand, links the game to the youth of America. It connects baseball to a military figure and provides it with rural origins (Crepeau 1980). As a result it helps to establish the link between baseball and core values of an older way of American life. It is an invented tradition but no less significant for that. Indeed, it was not until the 1920s and 1930s that the rural mystique that surrounds the game began to lose some of its importance. By then, according to Mrozek (1983), baseball's claim as a national sport "did not depend upon its rural associations, which in any case were much more myth than fact" (172).

> Rather, baseball thrived because it had the same scientific and social
> inclusiveness that promoters saw in football and thus matched as well as
> molded the purported national character. (172)

It is certainly true, as Zingg (1988) observes, that "baseball's claim as the national pastime strikes home in ways that go well beyond its alleged connection to a legitimate folk heritage in the play and games of the American people" (355) It also reflected the spirit of capitalism, and prominent businessmen, most notably Albert G. Spalding, began to promote it as a marketable commodity. According to Pope (1997), "The invention of the American baseball tradition, like most other invented traditions during this period, was principally a middle- and upper-class endeavor" (77–78). Spalding, who had played baseball for the Boston Red Stockings and established a multi-million dollar sports equipment business, "worked tirelessly to exploit baseball as America's national game" (Zingg 1988, 355). In so doing, he and others like him sought to ensure the persistence of a bourgeois cultural hegemony that facilitated the interests of American capital.

"By the second decade of the twentieth century," according to Pope (1997), "claims about baseball's nationally unifying characteristics were ubiquitous in American social commentary" (77). Indeed, in the opinion of Crepeau (1980), between the two world wars, baseball established itself as "the undisputed National Pastime" (ix). It did so by reflecting and helping to strengthen American values—democracy, opportunity, fair play, individualism, team spirit, and competitiveness. Whether these values actually operated either in baseball or in American society as a whole and how far they can all even coexist are debatable issues. What matters, however, is that large numbers of Americans believed in these values and in their link to baseball. Baseball was the game of the common man, even though it was run as a profit-making concern by far from common men. The game reflected the principles of democracy and equality of opportunity upon which the American Dream rested. Thus, Crepeau (1980) submits, "as the National Pastime, baseball also became a means of expressing American nationalism" (x). According to Crepeau (1980), "Baseball and Americanism belonged together" (66). Baseball, in the words of Kimmel (1990), is "truly an American game" (65). Certainly the annual opening of the baseball season was and remains a matter of patriotic pride. The linkage of baseball with Fourth of July celebrations is almost as old as the game itself. According to Pope (1997), "Fourth-of-July baseball games since the Civil War both popularized the emergent game and linked it to the modern American character" (103). The singing of the National Anthem before matches, which has become a regular feature since World War II, further unites the game and the nation as does the pre-match appearance of High School color guards. Nor should one ignore the fact that so many American presidents have associated themselves with sport in general and baseball in particular, thereby establishing, in the minds of the American people, a link between baseball and the nation-state. Warren Harding, for example, used baseball as an electoral tool and by 1922 was being described as "the president of the fans" (Pope 1997, 75). As we have seen, however, with the Fourth of July rituals, government patronage was by no means the only way in which the interests of the nation-state were associated with baseball. As Pope (1997) points out, "National loyalty and patriotism were also promoted through sports rituals and pageantry that linked baseball and nationalism" (77).

During those interwar years, American society evolved from being predominantly rural-agrarian to becoming increasingly urban-industrial, resulting in problems and tensions that were reflected as much in the world of baseball as elsewhere in the United States. America's common response, writes Crepeau (1980), took the form of "holding onto the values of the rural past while, at the same time, embracing the new urban society" (x), and this was also "the most common response to change in the baseball world" (xi). Dyreson (1995) argues that "the increasing popularity of professional baseball in the 1920s furnishes some instructive insights into the changing role of sport in consumer culture" (217). There remained an identification with liberalism and some of the more traditional American values. At the same time, commercialism and sensationalism (the importance of the "home run" for example) began to take center stage. The Chicago White Sox match-fixing scandal of 1919 was a shattering experience for many Americans, and not only those who followed baseball. There was disbelief but also the widespread fear that the world clearly was in disarray. An example was required and, according to Crepeau (1980), "Baseball entered the Twenties preparing to defend standards, ethics, morals, patriotism, and the remaining eternal verities . . ." (23). The transformation of baseball, however, was rooted in more general trends in American society of which the growth of a consumer culture was only one of many. In this sense, there is much truth in Kimmel's (1990) description of baseball as "a metaphor for America" (55).

One of the most dramatic developments in modern America was the migration of huge numbers of people from rural communities to the rapidly growing cities. The game of baseball moved with them, not only physically but in some metaphysical sense as well. Indeed, for many young men, the game provided them with a sense of belonging otherwise absent from their new life experience. Thus, Story (1995) writes of "the surrogate family ambience of team sports" (132).

As Crepeau (1980) suggests, "Major-league baseball was an urban phenomenon and became a target for civic pride" (49). It assumed this role at an early stage. For example, Carter (1988) relates how baseball was a key element in the rivalry for "great city" status between St. Louis and Chicago in the 1860s and 1870s, and indeed becoming home to professional sports franchises, those of baseball included, has remained an important weapon in the arsenal of any city engaged in the modern process of civic boosterism. Baseball's other immediate function, although more debatable, is no less significant. According to Crepeau (1980), "It is possible that baseball served as a familiar point of reference to the rural Americans newly arrived in the city" (49). In this respect too, the game may have contributed to the construction of American national identity.

> The baseball press exhibited a certain amount of xenophobia. The city was portrayed by some writers as an alien element in American culture because it housed a large non-Anglo-Saxon immigrant population. (58)

The hope was, however, that baseball itself would help to "Americanize" these immigrants. In fact, baseball was able both to strengthen group identities (for example, that of the Irish Americans or those of German extraction) while simultaneously promoting Americanism (Gorn and Goldstein 1993). According to Pope (1997), "Baseball provided second-generation immigrants acceptance and identity as Americans" (73). Certainly, as Pope (1997) notes, "In an increasingly heterogeneous society, many Americans found it difficult to define the precise nature of national identity" (9). "Paradoxically," he continues, "the United States, one of the most clearly defined modern nations, faced a perplexing problem of national identity" (10). Undoubtedly, sport generally and baseball in particular were of considerable help in answering questions about what it meant to be an American, but only for certain sections of the population. For many years, for example, other groups were excluded from major league baseball. As Crepeau describes it, "Baseball was portrayed as a force for democracy, opportunity, and Americanization; it was a microcosm of the great American melting pot" (163). Yet, the Ku Klux Klan were active in the National Pastime and "if American baseball was a melting pot, the Jew had difficulty melting and the black American never got into the pot" (Crepeau 1980, 165), or at least not until after World War II. Up to that point, as Riess (1988) argues, "baseball's democratic ideology did not extend to Black Americans, who were completely excluded from professional baseball because of racial prejudice" (262).

Informally baseball's National League had enforced a "color ban" aimed at both players and clubs since its formation in 1876. But some black players played for professional teams in other leagues. However, one such organization, the International League, under pressure from journalistic opinion and the protests of certain white players, decided, in 1887, to prohibit the admission of additional black players to its organization. In the course of that year, moreover, the situation worsened until African Americans found themselves excluded from all "white" professional teams (Rader 1996). This situation was to persist until after World War II. Indeed, it was not until the arrival of Jackie Robinson with the

Brooklyn Dodgers in 1947 that the exclusion of African Americans from major league baseball finally came to an end.

That this event happened was again a reflection of changes in American society. First, the contribution of African Americans to the war effort had helped to enhance their status as true Americans. Second, countless numbers of African Americans had flooded into the cities that were home to major league franchises. What better way to tap the potential new market than to start to sign African American players. In return, however, the latter, including Robinson himself, were expected not to rock the political boat with controversial statements on race issues.

In various ways, therefore, baseball attuned itself to the modern age. In recent years, however, it has been obliged to confront a further range of problems. According to an article in *Time* magazine (27 July 1998), in 1998 "baseball accidentally saved itself, with a mixture of talent and nostalgia" (42). The background against which this claim must be understood is one of conflict between management and players, resulting in a strike that brought the 1994 season to a premature end, and of a product that had become increasingly difficult to sell to a public that appeared far more attracted to the instant fix of a sport such as basketball than the slow ebb and flow of what had once been regarded without any shadow of doubt as America's national pastime. Some extremely gloomy forecasts were made.

> [W]hatever happens, the game will have lost its special, almost mythological, standing in America. Baseball will return someday. The national pastime, though, is dead. (Verducci 1995)

During the summer of 1998, however, the American people rediscovered baseball. Here is the game of one's ancestors and a constant reminder of an earlier, more pastoral period in American history. Even in the great cities, to go to the ballpark is to return to some half-remembered world far removed from the downtown skyscrapers and busy freeways. This is epitomized in the words of the game's own anthem, "Take Me Out to the Ball Game," and testified to by the fact that crucial to the design of new baseball stadia is the attempt to recreate the past while at the same time merging it with modern (or postmodern) consumerist demands. The seventh inning stretch and the singing of baseball's anthem are as much part of any game as the pitching, batting, and other onfield activities, as indeed is the consumption of favorite baseball foods. The juxtaposition of ivy clad walls and shopping malls becomes a potent marketing combination. The Baltimore Orioles' $105 million Camden Yards ballpark, for example, has become a tourist attraction precisely because of the combination of nostalgia and present-day consumerism, with even its ushers wearing bow ties and suspenders (Pope 1997).

Similarly, the contest between Mark McGwire of the St. Louis Cardinals and Sammy Sosa of the Chicago Cubs to beat Roger Maris's record of home runs hit in a single season helped to bring the crowds back to baseball in 1998. While this was a contest that was acted out in the present, it also evoked memories of baseball in the past, particularly during that period when the "homer" first became one of the game's major selling points (Crepeau 1980). The race for the record number of home runs in a season was somewhat clouded by the revelation that one of the front runners, McGwire, had taken androstenedione which is directly converted by the body into testosterone, elevated levels of which help athletes to train harder, recover more quickly, and increase power and muscle for quick-burst athletic activity (*USA Today*, 26 August 1998). To all intents and purposes, however, McGwire's admission of "guilt" could scarcely compete in the battle for news time with the American passion for record breaking in the National Pastime.

In any case, there was perhaps another issue involved, one that sheds further light on the relationship between sport and being American. Although McGwire and Sosa were inextricably linked in the contest to set a record in the National Pastime, only one of them, McGwire, was truly an American, at least in the eyes of many baseball fans. In 1998, Sosa was one of eighty-five players from the Dominican Republic currently involved in major league baseball in the United States. He was born in San Pedro de Macoris, sold oranges and shone shoes on the streets as a child, and grew up unaware of the history and tradition associated with baseball in America. McGwire, on the other hand, epitomized the white, working-class hero—"a hoe-down, home-town American slugger" (*Observer*, 6 September 1998). When McGwire won the race to beat the Maris record, therefore, it was a genuine American achievement as opposed to simply an achievement in an American sport. He subsequently went on to set a new record of seventy home runs for the season. Afterward McGwire observed, "I'm glad I've been associated with Sammy Sosa. It's been a great year for everyone. I'm absolutely exhausted. I don't think you can use your mind any more playing baseball. I've amazed myself that I've stayed in a tunnel for so long. It just proves to me I can overcome anything with the strength of my mind" (*Guardian*, 29 September 1998). Sosa's assessment of the season had been rather more cryptic but no less instructive. Speaking about his own personal achievement, he is on record as saying, "My country is happy" (*USA Today*, 9 September 1998). He did not mean the United States.

Baseball's place in American hearts is also testified to by the number of creative writers who have given the game prominence in their work. Bernard Malamud's *The Natural* (1952), Robert Coover's *The Universal Baseball Association, inc. J. Henry Waugh, PROP.* (1992), and Philip Roth's

The Great American Novel (1973), to name but a few, all feature baseball as a central motif. According to Messenger (1990), "Baseball fiction has been the most supple and imaginative of all sports fiction, allowing the authors the greatest range of imaginative inter-play" (24). Certainly through his central character, J. Henry Waugh, Coover offers us a range of insights not only into Americans' relationship with baseball but also into the American psyche more generally (Bairner 1996c).

Moreover, not only writers of fiction but intellectuals more generally have been captivated over the years by baseball's central location in American culture. As Pope (1997) observes, "To this day, baseball's preferred ideology runs untrammeled throughout the nation's cultural landscape." Thus, "journalists, popular intellectuals, and filmmakers continue to stoke the flames of baseball's 'innocent,' mythical past" (80). Indeed, as Pope (1997) claims, "the search for an idealistic, pristine national identity in the lexicon of baseball is a uniquely American tradition" (82).

The early 1990s was by no means the first time when baseball's future was thought to be threatened. Indeed, despite its popularity in the interwar years, its demise was already being predicted. This was based on a belief that "a slow and dull game could never sustain itself in a society that was increasing its speed and could ultimately find meaning only in intense activity" (Crepeau 1980, 107). This ignored the fact that one of baseball's great charms had always been its timeless quality. However mythic the idea of baseball's origins and the portrayal of its links to a rural idyll, the success of the game has not simply been the result of successful marketing from Spalding onward. Indeed, as we know, myths are of vital importance in the construction of links between cultural phenomena and national identities. As Zingg (1988) points out, "Throughout their history, Americans have appeared unusually eager to embrace fact and fiction with equal enthusiasm—and often little discrimination—in the name of national pride" (356). For that reason, "artificially conceived, vigorously defended, ostentatiously celebrated, baseball is the quintessential American game" (Zingg 1988, 356). Yet concerns about the its future have remained.

The pessimistic prognosis, however, was premised, in part, on a feeling that baseball was ill suited to the new economic order and its links to sport. As Crepeau (1980) comments on one of baseball's all time greats, Babe Ruth, "He was a celebrated and endangered species in the emerging corporate America" (82). There was also a belief that, in terms of sport's entertainment value, speed and the clock had become the key characteristics, as they were of modern American life in general, and that these were more adequately reflected by both American football and basketball than by baseball. Nevertheless baseball's influence on the development of the broader American professional sporting tradition had already been profound (Pope 1997).

American Football and National Identity

American football emerged in colleges in the late nineteenth century and has subsequently made a major impact on American society while simultaneously reflecting important social developments (Gorn and Goldstein 1993). Football was being played in America from as early as the 1850s. At that time, however, and during the two decades that followed, there were significant overlaps between the sport being played at universities such as Harvard and Princeton and the British pastimes of association football (soccer) and rugby. In 1876, representatives of Harvard and Yale agreed to rules that spelled the beginning of the sharp decline of soccer in the United States and the consolidation of the game that more closely resembled rugby. It was this which evolved into American football as we now know it.

Given the game's origins in the Ivy League schools, it is hardly surprising that it was originally regarded as an elite sport. As Gorn and Goldstein claim, "Far more than academic achievement, the experience and culture of football linked different generations of American leaders in a collegiate socialization process that helped provide class cohesion for the children of the American upper classes" (164). It emphasized institutional loyalty and teamwork, valuable qualities in the emergent corporate world. But its relationship to developments in American society went deeper than that. Indeed, in the 1890–1950 era, intercollegiate football revealed its capacity to inspire fan loyalty far beyond the confines of the colleges themselves and the social classes most associated with them (Rader 1996). Collegiate football spread rapidly from the Northeast where it had begun to the Midwest, the West Coast, and the South (Pope 1997). Like baseball's Fourth of July rituals, football managed to impose itself on another important date in the American calendar—Thanksgiving Day. There emerged a practice of staging important games to coincide with Thanksgiving celebrations, thereby linking the game in the popular imagination to the emergence of the nation. As Pope (1997) describes it, "This newly invented Thanksgiving sports tradition connected an Americanized game with the sacred ideals and customs of a nation just one century old" (85).

According to Gorn and Goldstein (1993), "College football, as a consuming phenomenon in institutions of higher learning, stood at the center of the cultural transformations of the late nineteenth and early twentieth centuries" (169). These included a redefinition of American middle-class and upper-class masculinity, the preeminence of sport in many educational institutions, a form of corporate and quasi-military combat for the sons of national and local elites, and the public spectacle

of upper-class display. There is certainly no denying that, as the twentieth century has advanced, American football fandom has been extended
well beyond colleges and their alumni. This is partly due to the emergence of the National Football League and professional franchises. But in
smaller states, denied major sports franchises, the state university football team can attract widespread support even among those who have no
direct contact with university life. The adverse impact of collegiate sport
on the academic life of universities and also on the lives of actual recipi-
ents of sports scholarships (in basketball as well as in football) has
attracted considerable attention. Moreover, football has never managed
to take from baseball the title of National Pastime. Nevertheless, in certain ways it does appear to have been well suited to Americans at a particular stage in their nation's economic and social history. As Oriard
(1993) suggests, "For the cultural scholar, football in the 1990s as in the
1890s can open a window into American culture, in all its complexities
and diversity" (280). It may well be only a game. But, as Oriard (1993)
argues, "it also remains, for all Americans who follow the game, a cultural text in which we read stories about some of the most basic issues
that touch our lives" (282).

   If baseball can be characterized as a premodern sport rooted in
America's rural past, then American football is surely the modern sport
par excellence, linking, as it does, sport and the bureaucratization of physical activity (Gorn and Goldstein 1993). The inspiration came from Walter
Camp, who modelled his Yale University teams on the new Taylorist
structure of industrial production and scientific management. As Oriard
(1993) indicates, "Camp consistently interpreted the game's meaning and
significance from what is essentially a managerial and technocratic perspective" (37). According to Gramsci (1971), Frederick Taylor expressed
the purpose of modern American society as, "developing in the worker
to the highest degree automatic and mechanical attitudes, breaking up
the old psycho-physical nexus of qualified professional work, which
demands a certain active participation of intelligence, fantasy and initia-
tive on the part of the worker, and reducing productive operations exclusively to the mechanical, physical aspect" (302). It was this set of attitudes
that Camp brought to football. At its harshest, according to Oriard (1993),
"Camp's interpretation of football's cultural text makes the sport seem a
model of social control" (47).

   In addition, partly due to its origins but also as a result of its inherent
characteristics, the game had manifest military implications, combining
both the order and chaos of the battlefield. As Don DeLillo (1986) writes
in his novel *End Zone:* "The special teams collided, swarm and thud of
interchangeable bodies, small wars commencing here and there, exalta-
tion and first blood, a helmet bouncing brightly on the splendid grass, the

breathless impact of two destructive masses, quite pretty to watch" (111). According to Pope (1997), "Pre-World War I discussions about physical fitness and national preparedness had a profound influence on the American sporting culture" (121). Indeed, "between 1917 and 1919, the armed services made sports and athletic training a central component of military life" (139). Some sports, of course, were regarded as more appropriate than others to the exigencies of the military and there is certainly plenty of evidence that many high-ranking officers regarded football as an ideal preparation for war. As Wakefield comments, "Ball games, of course, taught young men how to throw a grenade, but even more significantly ball games, especially football, were believed to teach young men how to persevere in the face of exhaustion, pain, and fear" (103).

Despite its elite origins, its militaristic connotations, and its scientific dimension, football's popularity has spread throughout a wide cross-section of the American population. According to Gannon and Kanafani (1994), "A sport that captures many of the central values of American society, football has steadily become an integral component of the community" (303). Even becoming a football cheerleader is something to be valued by many, irrespective of its negative image in other quarters. As Gannon and Kanafani (1994) suggest, "In the United States, football is not only a sport but also an assortment of common beliefs and ideals; indeed, football is a set of collective rituals and values shared by one dynamic society" (303).

Both football and baseball, according to Mrozek (1983), were "taken to embody qualities that were quintessentially American, even if these qualities were readily discernible in other cultures or might even be regarded as defects by a twist of taste and judgment" (175). They combined teamwork and individualism. Indeed, given that both are team games, the amount of attention paid to individual statistics is truly remarkable and is indicative of a society in which the individual is always celebrated even in the most corporate of enterprises. The games also spoke to the extreme differences in the American landscape (Mrozek 1983). Both the gridiron and the diamond conjured up images of the "wilderness" in the midst of the city. Baseball and football possessed national distinctiveness together with geographical extensiveness. They were truly national games and, as such, "shapers of American nationalism" (Mrozek 1983, 175). But there is one other team sport that makes up the United States' great triumvirate.

Basketball: The New Kid on the Block

How far the argument can be pursued such that, if baseball is premodern and American football modern, basketball can be portrayed as postmodern is open to question. What cannot be denied, however, is that basketball has been America's sporting success story during the last two decades of the millennium. In particular, it has become the urban, African American sport *par excellence*. Invented in 1895 by James Naismith, a Canadian who was a student and part-time instructor at the International Young Men's Christian Association (YMCA) Training School in Springfield, Massachusetts, basketball was a product of the "muscular Christianity" movement. But it spread rapidly beyond the confines of such bodies as the YMCA as "part of the Progressive, professional, middle-class effort to channel, guide and Americanize immigrant youth through elementary and secondary extracurricular activities" (Gorn and Goldstein 1993, 175). However, although implicated from the start in the construction of an American national identity, by becoming the preferred sport of many working-class ethnic communities, basketball, ironically, contributed simultaneously to the process whereby homogenization could be successfully resisted to some degree. Its appeal, of course, derived from the fact that it was well suited to the urban landscape although, as time has gone on, it has also been aided by its speed and its capacity for instant gratification through regular scoring. It has also provided African Americans with a team sport with which to identify at a more personal level than is the case with either baseball or football. Ironically, however, but arguably unsurprisingly, although played at the highest level by disproportionately large numbers of African Americans, the live matches in the NBA continue to attract predominantly white audiences. This can be interpreted in part with reference to inequality and the high prices of tickets. But it also alerts us to the very real possibilty that in the United States sport continues to represent an arena in which black people entertain their white compatriots. For every Michael Jordan, moreover, there may be thousands of young African American men whose lives have been blighted by a mistaken belief that sport alone affords them a way out of poverty and a point of entry into a white-dominated world (Hoberman 1997). This is a dismal assessment particularly if one is looking to sport as a mechanism for social harmony and genuine personal advancement. When one turns one's attention, however, to the experiences in American sport of First Nation people, one finds plenty more compelling evidence that social exclusion rather than cross-cultural reconciliation remains a fact of life.

AMERICAN SPORT AND NATIVE AMERICA

Indeed, before going on to look at the impact of globalization on American sports culture, it is worth remembering that the aboriginal peoples are also part of the American way of playing sport. In terms of high profile sporting activity, however, the influence of native Americans has been strange to say the very least. The Atlanta "Braves," the Cleveland

"Indians," the Washington "Redskins," and the Kansas City "Chiefs" are all names of major league franchises. Even college teams adopt similar derivative names—for example, Florida State University "Seminoles" and the University of Illinois "Fighting Illini." The names are accompanied by crowd gestures, including the "Indian Chant" and the "Tomahawk Chop." So what is this all about in terms of the construction of an American national identity? Many native Americans have argued that it is part of a racist discourse that in general seriously undermines their status in contemporary American society (Churchill 1993). The response by the sports authorities has been to argue that, in fact, the use of such names and practices honors native people and involves them more in American national identity. But as Churchill (1993) has asked, how honored would African Americans be by a team called the "Niggers"? He proceeds to conjure up numerous similar names, all of them "honoring" some section of the American population—the Kansas City "Kikes," the San Leandro "Shylocks," the Fresno "Faggots," the San Diego "Spics," and the Baltimore "Beaners," among others. Their very absurdity forces us to consider why the "Redskins" is an appropriate title and the answer is obvious. Native Americans are pre-Americans and count for far less in terms of the construction of what it is to be American than do Italians, Jews, and even Mexicans, all of whom have been in the melting pot however imperfectly that has been stirred. The native peoples, however, are the true other and can be denigrated in this way without giving serious offense to most American people. Some progress has been made in this respect. Stanford University, for example, has dropped the name "Indians" from its sports teams. But most Americans continue to see the campaign to change the names of leading franchises as the result of an excess of political correctness. Whether they would regard attempts to marginalize their own particular group of ethnic origin is an entirely different matter.

SPORT, AMERICAN SOCIETY, AND GLOBALIZATION

It is undeniable that the development of American sport has followed the contours laid down by developments in American society. In particular, the idea of the major sports franchise that can be uprooted and reconstituted in a different metropolis would be unthinkable were it not for the massive urbanization of the United States. As Rader (1996) observes, "aided by jet air travel, sports entrepreneurs moved to exploit the new population centers" (224). This trend has had a particularly significant impact on the Sunbelt states of the South and the Southwest where professional sports franchises have been established often at the expense of cities in the Northeast. The result has been to integrate even more

Americans into a national sports system while simultaneously providing them with greater opportunities to celebrate the uniqueness of their own cities and regions. Thus, the World Series unites the American people and, at the same time, provides an experience which is quasi-international in its appeal. But what about America's links to the outside sporting world?

If one were to equate globalization with Americanization, it would be meaningless to ask how successfully American sport has resisted the former. On the other hand, if globalization derives from a multiplicity of sources and travels in many directions, it is reasonable to examine its impact on the United States. Although clearly among professional team sports basketball has experienced the most rapid growth, in terms of viewing figures, crowds, salaries, and sponsorship deals, the fastest growing participant sport is arguably soccer. The question, "why?" must be prefaced by some comments on soccer's failure to establish roots in American society during the earlier part of the twentieth century when it was spreading throughout the world. It should be noted at once that areas that were relatively immune to the spread of soccer included, ironically, many of Britain's former colonies. In this respect America was no exception despite the fact that the absence of top-level soccer has been described by one author as an "American exceptionalism" (Markovits 1988). Markovits focuses on "the 'crowding out' of soccer in America's 'sports space' as a consequence of the development of indigenous American sports which had already become entrenched in American culture by the time Britain's game of soccer reached the rest of the world" (125). According to Markovits, "Bourgeois America created a new identity which prided itself on being explicitly different from that found anywhere in aristocratic Europe" (128–129). American football and baseball established themselves as American sports *par excellence* and occupied the space into which soccer might otherwise have entered. According to Markovits (1988), "It is particularly America's bourgeois hegemony and legacy of the 'first new nation' which contributed substantially to the continued absence of the world's most popular team sport as a major presence in American popular culture" (125).

Yet, according to Sugden (1994), "In terms of longevity and international competition soccer is the elder statesman of American sport" (219). For example, U.S. representative teams played a series of games against Canada in 1885 and 1886. The ruling body of American soccer, the United States Football Association (USFA) was formed in 1913 and became affiliated to FIFA the same year. In addition, with the exception of 1938, America has participated in every World Cup since 1930 and has reached the final stages on six occasions (1930; 1934; 1950; 1990; 1994; 1998). Despite this proud history, however, the game has never managed to establish itself in the mainstream of American sporting culture. This paradox raises two interesting questions. First, why, despite its American advocates, has the game failed to impact upon the nation's sporting psyche? Second, is the status of soccer changing in the United States as a consequence of globalization?

There has never been any lack of people interested in playing soccer in the United States. Of crucial significance, however, is the nature of the people involved. During the late nineteenth and early twentieth centuries, successive waves of European immigrants brought with them what Sugden (1994) calls, "their distinctive and alien cultural preferences, including a knowledge of and liking for soccer" (237). As a consequence, by the 1920s, many "Americans" were playing the game in organized competitions. As Sugden (1994) relates, "Largely outside of the public gaze, soccer in the 1920s and 1930s enjoyed a growth phase within immigrant communities from industrial and commercial centres such as New York, St. Louis, Chicago, Milwaukee and Fall River" (237). Furthermore, ethnic soccer clubs played an important part in maintaining subgroup identities and resisting assimilation. Against this, however, was the desire of many immigrants to forget their past and acquire a new, American identity. Since playing soccer could be construed as being un-American, it was increasingly eschewed even by newly arrived immigrants who chose instead to embrace the sports culture of their new home. Thus, we have seen the extent to which baseball was involved in the assimilation process. Once again, soccer was crowded out.

Since the 1960s, however, participation levels have increased rapidly and the new soccer constituency differs markedly from the old, working-class ethnic communities. Today it is the fastest growing sport among the American suburban (primarily but by no means exclusively white) middle classes. It is much less violent than American football, requires less equipment and organization than baseball, and is accessible to both females and males. It is these factors that explain why soccer's popularity in high schools and colleges has grown so markedly. The same factors, however, also help us to understand why there has been no such concomitant growth at the level of professional participation. Those groups in American society who regard sport as a possible route to material success are not yet involved in soccer's boom and are unlikely to become so unless professional soccer starts to compete financially with the other major team games. That it is unlikely to do so, however, without the involvement of deprived, inner-city youngsters means that American soccer finds itself in a Catch-22 situation. The sport's recent success ironically represents a major obstacle to its further advance.

As Sugden (1994) comments, "The current popularity of the game at youth and intercollegiate levels belies the fact that soccer has gained little ground in blue-collar America, is all but ignored by Afro-Americans and, outside of recent émigré enclaves, has a very low profile in the inner cities." He continues, "The fact that the game has been so successfully appropriated by women serves to confirm, both in the mind of the dis-passionate observer and in the mind of the average American sports fan, that soccer is an inappropriate sport for healthy American males" (249). First it was an immigrant game and now it is a game for women and chil-dren. In either case, soccer remains outside the dominant value system of American sport. Thus, the United States remain the international football organization's "final frontier" (Sugden and Tomlinson 1998). This does not mean, however, that the American sports culture has totally resisted this particular element of the global sports culture. The fact that many Americans now play the game albeit in different ways from their coun-terparts elsewhere (for example in co-ed teams) is at the very least an indication of glocalization if not globalization. Moreover, as Sugden and Tomlinson argue, "world soccer culture penetrated only partially and unevenly the sports cultures and space of the USA, but analysis of the impact of World Cup '94 is also a reminder that central to some major trends in the globalization of world sport is a political economy that merges the interests of trans-national bodies such as FIFA, multi-national corporations, and national and regional elites" (219–220). Thus, America has failed to resist the global spread of soccer although it is undeniable that the game has never played a significant part in the construction of American national identity, except negatively perhaps by revealing what real Americans are not.

AMERICAN SPORTING NATIONALISM

However, there is certainly no denying the role played by other sports in the construction of American national identity. As Sage (1990) claims, "National loyalty and patriotism are fostered through sports rituals and ceremonies that link sport and nationalism" (76). He continues, "Impor-tant national and international events like the Super Bowl and the Olym-pic Games are incorporated into a panoply of political ritual that serves to remind people of their common destiny" (76). According to Pope (1997), "The Olympics provided an arena in which certain Americans could invent and popularize symbols of their political and sporting cul-ture by linking athletic prowess to national mythology" (40). American sport is inextricably linked to competition, business, masculinity and so on (Wilcox 1994). As a result it helps to maintain a system that finds favor with countless American citizens. Events such as the Olympics have, at various times, afforded the American people considerable opportunities to feel good about their athletic prowess and, thus, about themselves and this pattern continues even at a time in history when increasing numbers of American citizens are far more likely to suffer from the consequences of obesity than to participate in exercise. By being so supportive of the nation's dominant value system, however, sport is also implicated in creating and reproducing divisions among the American people.

According to Sage (1990), "Sport is a powerful contributor to the ideology that legitimizes the social inequalities of class stratification on American society and promotes the notion of social mobility based on effort" (41). It has also played a major part in perpetuating the ideology of male superiority and dominance (Sage 1990). In addition, while its impact on race relations has been arguably more subtle than on gender, it has nevertheless served to maintain different forms of segregation. As Sage (1990) describes it, "Unlike the patriarchal ideology that has barred most women from sport, the ideology underlying racism is not incompatible with black sport participation, but it has dictated that black athletes be subordinate and in certain times and places totally segregated from playing with whites" (56). Furthermore, as Hoberman (1997) has controversially argued, even when African Americans have been permitted to enter into the world of professional sport in increasingly and disproportionately large numbers, the effects may still be harmful inasmuch as the pursuit of sporting success is carried on to the neglect of black advancement, particularly by men, in other areas. According to Hoberman (1997), "Confinement within the athletic syndrome is maintained by powerful peer-group pressures which ridicule academic achievement while stigmatizing blacks who do not beat 'whitey' at whichever game is at stake" (xvii). For Hoberman (1997), "The entrapment of African Americans in the world of athleticism is the result of a long collaboration between blacks seeking respect and expanded opportunity and whites seeking entertainment, profit, and forms of racial reconciliation that do not challenge fundamental assumptions about racial difference" (4). Hoberman's thesis has been widely criticized. The fact remains, however, that whether or not African Americans have been complicit in the process whereby sport is presented as an appropriate career path for black males while academic attainment is not, the extent to which success in sport has empowered them is open to question.

In general, it is clear that, although sport plays a significant part in creating a sense of what it means to be American, it also represents a domain in which dominant groups seek to maintain their authority and their subordinates practise forms of cultural resistance. On occasions, resistance through sport assumes particularly dramatic forms such as the Black Power protest of Tommie Smith and John Carlos during their medal ceremony at the 1968 Olympic Games in Mexico City. At other times, it is a long term process that eventually results in gains, for exam-

ple Title IX (of the Educational Amendments Act of 1972), which out-
lawed sexual discrimination by school districts and institutions of higher
education in receipt of federal aid. Whatever the success of such resistance to date, however, much remains to be achieved before one can claim
that the American people are truly united by sport. For the time being,
the control of sport is still in the hands of capital in general and of rich,
white men specifically. To the extent to which this remains equally true of
American society as a whole, of course, it is appropriate to speak of sport
as being a fair reflection of the nation's identity as a whole. Furthermore,
this does not mean that sport simply reflects the nature of American society. Rather, it has consistently been implicated in making America the
sort of place that it is. Commenting on the formative years of modern
sport in America, Mrozek (1983) argues, "More than a microcosm of other
elements, sport was a new pattern in the social fabric, novel as an institution, with so many open ends, and so many raw edges that it could
grasp hold of the double-faced entity that was the American experience
and the American mentality" (235).

During the Cold War, sport clearly had a part to play in the promotion
of American values. International events, such as the Olympic Games,
acquired a new significance. For much of that period the contest between
the Americans and the Soviet bloc was unequal for two related reasons.
First, the representatives of the United States who travelled to the Olympics remained truer to the amateur ideal than did their "communist"
opponents who were stigmatized by the Western media, not without evidence, for their "shamateurism." Indeed, despite the achievements of
countless American athletes, before, during, and after the Cold War, track
and field has consistently been something of a poor relation in the
nation's sports culture in terms of spectator interest and, indeed, financial
incentives. In fact, the second reason why American Olympic teams were
often at a disadvantage when competing against Soviet or East German
teams is directly linked to both money and the American sporting culture. Games such as baseball and American football remained quintessentially American. The former has now appeared at the Olympic Games,
but only since the cessation of Cold War hostilities. Furthermore, not only
are they American games, they also offer remarkably lucrative career
opportunities for the most successful players. Thus, whereas the Soviet
Union was traditionally in a position to call upon its very best sports people to secure Olympic victories and, thereby, promote the communist system, America's Olympics teams were bereft of much of the nation's athletic talent.

Despite America's difficulties in competing with the communist challenge, however, in the Olympics, the World Athletics Championships, the
Pan-American Games, and so on, track and field stars became (and

remain) potent weapons in the ideological arsenal of the United States, just as they had been on one previous occasion when competitors at the Berlin Olympics (and, in particular one athlete, Jesse Owens), temporarily undermined the myth of Aryan superiority upon which the Nazis' ideological edifice had been constructed. Even since the ending of the Cold War, indeed, by virtue of the fact that they compete in high profile, global events against the representatives of other nations, track and field winners have been the most likely American sports people to be seen waving the national flag. Golf and tennis are other sports that provide similar opportunities. The big American team sports continue to be associated, at least overtly, less with the nation than with city or even simply business rivalries. In spite of the introspection of much of the American sporting culture, however, it has impacted on other societies. As Rader (1996) argues, "In the second half of the twentieth century, track and field, golf and tennis, sports whose antecedents extended back to socially exclusive clubs, reflected a more general trend toward the internationalization of American sports" (290). In addition, the American approach to sport, if not some of the great American sports themselves, has clearly been influential well beyond the boundaries of the United States. This is seen in the increasingly close relationship between sport and the growing power of the media (particularly television). More generally, by playing a vital role in the process through which sport and business have become inextricably linked, the United States has helped to determine the character of sport's global political economy. It is a moot point, however, whether this represents evidence of Americanization as opposed simply to the worldwide triumph of capital. Indeed, to ascertain the extent to which any of these developments are indicative of the successful Americanization of sport what is required is an analysis of the actual experience of other societies. This question has already been discussed with reference to the sporting cultures of Ireland and Scotland. But if there is such a process at work, and if it has been successful, then one might expect to find the clearest evidence in the United States' English-speaking neighbor, Canada.

chapter six

Maple Leaf Americans

SPORT AND QUESTIONS OF CANADIAN NATIONAL IDENTITY

At least since the 1960s, Canada has become one of the most discussed countries in terms of the culture and politics of national identity. As this chapter reveals, there are numerous ways in which Canadians are culturally divided, but the specific issue that has attracted the most attention concerns the growth of a separatist movement claiming to represent the interests of the French speaking majority in the province of Quebec. Of the latter's seven million population, 83 percent are francophones although there are numerous large ethnic and linguistic minorities, the largest of which consists of 760,000 English speakers, a huge majority of whom support their province's continued place in a federal Canadian nation-state (Lawton 1995). The period since the 1960s has witnessed a number of inconclusive and increasingly acrimonious rounds of constitutional negotiations to satisfy the demands of French speakers generally in Canada and of the Quebecois in particular (Tully 1994). In the meantime, the sphere of identity politics in Canada has grown to include the voices of many other groups who are equally concerned about their place in Canadian society and, indeed, about what it means to be Canadian. In addition, all Canadians have been forced constantly to deal with the increasing cultural influence of the United States just as many of their ancestors were obliged to find ways to challenge the cultural hegemony of the British. As Jackson (1994) argues, "Perhaps more than any other nation Canada has been confronted directly with the issue of Americanization" (429). Like the debate between francophones and anglo-phones, this problem has a long history although arguably it has become increasingly pressing during the contemporary period. In all of this, sport has played its part.

IMPERIALISM, SPORT, AND THE CANADIANS

There is certainly no denying the importance of sport in Canada. As Hall et al. (1991) observe, "Most Canadians, even if they are not active partic-ipants, are touched in some way by sport" (11). In addition, "It is inextri-cably linked to the major social institutions that regulate Canadian soci-ety—government and politics, the economy and big business, the mass media and the educational system to name just a few" (Hall et al. 1991, 11). Until relatively recently, however, sport in Canada, as elsewhere, has been largely neglected by the academic community. For example, accord-ing to Metcalfe (1987), "Few Canadian historians have regarded sport as an integral part of the social history of Canada" (9). Similarly, Macintosh and Whitson (1990) bemoan the fact that "for most of Canada's history, sport was envisaged as an activity which provided diversion and amuse-ment for the general populace, but one which had little broader signifi-cance" (3). However, an ever-growing community of scholars has begun to reveal the extent to which sport has been intimately involved in help-ing to make Canada the sort of country that it is while simultaneously offering Canadians perceptions of themselves and of their relationship to their real or imagined nation.

Like most other societies, Canada first adopted modern sports as a result of having a relationship with Britain and, because Canada was a part of the British Empire, this relationship was particularly close. Indeed, in the years leading up to Confederation in 1867, the develop-ment of Canadian sport was dominated by the central role of British games (Metcalfe 1987). For example, cricket was played by immigrants, soldiers, and those native-born subjects who were imbued with British sporting ideology, many of them having attended prestigious private schools established in imitation of their English counterparts (Metcalfe 1987). Other sports that were introduced to Canada courtesy of the British included curling and golf, which were to remain closely associ-ated with their perceived Scottish roots. In addition, the colonial admin-istrators in Canada and, above all, a sequence of governors general played an important part in promoting an emergent Canadian sports cul-ture. Indeed,the governors general are still remembered in the names of leading trophies awarded in a variety of sports—the Connaught Cup (soccer), the Stanley Cup (hockey), the Grey and Vannier Cups (Canadian football), and the Minto Cup (lacrosse).

Lacrosse, of course, was indigenous, having been played for centuries by First Nations people who knew it as baggataway or *tewaarathon* and for whom there were around forty variations of the game (Metcalfe 1987). Ironically, given these native origins, lacrosse, along with baseball and a Canadian version of football, was to play an important role in helping native-born Canadians to counter British sporting hegemony with more peculiarly Canadian traditions. As Metcalfe (1987) puts it, "While accepting the value system and ideology of Britain, these young men *were* Canadian and looked to North America, not to Britain, as home" (30).

Much of the early activity both of those concerned to propagate the British ways of playing sport and their rivals who were seeking to mount a Canadian counterhegemonic challenge took place in the cities of Montreal and Toronto, with the former being widely recognized as the cradle of organized sport in Canada (Metcalfe 1987; Morrow 1989). Indeed, according to Morrow (1989), Montreal became "a kind of Mecca" for Canadian sport in the nineteenth century due to its geographical, economic, cultural, and commercial advantages (1). As early as 1807, the Montreal Curling Club had been established by twenty prominent Scottish-born citizens. This was to be followed by the setting up of cricket and hunt clubs in the 1820s, a demonstration of lacrosse in 1834, the Montreal "Olympic Games" in 1844, the building of specialized sports facilities during the 1840s and 1850s, the formation of the Montreal Lacrosse Club in 1856 and of the Montreal Golf Club in 1873 (Metcalfe 1987). Metcalfe suggests that only the Montreal Snow Shoe Club (established in 1840) included members of the French-speaking elite alongside their anglophone counterparts. All of the other early sporting initiatives in Montreal were the preserve of anglophones and of these only the wealthiest were able to participate.

Unlike Australia, New Zealand, the Indian sub-continent, South Africa, and the constituent parts of the West Indies, however, Canada was able to resist British sporting imperialism relatively successfully and evolve its own sporting culture, which drew upon indigenous pastimes together with the transformation of imported British games. It might be logical to assume, therefore, that having once challenged a globally influential cultural force, Canada is in a particularly strong position to mount national resistance to contemporary globalization or, if one prefers, Americanization. The flaw in this argument is that one of the main reasons why Canada was able to resist British sporting imperialism was that its close proximity to the United States, which had rejected British political control and, in so doing, developed its own distinctive sporting identity, enabled Canadians to tap into the most popular leisure pastimes of their more powerful neighbor.

AMERICANIZATION, SPORT, AND THE CANADIANS

Indeed, if contemporary globalization and Americanization can be equated in any meaningful sense, it would be easy to anticipate that the country most likely to be affected by this process is Canada. Its towns and cities look American. Its people dress like Americans. Its popular culture shares many significant features with that of the United States. None of this is surprising if for no other reason than that the two countries are neighbors. However, not only does Canada share a border with the United States but unlike Mexico, its counterpart to the south, it also has a common language—English. That the latter is not the only major language spoken in Canada presents no insurmountable problems for comparison given the ubiquity of Spanish in the United States together with a multiplicity of other smaller linguistic groups. Indeed, the presence of numerous aboriginal languages is apparent in both countries. Moreover, despite certain distinctive vowel sounds, the English spoken by Canadians is virtually indistinguishable from that of many Americans. Despite these similarities, however, there are striking differences between the two countries that are apparent even to the most casual of observers.

Anyone who has ever seen a young Canadian backpacker will almost certainly have seen the Maple Leaf emblem displayed in some form or another. Many Canadians clearly seek to distinguish themselves from Americans almost as a matter of course. Canada is a sovereign state that, despite close economic links with the United States and regardless of the wishes of some of its own citizens, is unlikely to move toward any kind of political union with its neighboring state. There exists undeniably a distinctive Canadian culture, one that is wholly or, at least, in substantial part, cherished by the overwhelming majority of Canadians.

SPORT AND THE CONTEST FOR CANADIAN NATIONAL IDENTITY

In the world of sport Canada's independence is underlined at the level of international competition not only at events such as the Olympic and Commonwealth Games but also in specific sports including those that remain as reminders of British influence, cricket, soccer, and rugby union. In addition, attempts to reform Canadian sport and secure greater international success have taken place under the overall heading of Team Canada. Thus, as Hall et al. (1991) argue, it is important to understand sport within a specifically Canadian context as opposed to North American society in general. As they remark, "Certainly there are similarities between organized sport in the United States and Canada, but there are also major differences" (Hall et al. 1991, 12). None of this is to suggest, however, that all of Canada's citizens are happy with the national identity that accompanies those sporting differences and complements the existence of the sovereign, federal state.

Although many citizens of the United States have Spanish as a first language, most think of themselves as American. In Canada, however, a significant French-speaking minority express serious reservations about their "Canadian" identity. It is they who, in the first instance, successfully demanded that French should be recognized alongside English as an official language and who have subsequently pressed for greater autonomy for the province of Quebec in which there is a French-speaking majority. This linguistic division has had obvious implications for the cohesiveness of Canadian engagement in international sport. Two examples relate specifically to the Olympic Games.

When the Olympics were held in Montreal in 1976, they performed two distinct, and potentially competing functions as regards the consolidation of national identity. As Kidd (1996) observes, "While cultural struggle has occurred at every Olympic Games, it was particularly acute at the time of the Montreal Games, when the very definition of the host nation and the purpose of the sports—both of which frame staging and interpretation of an Olympics—were openly and fiercely debated" (153). From the perspective of the supporters of federalism, these were Canada's games, held in a city that had played a crucial role in the early development of the nation's sporting culture. For the francophones of Quebec province, however, the games belonged to them and were regarded as recognition of their national distinctiveness. This difference of opinion was also manifest in events surrounding the 1984 Winter Olympics, held, ironically, in Sarajevo, which was itself soon to be gravely affected by the political repercussions of nationalist rivalry. At the games, Canada won two gold medals. Both were awarded to a Quebec francophone, Gaetan Boucher, whose achievement was celebrated by René Lévesque, the province's premier, in the words: "Quebec 2 Canada 0" (Macintosh et al. 1988, 173). Again the message was plain. In the eyes of separatists, two different nations had been involved, while for federalists there was a willingness, indeed a desire, to claim Boucher's triumphs for Canada as a whole. There is even evidence to suggest that francophones have far less enthusiasm than their English-speaking compatriots for representing Canada in international sporting competition. More recently, when Formula One World Champion Jacques Villeneuve was welcomed back to his native land on 5 November 1997, it was to the Molson Centre, the new home of the Montreal Canadiens hockey team, that he came to be greeted by a vast crowd of fans of whom only one appeared to be waving the Canadian flag and most of the remainder were saluting his achievement with Quebec's *fleur de lys*.

In addition to francophone disquiet about a Canadian national identity that, in their opinion, is dominated by the English-speaking majority in the country as a whole, many native Americans have never felt "at home" in the nation-state of Canada. Furthermore, the real or imagined Canada in which the supporters of federalism believe has come under increasing pressure from waves of immigrants, from eastern and southern Europe and, more recently, from the Middle East, the Indian subcontinent, the Caribbean, and South East Asia. Although some of these new arrivals share in the dominant Canadian culture experiences of a British imperial past, many more have little or no empathy with that aspect of Canadian identity and simply wish to maintain their own native traditions, opt for a generalized North American identity, or adopt a combination of the two.

Thus, what passes for Canadian national identity has been constantly under threat and arguably that threat has grown in intensity. On one hand, it is assailed by the hegemonic tendencies of American culture. On the other, it is challenged by internal divisions. This chapter examines the extent to which sport has helped to unify the nation regardless of the latter and the degree to which it has been able to contribute to a movement of resistance against Americanization in particular and the processes of globalization more generally.

LACROSSE: THE NATIONAL SPORT?

In first seeking to uncover the nature of Canadian sporting nationalism, I asked an Ontario native and sports historian about his sporting background. His answer was succinct and to the point: "hockey in the winter, baseball in the summer." Eager to learn more, I mentioned other sports I knew were played in Canada. At the mention of each, my informant repeated the magic formula—"hockey in the winter, baseball in the summer"—until it assumed the quality of a mantra. I suspected that there was more to find out, starting with the game of lacrosse, of which I knew little but for some reason associated with only two places—the British girls' boarding school and Canada.

No one would seriously claim today that lacrosse is the Canadian national sport. It is played by relatively few Canadians, is restricted to certain geographical areas and receives little public attention. In any case, since it originated among aboriginal people and, as a result, is played in what is now the United States as well, its links to the national identity that supports federal Canada might seem tenuous to say the least. Nevertheless, as history shows, it did play a significant part in the construction of anglophone Canada's sporting nationalism. Furthermore, as is argued in the concluding chapter, definitions of national sport are inevitably bound up with attempts to define the nation. If perceptions of the nation are inspired by concerns with uniqueness and exclusion, then sports and other cultural traditions that may have limited popular appeal can nevertheless serve a useful political purpose.

The expansion of lacrosse beyond its native roots was largely inspired by Dr. William George Beers, a considerable propagandist of all things Canadian who sought in particular to take advantage of the nationalistic fervor generated by the formation of the Canadian confederation in 1867. During the 1860s, having learned the Mohawk game of *tewaarathon*, Beers developed the modern form of lacrosse, providing it with a written set of rules and standardized equipment. In 1867, he was also instrumental in establishing a governing body—the National Lacrosse Association (NLA)—the first such institution to be formed in Canada (Kidd 1996). During that year, lacrosse was an event at many Dominion Day celebrations and the NLA banner proclaimed, "Our Country and Our Game" (Morrow et al. 1989). According to Morrow (1989), "The years between 1868 and 1885 were pivotal in the development and growth of lacrosse in Canada" (55). During that period, Beers organized three tours of Britain—in 1867, 1876, and 1883. In part, he was eager to sell the game of lacrosse to the people of a country in which the modern sporting revolution had first taken place and which, therefore, had been influential in the process whereby lacrosse was codified and structured despite its distinctly non-British roots. The tours, however, were also a showcase for Canada itself, with lacrosse performing the function of a national-popular activity and, as such, underlining the distinctive character of the new Canadian nation (Morrow et al. 1989). To further illustrate the point, it was during these tours that Canadian sportsmen first wore the maple leaf symbol on their jerseys. By the 1880s, lacrosse had reached its pinnacle as a national sporting symbol of Canada. But it had already played an important role in allowing a certain section of the population to turn their backs on the sports that had been exported to Canada from Britain and, therefore, to develop a specifically Canadian sporting nationalism. For the most part, however, it was now left to other sports to carry on the work begun by the pioneers of modern lacrosse. Whether they would be able to mount a successful challenge to the next phase of sporting imperialism, which was to come from an entirely different direction, remained to be seen.

AMERICAN SPORT AND CANADIAN IDENTITY

Other sports that have a larger following than lacrosse in today's Canada include baseball and basketball. According to some historians, baseball, the great American game, was not "invented," as tradition would have us believe, by Abner Doubleday either in Cooperstown, New York, in 1839 or anywhere else in the United States for that matter. In fact, a game using rules very similar to those that were to be adopted for baseball in New York in 1845 is recorded to have been played in Brockville, Ontario, as early as 1838 (Morrow et al. 1989). It is certainly undeniable that "between 1900 and 1920 baseball was Canada's most popular sport" (Morrow et al. 1989, 126) and had taken over from lacrosse as the nation's summer game. In addition, as Metcalfe (1987) records, it was "the only game played by all Canadian social classes" (93).

It can be argued, however, that baseball today plays more of a part in the process through which Canada is being Americanized than in helping to maintain a separate sense of Canadian identity. There is no denying that when the Toronto Blue Jays won baseball's World Series in successive years the achievement brought a sense of pride to many Canadians, particularly in the city of Toronto itself. Nevertheless, the victory was secured in what is universally regarded as an American sport, that is, one that "belongs" to the United States, and without the assistance of native-born Canadian players. Indeed, with the Montreal Expos as the country's only other presence in big-time baseball, Canada's participation at the highest level of competition is seriously at odds with the game's grassroots popularity.

It is a similar story with basketball, a game that was actually invented by a Canadian, James Naismith, but which has come to be regarded as the most successful example of an American sport that has become globally popular. Certainly it is a widely played sport in Canada. However, despite the game's popularity as a serious sport as well as a recreational pastime throughout the country, top level professional basketball is played in only two Canadian cities—Toronto and Vancouver—and again normally with teams made up predominantly of players born in the United States. Because neither franchise has enjoyed any marked success since entering the National Basketball Association, it is too early to say whether or not their achievements would impact greatly on Canadian sporting nationalism. But it is safe to postulate that these would have negligible repercussions beyond the host cities. Indeed, the immediate effect of the quest by Canadian cities to attract "world class" entertainment, NBA and professional baseball franchises included, has been to replicate the American pattern whereby jingoism in sport is more likely to involve devotion to particular teams than to representative national sides.

CANADIAN FOOTBALL AND AMERICANIZATION

Only in two major team sports can Canada be said to have retained a degree of autonomous sporting life sufficient so far to consolidate the identity upon which the continued existence of federal Canada depends. First, Canadian football remains distinct from its American cousin and the Canadian Football League (CFL) is contested by Canadian teams, none of which have so far had the desire or the opportunity to defect to the NFL, although, for a time, American cities became home to CFL franchises, having been denied access to more lucrative American-based competitions. A uniquely Canadian form of football first emerged in the cities of Montreal and Toronto (Metcalfe 1987). The game was developed as a result of the influence of rugby, which was growing in popularity in the British military garrisons, and also the growing tension between rugby and soccer (Metcalfe 1987). According to Metcalfe (1987), "By the mid-1880's Canadian football had acquired the characteristics that were to remain central to its development until 1914" (56). At this stage, according to Cosentino (1989), "It was a sport developing its own approach, somewhat removed from its British roots but consistently emulating the American—the typical Canadian compromise" (147). As it evolved, however, it adopted American practices to the extent that by 1915, in Metcalfe's opinion (1987), "It could not claim to be a truly Canadian game" (61). Nor was it ever a sport with mass appeal. It is ironic, therefore, that for a short spell the CFL actually expanded into the United States, with cities desperate for a professional football franchise willing to go along with the Canadian game if only, as history has shown, for a brief period of time. Yet even this "Canadian" sport is heavily dependent on American players. Moreover, it is doubtful if Canadian football has sufficient mass appeal in an evolving Canada for it to play a major role in the processes of identity formation. But another sport, hockey, has traditionally done so and may still be one of the major elements in maintaining a sense of what it is to be Canadian that not only transcends many, although certainly not all, of the country's cultural variants but that, partly as a consequence of this, also provides some weaponry for the struggle to save Canada from cultural absorption by the United States.

CANADA IS HOCKEY?

Hockey is a sport Canadians invented. As a result, according to Gruneau and Whitson (1993), "It is hardly surprising that of all the sports played in Canada hockey has long been celebrated as something unique" (3). Hockey, according to another group of Canadian sports sociologists, is "part of our image of ourselves" (Hall et al. 1991, 41). Simpson (1989) describes "the development of longstanding rivalries that cemented, in the minds of Canadians, the close relationship of hockey to the sense of Canadian identity" (195). Hockey did not attain its current status overnight. But, as Metcalfe (1987) reveals, "By the early twentieth century, [it] had become recognized as Canada's national winter sport and its roots ran deep into small-town community life" (168).

Hockey's contemporary symbolic power places it alongside such other national institutions as the federal government, the public health-care system, and the Canadian Broadcasting Corporation (Gruneau and Whitson 1993). The game and its symbols are constantly used in the marketing of Canada. Along with the Maple Leaf, the Royal Canadian Mounted Police, and native wildlife, hockey provides one of the most common representations of Canadian identity. This is not simply a matter of people wearing items of clothes that celebrate particular teams. More broadly, there are artifacts everywhere that suggest the equations, Canada is hockey and hockey is Canada. It is no coincidence that it was a Canadian rock band that chose to mention hockey's premier competition, the Stanley Cup, in one of their recordings. In their "Open Heart Symphony" album, the popular Canadian rock band Spirit of the West (1996) complain that, in the German city of Frankfurt, nobody knows the latest Stanley Cup scores. What is more, there are certain compelling reasons for accepting the legitimacy of this equation of Canada equals hockey. At the statistical level, it is the case that Canadians make up a majority, albeit considerably smaller than in the past, of players participating in the most competitive hockey competition in the world, the National Hockey League (NHL). In season 1998–1999, Canadians made up 61.4 percent of NHL players with Americans constituting 16.1 percent and Europeans most of the remainder (*Hockey News*, 6 November 1998). At least as significant, however, is the game's ubiquity throughout this vast country. Pick up games of hockey are played everywhere to the extent that it would sometimes seem as if this is the main pastime of Canadians in the long winter months. Small farming communities in the prairie provinces, fishing and mining towns in the Maritimes, isolated regions of the far north, and, of course, the great urban centers are all home to hockey teams, which in turn are frequently the main source of a particular community's collective identity. The game is played by natives. It is also played by many of the immigrants who have made the Canadian population an increasingly complex mix. Perhaps most significantly of all, hockey is played with equal enthusiasm by both anglophone and francophone Canadians.

In terms of nationwide popularity at the very least, therefore, hockey can truly be described as a national game that has played a key role in the production and reproduction of the type of identity upon which the federal idea depends. Although the game has long been widely played in the United States as well, this has not undermined its close relationship with Canada and Canadians. According to the memoirs of "a man who couldn't play the game," "Articles on hockey in mainstream sports magazines in the States up until the late eighties were not so often done because of a *love* of the game, but were done to *sell* the game" (Richards 1997, 45). For Richards (1997), "It is a Northern game, a violent game, and (though they don't know this really bothers them) a Canadian game. And in a way, the game is beneath them" (45). There is certainly a perceived Canadian way of playing the game that is celebrated as being in some manner indicative of a national character—rugged, honest, utilitarian. We have also noticed how the establishment in Canadian cities of "world class" baseball and basketball franchises help to create a form of civic jingoism that is at odds with the concept of sporting nationalism. This is equally true of hockey although, in a perverse manner, by endorsing the importance of local community in an increasingly small world, the game continues to preserve a certain element of Canadian national identity. In other ways, however, hockey's relationship to place raises serious concerns about its ability both to transcend divisions and to aid cultural resistance. Indeed, there are numerous indications that hockey is implicated in processes through which cultural divisions in Canada are maintained and even exacerbated. In addition, there is a serious question mark surrounding the sport's capacity to facilitate resistance to Americanization.

Hockey and the Politics of National Identity

Dealing first with the issue of internal division, hockey has frequently served to consolidate the difference between French and English Canada. This can be illustrated in a number of ways. The presence in the NHL of the Montreal Canadiens and for a short spell the Quebec Nordiques has provided francophones with top-level franchises with which to identify. The fact that, in the case of the Canadiens at least, support has also come from English-speaking Canadians has done little to undermine the symbolic importance to the francophone cause of these major teams. Indeed, as Ken Dryden (1993), a former goalie with the Canadiens recalls, the divisions within Canadian society became all too apparent in the course of a game in which he was involved when many of his team's French-speaking fans announced their support for separatism. Dryden describes the atmosphere during a match between the Canadiens and the St. Louis Blues, played at the Montreal Forum on 15 November 1976, the day on which the Parti Québecois (PQ) won a majority of seats in the Quebec Provincial Assembly. Specifically he recalls the moment when the final election result was flashed up on the scoreboard.

> No longer afraid to hope, thousands stood up and cheered and the Forum organist played the PQ anthem. And when they stood and cheered, thousands of others who had always stood and cheered with them stayed seated and did not cheer. At that moment, people who had sat together for many years in the tight community of season-ticket holders learned something about each other that they had not known before. The last few minutes of the game were very difficult. The mood in the Forum had changed. (21)

A victory for the Canadiens over any NHL opponents is something that gives pride to many francophones. But wins against the Toronto Maple Leafs, as representatives of English-speaking, federal Canada, are particularly pleasurable for the more ardent separatists. In the 1930s, according to Gruneau and Whitson (1993), "the Canadiens' rivalries with the Montreal Maroons and, later, the Toronto Maple Leafs provided for the regular dramatization of the French and English identities that were so much a part of the popular consciousness of the day" (101). Even the Canadiens' nickname—the Habs (an abbreviation of *habitants*)—evokes memories of the original French settlers in Canada. As Lévesque, founder of the separatist PQ, said of the people whom he claimed to represent, "We are the children of that society, in which the habitant, our father or grandfather, was still the key citizen" (Richler 1992, 13). All of this is somewhat ironic given the city of Montreal's historic role in the establishment and early development of an essentially anglophone Canadian sporting culture. But it can be partly explained in terms of demographic change, shifts in the balance of political power within the city and throughout the entire province and the upsurge in separatist sentiment since the 1960s.

Arguably it has become increasingly difficult to argue that in Canada, or anywhere else for that matter, major commercially successful sports franchises can act as vehicles for the celebration of cultural difference. As is discussed in the conclusion of this comparative study, it has become easier than ever before for people to identify with teams, clubs, and franchises far removed from their national or regional locales. It would be too simplistic to insist in the modern era, therefore, that the Canadiens and the Leafs carry with them all of the collective sporting ambitions of francophones and anglophones respectively. Nevertheless, hockey remains intimately bound up with the rivalry between the two nationalities.

For example, the affinity between francophones and NHL teams located in the province of Quebec was further strengthened when Eric Lindros, hailed as the new Wayne Gretzky, refused to go to the Nordiques who had chosen him in the draft system. Although the player and his family consistently maintained that his preference for another franchise (in the end he went to the Philadelphia Flyers) was prompted not by any animosity toward French Canada but simply because he wished to ply his trade in a more lucrative and high-profile market, there were hints that he was unwilling to go to a team where a sound knowledge of the French language would have been more or less obligatory. Whatever Lindros's real reasons, it was inevitable that his behavior was interpreted by francophones as but the latest in a long series of snubs by English speakers (Poulin 1992). According to Poulin (1992), "Ultimately, the Lindros story is the human tragedy of a young man whose education has taught him to be exclusively preoccupied with material concerns and pointed him in one direction only. He has learned to be rather narrow-minded and not at all open to the contemporary concept of the world as a global village" (xvii). By leaving Canada for the United States, however, Lindros was clearly a product of sporting globalization. But the fact remains that he could not feel comfortable with his native country's own multiculturalism. As Mordecai Richler (1992) suggests, "Short of trampling on the fleur-de-lis, Lindros couldn't have done more to set himself stage center in the national quarrel" (226). The fact that Quebec City subsequently lost its franchise to Denver, Colorado, was yet another blow to Québecois sporting nationalists who would not have failed to see the irony of a Stanley Cup victory secured by the new franchise, the Colorado Avalanche, made possible in no small measure by players who had previously represented the Nordiques, and secured as a result of the money and future considerations that could be traced back to the Lindros affair.

In contrast with the English-speaking Lindros, most young francophone hockey players aspire to a career with a team in Quebec, specifically the Canadiens. Yet the pressures on the ones who make this dream come true are enormous. Montreal-born Alexandre Daigle, formerly of the Ottawa Senators, has remarked on the fact that he has performed well on the road against the Nordiques and the Canadiens because of the fans who were watching him (MacGregor 1997). According to MacGregor (1997), all of the great Quebecois players have been conscious of where they are from.

> Béliveau understood, just as Lafleur came to understand, just as Alexandre is beginning to understand, that the pressures of being a francophone hockey player in, or even on the border of, Quebec are unlike the pressures known by any other Canadian athlete. (272)

When Quebec's future within Canada was put to a referendum in 1995, there was considerable concern about what separatism might mean for hockey both in Canada generally and, specifically, in what would have become a new state. Leading Quebec players were quoted as being relieved that the vote had gone against the separatists, albeit by a very small margin. Thus, Montreal-born Luc Robitaille, then a winger with the New York Rangers, commented: "We should never separate. I do not think it would be good in the long run for Quebec" (*Hockey News,* 17 November 1995). Similarly, Ray Bourque of the Boston Bruins, also originally from Montreal, remarked: "I feel Quebec is part of Canada. There has to be a way to work things out—some way" (*Hockey News,* 17 November 1995). It should be added that there is even a perception in some quarters that French Canadians play the game differently—more like Europeans.

It is apparent that nationalist tensions still impact upon hockey in Canada. For one final example, it is worth recording that, during an NHL game played on 27 December 1999, between the Montreal Canadiens and the Ottawa Senators, Patrice Brisebois, a Canadiens defenseman and French speaker from Montreal, was described as a "fucking Frog" by an opposing player (*Hockey News*, 21 January 2000). The fact that the latter was not himself a Canadian but a Czech, Vaclav Prospal, is perhaps significant. It is possible that messages concerning cultural diversity have actually penetrated the consciousness even of professional sportsmen in Canada to a degree unknown among their counterparts in other countries. It was also something of a blessing that the player involved was a European since the ramifications of his offensive remarks were consequently less serious. Nevertheless, Prospal himself made a half-hearted apology and was forced to attend a private session with the NHL-appointed divesity trainer, Zack Minor. Furthermore, many people connected with the sport felt that the Senators player should have been suspended or fined.

In terms of the relationship between sport and nationalist politics, it has been forcefully argued that what is increasingly revealed in Quebec is a form of civic sporting nationalism. According to Harvey (1999), the promotion of the Quebecois as an ethnic group has been played down by the separatists in recent years. Yet the Quebec nation is still identified as French-speaking, which in itself shows the extent to which civic nationalism can become involved in the politics of cultural exclusion. French speakers who have different ethnic roots from those of the Quebecois and who, more significantly, may have grown up in very different societies, could find it difficult in a separate Quebec nation-state to identify with national sporting causes despite a linguistic connection to the national majority. All the more difficult, one might imagine, will it be for English speakers and others, including native peoples, to identify with a form of nationalism that might well be civic in its characterization but that could be perceived as being at least as oppressive and exclusivistic as any expression of ethnic nationalism would be.

While the tension between anglophones and francophones is the most frequently debated internal division in Canada, hockey is a window through which other differences can also be observed. Indeed, these other sources of division have tended to affect both francophone and anglophone "nations" equally. For example, although aboriginal people have been little different from their fellow Canadians in terms of their enthusiastic adoption of this national game, this has not made the assimilation of native people into Canadian society any more easy. Rather, as we shall see, hockey has simply become an arena in which racist attitudes toward native people have been consolidated and reproduced.

Hockey and Race in Canada

According to MacGregor (1997), Ted Nolan, who was to become coach of the Buffalo Sabres, "never forgot the racism he faced as a native hockey player" (237). Indeed, given the large numbers of First Nations people who actually play the sport, it is remarkable how few of them have been able or encouraged to advance all the way to the NHL. As MacGregor (1997) noted, "Hockey is widely and enthusiastically played on the reserves, yet [in 1997] only six players in professional hockey came from the reserves, with another twenty or so native NHL and minor-league players having been raised and played their hockey off-reserve" (238).

One current NHL star, Gino Odjick, has tried to draw attention to the plight of Native Americans by using as his shirt number the number previously assigned to his own father at a Spanish reservation school (MacGregor 1997). Another native player, Chris Simon of the Washington Capitals, unintentionally allowed the spotlight to fall on the issue of racism in hockey when, during the 1997–1998 NHL season, he was accused of making a racist remark toward an African American adversary (*Globe and Mail*, 10 November 1997). Most of the resulting condemnatory statements drew attention to the guilty party's ethnic background, as if to suggest that he of all people should have known better, and consistently failed to remark on the widespread incidence of racist attacks on aboriginal players of the national game. For example, writing in the *Hockey News*, Bob McKenzie (1997a) highlighted the issue of racism in hockey without once mentioning incidents in which First Nation players were the victims. McKenzie (1997b) also drew attention to ethnic slurs directed toward French-speaking players, which now include the verbal abuse directed by Vaclav Prospal toward Patrice Brisebois, while mentioning only in passing the serious nature of racist insults aimed at native North Americans.

Despite being on the receiving end of racist and ethnic abuse, the francophones and the native Americans have taken up hockey just as enthusiastically as English-speaking Canadians. It is less likely that more recently arrived Canadians will seek to confirm their new national identity by chasing a puck. Bringing with them the sporting traditions of their countries of origin, they remain unimpressed by hockey's attractions. Soccer and even cricket are more likely options, setting the new Canadians at odds with a national culture that had rejected these pastimes in the course of forging a distinctive identity. This is just as true of the French speakers who have settled in Quebec as of those immigrants to the other parts of Canada. Indeed, it is instructive to note that in the most recent referendum to decide that province's future, there was considerable evidence that the more recent arrivals were ill disposed toward separatism and favored instead the continuation of the federal system. Thus, it was revealed how the new Canadians have not only refused to be as-similated into Canada's sporting culture but are also unhappy with aspects of the prevailing political culture as well.

However, Canada has proved to be an attractive destination for immi-grants, many of whom have arrived in recent decades from the Carib-bean. On occasion, sport has played a significant part in their integration, not, of course, if they have clung to the parental culture and continued to play cricket, but certainly when they have turned their attention to activ-ities such as track and field and boxing. This integrative process, how-ever, has not been without its difficulties. These became particularly acute in the wake of the revelation that Canadian athlete Ben Johnson had used steroids in his preparation for the Seoul Olympics in 1988 when he was initially awarded a gold medal for his world record–setting per-formance in the 100 meters final. As Jackson (1998) claims, "The tarnished legacy of Ben Johnson continues to influence the lives of Canadians, espe-cially those black athletes who are following in the former sprinter's foot-steps" (23).

In part, the Johnson scandal is tied into a range of considerations about sporting ethics and the demands of elite performance. If Canadians are to compete successfully on the world stage, how should they respond to the allure of performance-enhancing drugs? At this level, Canadian athletes have been drawn into a debate that also occupies the attention of their fellow competitors worldwide. But, because of its racial ramifica-tions, the Ben Johnson saga extends beyond that general concern. As Jackson (1998) observes, "Johnson's mediated representation during his reign as world champion, an achievement which brought Canada inter-national recognition and prestige, reveals a temporary displacement of his racial identity" (27). Johnson had become "Canadian," not "Jamaican-Canadian" far less "Jamaican." He was presented as being in possession of a "Canadian" work ethic and achievement orientation. In addition, his successes on the track had provided a basis for the strengthening of Canadian self-esteem and, hence, national identity. This changed imme-diately with the disclosure of Johnson's guilty secret. As Jackson (1998) describes it, "Following the initial shock, disbelief, denial, and shame, there appeared to be a wave of abandonment and resentment" (29). This led to an outbreak of serial racial stereotyping, which ultimately raised doubts about the entire basis of Johnson's Canadian identity (Jackson 1998). For example, according to Jackson (1998), "Media discourses that define Johnson as a Jamaican immigrant, represent him as an animal, and imply that he lacks intelligence are all ways in which his Canadian iden-tity is called into question" (35). It can be argued that, in the intervening years, a number of black athletes, many of them sprinters, have not only served to rehabilitate Canadian track and field after the Ben Johnson nightmare but, in the manner of their achievements, have also helped to lessen the damage done by earlier racist discourses. The fact remains, however, that, despite Toronto being recognized as the world's most ethnically diverse city, at one level Canada is still constructed as a white nation and sport has not been entirely successful in contradicting that view. As shall be shown in the example of Sweden, it is relatively easy for some people in multicultural societies to regard the success in certain sports, such as boxing, of members of ethnic minority groups as evidence that these are not appropriate pastimes for the hegemonic white population. Thus, those who achieve recognition in such pursuits are marginalized to the extent that their authentic citizenship—their belonging to the nation—is symbolically withheld. Ethnicity and race are not the only factors that serve to undermine the integrative capacity of hockey.

Hockey, Sex, and Gender

The game's image as being intensely masculine has also weakened the case. Only a minority of Canadian women would claim to have had their national identity confirmed by a sport that has traditionally been celebrated as a macho and, at times, explicitly violent presentation of manliness. For many, the game has meant little more for many women than a sense of neglect at best and, in some cases, feelings of fear. A substantial section of Canada's female population together with a healthy percentage of its men would balk at the proposition that hockey can be regarded as indicative of the nation's best qualities. With its fighting and its arguably related history of violence toward women as well against other men away from the ice, its close links with heavy drinking and drug abuse, and, as revealed most recently, a high incidence of child molestation by coaches, the game represents in the eyes of many of its critics precisely those things of which Canadians should not be proud. In general, serious involvement in hockey from an early age may be unhelpful in turning boys into socially responsible men. With reference to the star performers, Robinson (1998) writes, "Since they first stepped out on the ice as little boys and showed their extraordinary talent, they have held the coveted status of male hero in a culture that worships sports heroes of only one sex" (7). More generally, according to Robinson (1998), "Young men are put in a precarious position in this subculture" (2). Critics suggest that the game's practices are undemocratic and feudal and have the potential to destroy the lives of many youngsters who were innocently drawn to hockey as a beautiful and exhilarating sport.

For example, Graham James, a father figure and mentor as well as a coach to Western League players for more than a decade, was sentenced on 2 January 1997 to three and a half years in a federal prison on two counts of sexual assault (*Hockey News,* 17 January 1997). The equally high-profile sex abuse scandal at Toronto's Maple Leaf Gardens, which revealed that twenty-four boys had been sexually abused by a former equipment handler between 1969 and 1988, brought the game's darker side to an even wider audience (*Hockey News*, 14 November 1997). But numerous other cases have also come to light in recent years (*Hockey News*, 31 January 1997). Equally disconcerting is the fact that, as Robinson (1998) reports, "adults responsible for the well-being of young players, who would never themselves sexually abuse a young person, may allow the abuse to occur, not because they are unaware of it, but because they, like so many of us, see the athlete as a masculine commodity that serves them, despite their protests that they love the boys as their sons" (11). Financial scandals have also increasingly plagued the NHL and damaged hockey's image.

Hockey and Corruption

The most extreme example is provided by the career of R. Alan Eagleson, the game's most powerful figure for two decades who, in early 1998, became a criminal in the United States, where he was fined in a Boston court, and in Canada, where he was sentenced to eighteen months in prison. According to U.S. Attorney Donald K. Stern, Eagleson "dipped into the till and took money directly out of the players' pockets" (*Hockey News*, 23 January 1998). In many ways, therefore, hockey has found itself in the dock both in reality and metaphorically. Yet, for a majority of male Canadians, the less pleasant of the game's traits are conveniently ignored. Moreover, if it could be shown that hockey can help Canada to resist American cultural imperialism, then many more people might be prepared to turn a blind eye to its more sinister side.

HOCKEY, GLOBALIZATION, AND CANADIAN NATIONAL IDENTITY

Time and again, the cry goes up—hockey is Canada's game or, as the legend on countless T shirts would have it, "Canada Is Hockey." This is not to ignore the fact that it is played in numerous other countries. But implicit is the widely held belief that Canada and the Canadians have a special affinity with the game that is matched in no other country. For many years, it was also felt that the Canadians were undoubtedly the best hockey players in the world. By the 1960s, however, it had become apparent that the Russians as well as other Europeans and even Americans could also play a bit. The result was a period of national soul searching. Victory in a challenge series against the Soviet Union in 1972 provided temporary relief. Thus, according to Richards (1997), "Certain people will always make more excuses about why we won that series, than they would have if we lost. But I will tell you—we were and are better, then and now. It's everyone's game—yet it is *ours*" (212). He finishes triumphantly with the words, "If that's nationalism in sport, don't ever forgive me." Despite such expressions of certainty, however, the feeling remains that the Canadians have no automatic right to the status of best in the world and certainly Canada no longer provides the only stage (if it ever did) for the world's best players. According to International Ice Hockey Federation statistics, although Canada has 3.5 times more young people involved in organized hockey than do Sweden, Finland, Russia, the Czech Republic, and Slovakia combined, it is losing out to these other countries in terms of the production of great players (Robinson 1998).

Some comfort is still drawn from the sheer numbers of Canadians who play at the game's highest level in the NHL. According to one journalist, writing only partly with tongue in cheek, "Canada invented hockey, taught the rest of the world how to play it and will always be in a position of global superiority" (Campbell 1994). Brave words, but for Canadians the reality by 1998 had become very different. NHL professionals competed for the first time in the Winter Olympic Games, held in Nagano, Japan. Despite high expectations surrounding the Canadian Dream Team, which included Wayne Gretzky, the greatest of them all in statistical terms, the medals went to the Czech Republic, Russia, and Finland, the latter beating Canada in the playoff for Bronze. Furthermore, despite having won the World Championship in 1997, Canada's women also failed to secure anticipated gold medals at Nagano, losing in the final to the United States. Just as Canadians in the past had been faced with the need to reassess their standing in hockey's world order so Nagano ushered in another period of soul searching. In addition, there were now even more compelling reasons to indicate that hockey was no longer a Canadian possession.

Although Canadians continue to constitute a majority of players in the NHL as well as the many other leagues that operate in the United States as well as Canada itself, most NHL franchises operate in American cities and a number of those that are located in Canada are constantly under threat. In the eyes of some Canadians there is something wrong with hockey's claim to be a national game when not only has it been the cause of so many young Canadians having to leave their country in the pursuit of fame and fortune but it has also been more or less taken over by Americans in terms of its corporate identity. As regards the movement of players into the United States, much was made of Wayne Gretzky's decision in 1988 to leave the Edmonton Oilers and move to Los Angeles (Jackson 1994). If "the Great One" could desert his country for a city with no history of hockey involvement, then what was happening to the national game? More than that, what was happening to Canada? Americanization has long been a Canadian concern and, as Jackson (1994) suggests, "The 'loss' of Wayne Gretzky came to embody for many Canadians their worst fears regarding this American influence and domination" (435). If the greatest hockey player of all time, himself a native of Toronto, could not be persuaded to spend his entire professional career in Canada, then serious questions had to be asked about Canadian "ownership" of the game. As Jackson (1994) reveals, the Gretzky affair is only one element in a more general crisis of Canadian identity, which can be traced back to 1988. "Conceptualized as a 'conjunctural moment,'" he writes, "the intersection of a specific set of political, economic, and cultural events led some people to label 1988 as a year of crisis in Canadian identity" (431). Apart from Gretzky's departure to the United States and his no less significant marriage to an American actress, Janet Jones, there was the major political issue of the Canada-United States Free Trade Agreement which was regarded by its opponents as having the potential to lead to American domination of the Canadian economy. In both sport and beyond, the threat of total Americanization seemed all the more imminent. The prevailing intellectual discourse was one that was characterized by crisis.

In terms of ice hockey, this fear is given added poignancy each time a Canadian NHL franchise is lost. Apart from Quebec City losing out to Denver, the Winnipeg franchise has subsequently gone to Phoenix, Arizona, and the prognosis for the Edmonton franchise is not good. The NHL itself is based in the United States and during the industrial disputes of recent years the impression frequently given has been that of American business and capital at loggerheads with decent young Canadian men. For example, criticism of NHL Commissioner Gary Bettman has frequently been couched in anti-American terms, despite Bettman's consistent assertion that the game needs the Canadians. Writing in the *Hockey News*, Stan Fischler (1996), for example, drew his readers' attention to Bettman's involvement in "the de-hockeying of Canada." Certainly future expansion plans for the NHL are all about increasing the number of American franchises at a time when even even some of those currently operating in Canada are under threat. It is already planned that the NHL will have expanded to consist of thirty teams in the near future, with new franchises having been granted to the cities of Nashville, Atlanta, Columbus, and Minneapolis-St Paul (*Hockey News*, 31 July 1997). This would mean that there would be twenty-five NHL teams operating in the United States and only five in Canada, with the Edmonton Oilers having been relocated to the United States.

Furthermore, those business interests that exercise ultimate control over the NHL are determined that professional ice hockey should expand beyond North America into the potentially lucrative markets of Europe and Japan. The first tentative steps to conquer the Asian market were taken on 3 and 4 October 1997 when the NHL's Mighty Ducks of Anaheim (whose connections with the Disney industry further underline the extent to which the game has been penetrated by global and/or American influences) and the Vancouver Canucks played a two-game series in Japan. This was the first occasion when NHL regular season games had taken place outside of North America and coincided with claims that an Asian super league would be established within the next ten years (*Hockey News*, 24 October 1997). Ensuring that the leading players would compete in Nagano was also part of a strategy to widen the appeal of hockey (*Hockey News*, 13 September 1996).

It is inevitable that Canadian-born players will play a major role in this process of expansion just as they have already helped to improve standards in Europe. According to Gruneau and Whitson (1993), one effect of NHL expansion would be to make hockey appear even less distinctively Canadian. On the other hand, they recognize that the fact that Danish and Irish soccer professionals ply their trade beyond their native shores has not necessarily weakened the national identity of their respective countries. Indeed, hockey players could actually help to increase international awareness of Canadian distinctiveness. Moreover, the globalization of soccer has done little to diminish its popularity in those countries, most notably of the United Kingdom, in which it was first played.

To what extent then, if at all, can hockey play a part in helping Canadians to resist globalization, which in this instance at least can be characterized as Americanization although one should not overlook the degree to which cultural flows have impacted in a variety of ways on the country's sports culture? Steve Dryden (1996), as editor in chief of the *Hockey News*, has sought to offer a realistic appraisal of the likely relationship between hockey and Canadians in the future. Dryden notes that "hockey is a Canadian birthright and it will never be anything else." It cannot acquire the same standing in the United States. On the other hand, Dryden recognizes that playing standards in the United States and elsewhere will continue to rise. But Canada will still be able to compete successfully at international level and, as a direct result of the growing strength of the game internationally, victories will be all the more commendable and will, thus, strengthen national self-esteem. Moreover, it is possible that hockey's capacity to reproduce a specifically Canadian identity will increasingly spring from its status within popular imagination. It will continue to remind Canadians of a simpler age as yet unfamiliar with the global pressure to conform. As Gruneau and Whitson record, "Hockey continues to have a powerful grip on the imaginations and collective memories of Canadians" (3). Furthermore, "Reminders of hockey's significant presence in Canadians' collective memories help to keep alive the idea of a national common culture" (Gruneau and Whitson 1993, 277).

Ironically, to this extent the game itself starts to pale into insignificance when compared with a variety of spurs to the imagination, including collectables, commemorative stamps, art galleries, advertising campaigns, that use hockey as a central motif and, of course, Halls of Fame. Nostalgia is also a key element in terms of the sales of books about hockey. One publisher is quoted as claiming that "the sentiment behind the nostalgia in Canada—still the heart of hockey readership and publishing—is the belief the NHL is abandoning the game's birthplace for the U.S." (*Hockey News*, 19 December 1997).

"The mystique of Canadian hockey," according to Gruneau and Whitson (1993), "threatens to be reduced—like so much of the heritage industry itself—to the marketing of nostalgia" (280). On the ice itself, the best hope may yet lie in small town hockey where community and tradition can still be celebrated around real hockey games as opposed to the hyperreal productions of the NHL, which, in any case, are priced out of the reach of many ordinary Canadians. The problem is that this is only one aspect of hockey in Canada. In the cities of Toronto, Montreal, and Vancouver the aim of corporate interests is to attract world-class entertainment, and if that involves breaking Canada's traditional link with hockey so be it. Civic boosterism has scant interest in traditional values and a historical sense of the Canadian virtues. Consumption and commodification become the key determinants and to that extent at least it would appear that the United States leads and big-city Canada follows.

In many ways, therefore, and not least in the world of sport, it is apparent that Canada has found the pressures of Americanization difficult to withstand. Hall et al. (1991) claim, however, that "organized sport is different in Canada because Canadian society is unique" (13). Despite its difficulties, it has managed to maintain a separate sporting identity. Furthermore, with the CFL's brief excursion into the American market and, above all, by virtue of the fact that without Canadian players and the national passion for the game of hockey, it would have been simply impossible for the NHL to expand to such an extent in the United States, Canada has even managed to exert its influence on American sports culture. The fact that it has been able to do so against such difficult odds is further proof of the degree to which globalization, if it is to have any explanatory value, must always be seen as a multidirectional process and never unilinear. We shall consider, in the next chapter, whether this is equally apparent in a society in which until relatively recently there has been little obvious threat to a well-established and secure sense of national identity. The example of Canada, however, also provides us with clear evidence that, during the process of so-called globalization, as Maguire (1999) suggests, space is opened up for the increased articulation of demands by identity groups that had previously lain dormant. Thus, while sport has provided Canadians with a terrain on which to engage in a resistance struggle against the pressures of American cultural imperialism, it has also become part of the battleground on which other politico-cultural wars are being fought out. On one hand, therefore, sport has helped to unify certain Canadians and to make them more certain of who they actually are. On the other hand, many more recognize in sport a mirror image of the deep social, cultural, and political divisions that afflict the country and consequently are demanding changes in the world of sport to complement those they seek in other aspects of Canadian life. The next chapter examines the relationship between sport and national identity in Sweden and also allows us to consider whether or not similar developments have taken place in a country even less well known than Canada for social cleavage.

chapter seven

Sporting Nationalism for Beginners

SPORT AND NATIONALISM IN SWEDEN

For many years, the issue of national identity in Sweden was largely ignored, particularly in English-language publications. There were no important examples of nationalist movements operating within twentieth-century Sweden (Elklit and Tonsgaard 1992). No groups wished to secede from Sweden and the Swedes had no territorial ambitions. Furthermore, the country as a whole had apparently eschewed the worst excesses of nationalist politics by way of a policy of neutrality. Thus, scholars chose to examine the Swedish polity with reference to its social democratic theory and practice rather than the reproduction of a national identity. Not surprisingly, therefore, the relationship between sport and Swedish national identity was also largely neglected, at least until relatively recently (Bairner 1994b; Bairner 1996b; Meinander 1998; Sörlin 1996).

In this respect, there is a marked difference between Sweden and neighboring Norway where the relationship between sport and national identity has been well established and discussed at some considerable length. As Goksøyr (1998) suggests, most attention has been paid to the late nineteenth and early twentieth centuries when Norwegian national identity was under construction. But he himself has discussed the ways in which the links between national consciousness and sport were consolidated during the twentieth century, and Hoberman (1993) has indicated how the official nationalism of the Norwegian government has impacted on sport in the 1980s and 1990s. One reason for the obvious sporting nationalism of the Norwegians may reside in the fact that Norway's history, so much of it spent under foreign rule, has simply made its people more nationalistic in general and this sentiment has simply been transported into the world of sport. Certainly the sporting rivalry with their larger and historically more powerful neighbor, Sweden, has traditionally been far more keenly felt by Norwegians than by the Swedes. But as this chapter reveals, it would be foolish to presume that Sweden has somehow been isolated from nationalism through a specific set of historical circumstances.

Goksøyr (1998) points out that two different styles of nationalism may be involved. "Historically," he writes, "the most aggressive Norwegian nationalism has been left-wing oriented and relatively democratic, while the most aggressive Swedish nationalism has been strongly right-wing oriented and authoritarian" (102). This description of Swedish nationalism is arguably too general to do justice to its complexities. It is undeniable, however, that the national identity of the Swedes has tended to be closer to that of other major powers, as has befitted its status as the biggest nation-state in the Nordic region, whereas Norwegian nationalism is rooted in ideas about small countries taking on the mighty. According to Goksøyr (1998), modern Swedes have developed a peculiar attitude toward nationalism and nationality. He argues that "in the former Nordic Great Power, Sweden, until about 1990 there was a self-conception of being Nordic in Europe and a diminution in the importance of a national identity" (102). He refers to the saying, "to be Swedish is unSwedish." As this chapter reveals, however, comments such as this actually offer an insight into Swedish national identity. Far from being linked solely to a conservative vision that is either inward looking or looks at the rest of the world as virtually untouchable, Swedish national consciousness in the twentieth century has been inextricably linked to a desire to be internationalist in certain clearly defined ways. Elitist ideas about being Swedish have remained and, indeed, been merged with social democratic internationalism. In addition, the modern period has witnessed the emergence of a type of right-wing nationalism that owes more to small-nation thinking than to ideas about national superiority. But this merely serves to emphasize that there is such a thing as Swedish nationalism and that this phenomenon cannot simply be categorized as belonging on a certain point of the ideological spectrum.

This chapter addresses the unwarranted neglect of Swedish nationalism in general and sporting nationalism specifically by arguing not only that Sweden is a sporting nation but also that sport has reflected and contributed to shifts in Swedish national identity and has played an important role in the way in which the Swedish nation has been presented on the international stage. Moreover, it will be argued that this dynamic involving sport and nationality is continuing despite the impact of the forces of globalization.

SWEDEN: A SPORTING NATION

There are four main reasons for regarding Sweden as a sporting nation. First, we have the perceptions of Swedes themselves. For example, young Swedish people have been shown to associate their country with sport to a greater degree than with any other phenomenon, with the exception of stress (Daun 1994). In addition, particular areas of the country are linked in the public mind with specific types of sporting activity, hence the equation of Leksand in Dalarna with ice hockey (Aldskogius 1993).

Second, Swedes have achieved remarkable sporting success over many years, particularly given a population size of less than nine million. Following in the footsteps of Björn Borg, a succession of Swedish tennis players have graced the world's courts. More recently, international golf has witnessed the emergence of a growing contingent of Swedish professional players, both male and female. In skiing, one of the all-time greats, Ingemar Stenmark, won eighty-six World Cup titles. Between July and August 1942, a Swedish middle-distance runner, Gunder Hägg, broke six world records. But it is not only as individuals that Swedes have made their mark on international sport. In team games, Swedish footballers have enjoyed some notable successes, not least a third place in the 1994 World Cup Finals in the United States. Moreover, Sweden's ice hockey players have fared even better, winning World and Olympic titles, with many of the star performers, from Börje Salming to Mats Sundin and Peter Forsberg, going on to become highly paid professionals in North America's National Hockey League. The list of Swedish sporting achievements could be continued for some time. But perhaps the most remarkable of all was that of Ingemar Johansson who became world heavyweight boxing champion in 1959, only a few years before professional boxing was to be banned in his native country. Even allowing for the fact that Sweden is a prosperous country, which might be expected to achieve more sporting success than an impoverished, developing nation, whose sporting achievements actually may be greater in relative terms, the fact remains that Sweden is a sporting nation in part because Swedes have performed consistently well at the highest level in a variety of sports. For a feature in a British newspaper (*Observer*, 4 October 1998), three journalists were asked to identify "the best sporting nation on the planet." They each chose relatively small countries that have achieved disproportionate sporting success. Two of the countries selected were Croatia and Jamaica. The third, picked by Jon Henderson, was Sweden. He observes that "Sweden's sporting reputation up until quite recently was based mainly on the feats of their footballers and winter sportsmen and women, plus occasional and unexpected contributions such as that of heavyweight boxer Ingemar Johansson." More recently, however, there has been a dramatic upturn in the fortunes, first, of Swedish male tennis players and, then, by men and women golfers. As Henderson reminds us, "Sweden's rise as a golfing nation followed the tennis revolution, but has been no less inexorable."

A third reason for describing Sweden as a sporting nation relates to the involvement of Swedes in the organization of international sport, to attempts to export the Swedish approach to sport to other countries, and to a constant willingness to play host to international sporting events. Swedes have represented their country on countless international sporting bodies, with Lennart Johansson, the president of the European football union (UEFA) being the best-known current example (Johansson 1998). Also in an internationalist spirit, the Swedish sports movement has sought to influence sports policy in countries as far apart as Tanzania and Latvia (Feldreich 1993; Hedlund 1984; Johansson 1986). In addition, since the Olympic Games were held in Stockholm in 1912, Sweden has hosted numerous international sporting events, including the World Cup Finals in football in 1958 and the world championships in athletics, ice hockey, and women's football in 1995 alone. But it is not only elite international competition that is welcomed to Sweden. Thus, youth football tournaments bring hundreds of boys and girls to the cities of Gothenburg and Stockholm every summer. For these young visitors, the image of Sweden as a sporting nation leaves a definite lasting impression.

A final reason for associating Sweden with sport is prompted by the close relationship that has existed for most of the twentieth century between sports policy and the general organization of Swedish society at the height of the so-called Swedish model. Sport has been prized for many years in Sweden because of the contribution that it is believed to make not merely to the physical well-being of the population (although that would be important enough) but also to the fabric of Swedish society. The extent to which this has implicated sport in the construction of a particular version of Swedish national identity shall be examined later in this chapter. It is already apparent, however, that sport is important in Sweden and that Swedes themselves take the role of sport in their society very seriously indeed (Andersson 1991). But the nuances of Swedish sport remain largely unknown to English-speaking audiences.

SPORT AND SWEDISH IDENTITY

According to Ehn (1993), "Sport in twentieth century Sweden has become one of the most emotional and expressive areas for nationalism" (204).

Indeed, he suggests that "in Sweden there is scarcely another field where love of fatherland is expressed so strongly in unison by so many" (206). Despite the accuracy of these observations, however, when the relationship between sport and national identity is explored, Sweden has seldom figured in the discussions. There may be sound historic reasons for this neglect. Changes in Swedish society and the relationship between Sweden and the outside world have been such as to make earlier explanations for ignoring the issue of national identity unsustainable. In any case, they have simply helped to obscure important aspects of Swedish history.

It was not until 1905 and the dissolution of the Union with Norway that the modern boundaries of Sweden were established. Moreover, late-nineteenth-century Swedes were conscious of the importance of developing a distinctive national identity. Second, although the Social Democrats who have governed Sweden for most of the twentieth century were highly successful in their attempts to avoid involvement in the major international disputes that directly affected much of the rest of the world while simultaneously developing a significant international status by virtue of neutrality, it can be argued that their policies were instrumental in the reshaping of Swedish national identity. Indeed, these resulted in a particular representation of Swedishness that was apparent in the affairs of the sports movement as well as in other areas of life, and which may well remain dominant today. But, thirdly, although it is undeniable that, for most of this century, Sweden has managed to avoid both ethnic division and also the worst excesses of chauvinistic nationalism, it is worth asking if it can continue to do so into the next century. The end of the Cold War rendered Sweden's neutrality a less important characteristic in terms of the construction of national identity. In addition, challenges to a cohesive sense of Swedishness have arisen as a result of the country's membership in the European Union and high levels of immigration, which have weakened substantially the relative homogeneity of the Swedish population. These changed circumstances are at the root of the growth of more chauvinistic nationalist rhetoric in Sweden. Among other things, this chapter considers the extent to which sport is likely to be involved if a more exclusive version of what it is to be Swedish becomes a significant political trend.

According to Eichberg (1989), "The history of Scandinavian sport suggests the presence of a specific identity, which is not merely a copy or variation of international 'normality'" (1). Indeed, he suggests that Scandinavian sport has contributed to the construction of a "Nordic regional identity." There is certainly some truth in this insofar as winter sports and a variety of outdoor activities, such as orienteering, are evocative of a Nordic way of life. Physical activity in the Nordic region has a long and diverse history, spanning the Viking era, the early Middle Ages, and the

Renaissance. Only some of this activity, however, was in any way peculiar to the Nordic peoples. For example, many of the games that were
played by the Vikings had been adopted as a result of contact with the
Celtic peoples of Scotland and Ireland. In addition, the aristocratic sports
played in Scandinavia in the Middle Ages were largely indistinguishable
from those enjoyed in other parts of Europe. Some attempts were made,
however, to associate sporting prowess with the Norse gods, although
even these can be likened to the linking of mythology and physical activity that is apparent in the construction of Irish sporting nationalism (Blom
and Lindroth 1995). One form of physical activity, however, did have
very real roots in the Nordic region and was to assume critical importance in the construction of Nordic identities.

SKIING AND THE SWEDES

Skiing has played a prominent part in the life of Nordic peoples for centuries (Sörlin 1996). A ski from Kalvträsk, dating from around 3200 B.C., is
one of the oldest preserved artifacts from the area, and various writers,
including Procopius, Paulus Diaconus, Adamus Bremensis, and Saxo
Grammaticus, have left us descriptions of skiing (Sörlin 1996). Despite its
shared Nordic history, however, by the 1880s skiing began to assume the
status of a Swedish "national" sport. According to Sörlin (1996), "It is
hard to escape the impression that skiing became, in a general sense, part
of a national mobilization, triggered by competition among the leading
countries in the era of industrialization" (149). As a consequence, the
Swedish Association for the Promotion of Ski Sports was established in
March 1892. What then were the qualities that at that time made skiing a
suitable vehicle for Swedish national mobilization and for establishing
the foundations of Swedish sporting nationalism?

Sörlin (1996) suggests four reasons why skiing was used in this way.
First, it was virtuous, associated with snow, winter, purity, and wilderness. Second, skiing was manly, described constantly as a masculine
activity like hunting, sport, and war. Third, it was heroic, connected as it
was to polar exploration and great journeys. Finally, and most relevantly,
it was Swedish, not least because the king who had founded the country
has arrived on skis (150). Skiing, however, was only an element in the
process through which Swedish sporting nationalism began to be developed toward the end of the nineteenth century.

Skiing was not, of course, the only form of physical activity that established itself at an early stage in Sweden. However, as Hellspong (1998)
observes, "The earliest references to agrarian sport in Sweden appear to
be a mixture of myth and reality" (11). In addition, he warns that "to discover the origins of many indigenous sports is a hopeless task when con-

sidering simple and popular pastimes" (13). What is significant, however, is the fact that "in the main, Swedish traditional games were not greatly concerned with results" (Hellspong 1998, 17). They also tended to be played without spectators. Overall, Hellspong suggests, "Swedish traditional sport was both similar and dissimilar to European sport in general" (19). The main concern of this present discussion is to consider the extent to which, despite manifest similarities with what goes on elsewhere in the world, the Swedish approach to sport has remained different in crucial respects.

SPORT AND THE SWEDISH NATION

Irrespective of a shared Nordic sporting heritage, in the case of Sweden, sport has been central to a process through which a particular Nordic country has sought to differentiate itself from its neighbors and to construct a particular national identity or, more accurately, a series of distinct national identities. This chapter explores the contribution made by sport to the construction of Swedish national identity in three separate periods:

1. from the origins of Swedish sport in the late eighteenth century to the end of World War I;
2. from the 1920s until the 1980s;
3. from the 1980s to the present.

In each of these periods, sport not only reflected the contemporary articulation of Swedish national identity but also played an important part in the construction and consolidation of the particular sense of identity being expressed.

As Sandblad (1985) suggests, "In Sweden, one way of compensating for the political defeat of 1809, involving the loss of Finland, was the dream of reviving the ancient Norse spirit and strength" (394). Not surprisingly, therefore, physical activity in early-nineteenth-century Sweden was closely linked to nationalism and militarism (Patriksson 1973). Indeed, virtually all physical education in Sweden from the mid-nineteenth century until the time of World War I was intended, first and foremost, to serve the interests of the military (Meinander 1992). Given these objectives, it was perhaps inevitable that Swedish physical exercise would be dominated by gymnastics. But there was an added nationalistic dimension to this preference inasmuch as the particular form of gymnastics that dominated Swedish physical education had been devised by a Swede, Per Henrik Ling (1776–1839). As Sandblad (1985) observes, "In Sweden, as in most other Scandinavian countries, modern sport was in part an outgrowth of Ling's system of gymnastics" (397). To begin with, however, the main quasi-political function of Lingian gymnastics was actually to resist the encroachment of the modern sports movement, which had originated in Britain. Thus, in two ways the Lingian system served the interests of conservative Swedish nationalism—by contributing to military training and by seeking to maintain a distinctively Swedish approach to physical exercise. The conservative bias of Swedish sport at that time was enhanced, furthermore, as a result of enthusiastic royal and upper-class patronage of athletic activities (Sandblad 1985).

The conservative and nationalist approach to sport was given added impetus at the end of the nineteenth century by the emergence of the Romantic movement and, in particular, by the influence of "Gotianism" or "political Scandinavianism," as Meinander (1998) calls it. This new trend in political thinking sought to systematize a widespread interest in and admiration for the ancient Nordic past with its emphasis on manly vigor and military virtues (Sandblad 1985). There are clear signs of the influence of "Gotian" ideas in the early stages of the development of the modern Swedish sports movement, for example in the choice of names for sports stadia (Walhalla and Ullevi, both in Gothenburg) (Sandblad 1985). Sandblad (1985) refers to "the ancient 'Gotian' ideal of manliness, which provided a source of inspiration—of which they may not always have been fully aware—for the athletic pioneers" (403). All in all, therefore, "Throughout the 19th century," as Sandblad (1985) claims, "the Swedish interest in physical exercise was accompanied by a conservative brand of patriotism" (403).

One important innovation during the later years of this period was the creation of the Nordic Games. Despite their name, these were "primarily an event by and for Swedes" (Yttergren 1994, 500). Indeed, they may well have represented a last-ditch attempt by Swedes to impose their hegemony over neighboring Nordic countries and especially over Sweden's last formal political partner, Norway. As Yttergren (1994) comments, "It was Sweden that was the driving force in the creation of a Nordic identity, and this was also the case with the Nordic Games" (496). Support for the Games was particularly strong in Sweden as a byproduct of opposition to proposals for a winter version of the Olympics. It was felt by many Swedes (and by Norwegians too) that the Winter Olympics would be too closely linked to the modern sports movement. The Nordic Games, however, were intended to be closer to the spirit of a more traditional approach to physical activity and would include parties, theatre productions, and other celebrations consistent with a bourgeois way of life (Yttergren 1994). The Games were first held in Stockholm in 1901 and two years later they took place in Oslo. Thereafter, Stockholm was again the venue in 1905, 1909, 1913, 1917, 1922, and 1926. Subsequent games were planned for 1930 and 1934 and, most controversially of all, in 1942, at a time when Norway was caught up in the travails of World War II and Sweden was continuing to declare its neutrality.

Gradually, however, the emphasis placed by Swedes on the Nordic Games and indeed on romanticized Gotian ideals began to wane. On the political front, the union with Norway was dissolved in 1905 and the two countries became more serious sporting rivals than ever before (Lindroth 1977). In fact, three years after the dissolution of the Union, the principal concern of Sweden's sports leaders was that Norway's representatives should not perform better than Swedish athletes at the 1908 Olympic Games in London (Holmäng 1988). As their concern would indicate, another important change had taken place in the early years of the twentieth century, with Sweden becoming far more involved in the modern international sports movement.

According to Holmäng (1988), "Right from the start Sweden took part in international sports interchanges to a prominent degree both through competition and leadership" (5). But this does not tell the whole story. In fact, Sweden was relatively slow to develop a modern sports movement, with a national federation (the Central Association for the Promotion of Sports) not being established until 1897 and the prototype of the present ruling body of Swedish sport, *Riksidrottsförbundet* or RF (the Swedish Sports Confederation) only being instituted in 1903. Early examples of modern athletic competitions had been held in Sweden in 1882 (Sandblad). But the emergence of a national sports movement was delayed as a result of continuing support for the Lingian tradition and also rivalry between the cities of Stockholm and Gothenburg, with support for the traditional approach to physical education remaining strong in the former whereas the ideas of the modernizers had come to dominate discussions about sport in the latter. Liberals were particularly keen to take control of sport out of the hands of military and commercial interests (Meinander 1998). There were also generational differences in terms of attitudes toward sport and the way was open for Swedish sport to be taken in interesting new directions. The one man most directly responsible for altering the trajectory of Swedish physical activity at that time was Viktor Balck.

Opinions remain divided as to how progressive Balck himself actually was. He became president of Sweden's national sports federation at its inception in 1903. According to Sandblad (1985), he was influenced by Gotian ideas and made frequent references to the physical prowess of the norsemen. As Meinander (1998) points out, Balck learned much from the ideas of his friend Frithiof Holmgren who was Professor of Physiology at the University of Uppsala. Holmgren's two main themes were those of the Vikings as role models and Darwinism as reality and these he applied to an understanding of sport as being necessarily competitive. Underlying all of this was an essentially conservative view of human society.

Indeed, Sandblad (1985) suggests that Balck and his supporters "used sport for political purposes, in a conservative direction, even though they did not themselves conceive of it as anything but pure patriotism" (405). In Sandblad's view, little actually changed as a consequence of Balck's assuming control of the national sports movement. He argues that "in Swedish national politics, the sports movement was given its most vigorous support by the Right, with its commitment to a strong military defence" (405). Yttergren (1994) also refers to Balck as a nationalist and a conservative. But there are other very different views on Balck.

Patriksson (1973), for example, is in no doubt that, at least in terms of sport, Balck was a modernizer. To understand how such wildly differing assessments have come about, one turns to Lindroth, one of the leading historians of Swedish sport. Lindroth (1981) does not deny Balck's patriotism nor his conservative ideas about the relationship between sport and moral development. Indeed, he suggests that Balck's high estimation of sport related to the beneficial effects he believed it to have on the mind and character of each participant. He paid little attention to any physical benefits playing sport might have. However, Lindroth also points out that at a fairly early stage Balck had become an admirer of English sportsmanship and he was certainly opposed to the dogmatic and narrow views about physical exercise that were exhibited in the gymnastics system developed by P. H. Ling's son, Hjalmar. Sandblad (1985), too, admits that not only Gotian ideas but also principles drawn from neoclassicism affected Balck's views on sport and these may well have influenced him to play a modernizing role, in spite of his political conservatism.

There is certainly no denying Balck's commitment to Olympism and through that to international sporting competition. Others were adopting a view of sport which owed more to arguments about the liberation of human potential (Meinander, 1998). But it is clear that while Balck may have successfully distanced himself from the cultural conservatism inherent in the defense of Ling gymnastics, he nevertheless advocated the idea of competition and, thereby, stood opposed to theories of sport and recreation that focus primarily on the intrinsic development of the individual. He found it difficult, however, to win over his country's sporting establishment to this idea. As Jørgensen (1998) notes, "Even though Balck was an enthusiastic advocate of the Olympic idea, he did not have immediate success in obtaining the backing of his native country, and only one sportsman from Sweden participated in 1896" (70). Lingian isolationism was still a potent force.

It is important to recognise that, during the opening decades of the twentieth century, Sweden itself, and not just Swedish sport, was undergoing major changes, which fundamentally altered the context within which sport together with a range of other activities was organized. As Sandblad (1985) puts it, "By the end of the First World War, other political and social forces were taking over, political democracy emerging victorious in Sweden as well as in many other countries" (400). In particular, the Social Democrats were becoming a dominant political force in Sweden and, significantly, for the very first time, they were beginning to take an interest in sport. As a result, the transformation of the Swedish approach to sport owed as much, if not more, to the changed political and social conditions as to the modernizing tendencies of a few individuals, most notably Balck.

Whereas previously conservatives had exercised more or less total control over sport and physical education in Sweden, the Social Democrats, under the leadership of Hjalmar Branting, began to participate in the sports movement and to initiate a social role for Swedish sport (Holmäng 1988). Branting himself regarded sport as one of the cornerstones of civilization (Horney 1960). In part, his enthusiasm for sport sprang from a genuine humanitarianism and a strongly held belief that sport can help to foster more harmonious international relations. More opportunistically, however, Branting also understood that in the light of the increasing popularity of modern forms of sporting activity among manual workers, it was politically judicious for socialists to reverse their traditionally hostile attitude toward sport (Sandblad 1985). With Branting's guidance, therefore, the Social Democrats endeavored to reform Swedish sport from within as opposed to condemning it from the sidelines (Liljegren and Wallin 1985). So successful was this tactical change that, as Sandblad (1985) observes, "one result of Branting's reformism was that, unlike several neighbouring countries, Sweden never had a strong separate workers' sports movement" (405). Instead, RF, while cherishing its autonomy, came to play the key role in developing an approach to sport that complemented the Swedish Model which the Social Democrats were in the process of constructing.

From the outset, RF sought to secure economic independence and, thus, autonomy from party politics (Lindroth 1974). Whether it succeeded in being apolitical is a different matter. According to Lindroth (1974), the Swedish sports movement can be compared with other popular movements in Sweden, including the trade unions, the temperance organizations, and the free church movement. These popular movements have been contrasted with middle-class associations that frequently operated alongside the state, sometimes actually providing services the latter was unable to offer (Norberg 1998). In reaching the conclusion that RF can be described as a popular movement, Lindroth applies a number of criteria—voluntariness, independence, permanence, organizational structure, large membership, geographical spread, dynamism, and an ideological component. He suggests that it is only in relation to ideology that RF's right to be described as a popular movement can be contested. We might add, however, that at various times in its development, RF has enjoyed a far closer relationship to the state than would normally be expected of a popular movement. Indeed, this helps to explain how, whether intentionally or not, the Confederation has managed to play a significant role in shaping modern Sweden and, as shall be argued, in constructing a particular version of Swedish identity.

RF quickly assumed a dominant position in the world of Swedish sport comparable with the preeminence of the Social Democrats in the wider society (Norberg 1998). Its membership grew from 93,000 in 1919 to 390,000 in 1939 (Lindroth 1987). In the process, RF successfully resisted the challenges of other general sports organizations, most notably that of the Swedish Workers' Sports Federation, formed in 1929. During the early 1930s, indeed, RF assumed the role of administrative guardian of Swedish sport (Norberg 1998). Today, there are sixty-three specialist national federations and 22,000 affiliated clubs under the general control of RF, which has close to three million members, of whom around two million are actively involved in playing sport (Riksidrottsförbundet 1994a). It is no exaggeration to describe the sports movement as the most successful of Sweden's popular movements in the modern era.

"In Sweden," Norberg (1998) argues, "corporative administration of relations between the sports movements and the state was established earlier than in the other neighbouring Nordic countries" (126). During the period from 1955 to 1970, however, the question of who should control Swedish sport was regularly discussed, even at the level of state commissions. Yet by the mid-1970s, RF's guardianship role and most favored position vis-à-vis the state remained secure and RF has continued to play a dominant role in the leadership of Swedish sport to the present day.

Today, RF has a number of separate but related functions. In general terms, it offers leadership to Swedish sport. It acts as sport's main pressure group, proposing legislative changes and canvassing for greater financial support, from both public and private sources. It also decides on the specific allocation of funds provided by central and local government and, to some extent, money raised within the private sector. In addition, RF acts as a training body for sport administrators and coaches and as a research establishment for the study of the social and physiological implications of sport. It must always be remembered that, as Henderson (*Observer*, 4 October 1998) notes, "embedded in the Swedish psyche is the idea that sport is, first of all, a means of maintaining physical well-being."

Sport and the Swedish Model

To appreciate the degree to which the sports movement has also contributed to the construction of Swedish national identity, it is essential to recognize that much of the sports movement's success has been due to RF's capacity to draw upon the values that lie at the heart of the Swedish Model—moderation, public-spiritedness, internationalism, and a blending of public and private initiatives. The Swedish Model is reformist, according to Meidner (1993), "In the sense that private ownership and free markets are accepted to a large extent" (219). Thus, private enterprise, in whatever field, has always been permitted by the Social Democrats to the extent that it has been regarded as contributing to the quest for the twin goals of equality and efficiency. As Therborn (1991) comments, "The paradox of an extensive Social Democratic Welfare State and vigorous private capitalism, which has so baffled or impressed perceptive foreign observers, makes sense, when the possibility of a confluence of welfare and international competitiveness is acknowledged" (209).

It is in the context of a mixed economy with equality and efficiency as its main objectives that the relationship between RF, the Swedish Model, and a particular expression of Swedish identity has to be understood. In a sense, RF has managed to draw upon the key elements of the Swedish Model. Its success has been due to the public-spiritedness of its membership and also to financial support from public and private sources. Thus, the reasons for RF's success replicate those very factors that made the achievements of the Swedish Model possible.

Certain key concepts, which recur in most studies of Swedish social democracy, are equally relevant to an assessment of the Swedish way of playing sport. For example, a word that appears at regular intervals in analyses of the so-called Swedish Model is *lagom*, which can be roughly translated into English as meaning "in moderation" or "just right" (Milner 1990, 49). The relevance of this concept to Swedish sport can best be illustrated by reference to two episodes in the history of the national soccer team (Bairner 1994b). Although writing with the benefit of hindsight and no doubt bitterly disappointed at the time, Orvar Bergmark's description of what it felt like to be a member of the losing team in soccer's 1958 World Cup Final, played in the nation's capital city, Stockholm, exemplifies the application of the idea of *lagom* to the world of sport. According to Bergmark, "The Swedish team had done more than people had wished for: it had got to the World Cup Final" (cited in Nilsson 1979, 191). The collective sense of *lagom* ensured that most Swedes were satisfied by the achievement of their players and this, in turn, prevented any widespread national mourning over the eventual defeat in the final itself at the hands of Brazil. Indeed, the Brazilian victors were shocked by the

Swedes' warm response to their triumph. As Oliver (1992) reports, "They won the admiration of all of the Swedes in the stadium and as a gesture paraded a huge Swedish flag around the stadium at the end" (19). It is not every nation that can be as magnanimous in defeat, particularly when such a significant sporting trophy is involved. Even in the arguably more polite 1950s, it is doubtful if many other home crowds would have been quite so charitable toward the conquerors of their own national team in a World Cup Final. In addition, this Swedish attitude toward sport appears to have survived in even more competitive times. The author personally observed the continuing relevance of the concept of *lagom* during the summer of 1994, during which the Swedish people watched their national soccer team progress to the semifinal stage of the World Cup Finals in the United States. The overall impression was of a people satisfied, and somewhat surprised, by the progress the Swedish players had made. When Sweden failed to reach the final there was no period of national mourning. In fact, the Swedes went out into the streets and celebrated. One fan of AIK even ventured the opinion to the author that it would have been embarrassing had either Sweden or Bulgaria, the other beaten semifinalist, reached the World Cup Final at the expense of their conquerors, Brazil and Italy.

At one level, these responses to Sweden's failure to win the World Cup can be interpreted as the logical consequence of a realistic world view of the nation's status in the football world. Sweden is a small nation with a semiprofessional domestic league structure. It would be foolish in the extreme to expect the national team, despite the overseas experience of many of its players, to compete successfully with the Germans, Italians, or Brazilians. Realistic or not, however, this is not the view taken by fans in countless other smaller footballing nations, including Scotland, where the expectation levels are frequently unrealistically high. This leads one to suppose that there has been something distinctive about Swedish culture in general that has permitted realism to flourish. *Lagom* is an obvious element in this to the extent that it instils in a population the capacity to accept graciously what has been achieved and not to become too depressed by the occasional reverse. Another concept that recurs in analyses of Swedish society, and which has pertinence to the whole issue of the relationship between sport and national identity in Sweden, is that of *Jantelagen* (or Jante's Law).

This *Jantelagen* is an unwritten law that is peculiar to all of the Nordic countries and not specifically to Sweden. According to Jante's Law, people are expected to be modest and humble about their achievements. The application of the law to Swedish sport means that elite performers are ill advised to dwell on their own personal success. Stars are not welcome. Indeed, some former top class soccer players have expressed the view that they are ignored in their native Sweden whereas their contemporaries from other countries have been virtually deified (Bairner 1994b) There is also a beneficial side, however, to the application of Jante's Law to Swedish soccer. In domestic competition, for example, teamwork is something that almost appears to be second nature to Swedish footballers. There is also an advantage to the national team inasmuch as highly paid professionals, plying their trade in some of the richest leagues in the world, are expected to play alongside part-time players from Swedish clubs. In some instances, this could be a recipe for disaster, with the home-based players being either awestruck, resentful, or both and the stars from overseas regarding it as being beneath their dignity to have to perform on the same team as men who spend much of their working week in banks or school classrooms. The informal application of *Jantelagen*, however, at least partly explains why it is relatively easy for players with such disparate experiences to bond together in the national interest. None of the highly paid exports would scorn the opportunity to represent their country regardless of the composition of the team and, unlike some of the star performers in other countries, neither would they dream of selling their stories to the press and thereby taking advantage of their celebrity status. Egalitarianism, at least on a temporary basis, is the essence of the national team and its players. The team in this regard is meant to be like Swedish society as a whole. It is an organic entity in which each element has a vital part to play and should be respected accordingly. Indeed, this evokes yet another concept that is a constant feature of discussions about Swedish social democracy—namely, *folkhemmet* or, in English, the People's Home.

The idea of the People's Home has been central to the construction of a social democratic society in Sweden. The Swedes have been invited to behave in a socially responsible way toward their compatriots in precisely the same fashion as people are generally expected to fulfil their obligations to their fellow family members. For the most part, the principle has worked well although there is extensive debate as to whether its success is attributable to the ideological appeal of social democracy or to a well-established Swedish political culture which is receptive to the values inscribed in *folkhemmet*. Whatever the past has revealed, however, Sweden has changed sufficiently in recent times for doubts to emerge concerning the long term relevance of *lagom, Jantelagen, folkhemmet*, and, by implication, the Swedish Model.

Commenting on the current problems faced by the Swedish Model, Lane (1993) highlights findings that suggest that "involvement in broad citizens' organizations was high in terms of formal membership (94 percent of a national sample) but the real level of participation by ordinary people was very low" (318). In this respect, the future of RF is arguably brighter than that of the Swedish Model as a whole. Not only are large numbers of Swedes active members of the sports movement, some 500,000 of them participate on an unpaid basis as coaches and officials. As Henderson (*Observer*, 4 October 1998) records, "There are virtually no full-time professionals in any sport—those who want to earn a living, kicking a football or slapping a puck, go abroad—while the national sporting structure is supported by volunteers, an estimated half a million of them." These volunteers make an immense contribution to Swedish sport, not least when one considers that, if they were to be paid at the same rates as youth leaders in the public sector, the cost to taxpayers would be in the region of £1,500 million per annum (Riksidrottsförbundet 1994a). Needless to say, however, even with the considerable efforts of these volunteers together with increased levels of private investment in sport and leisure, RF could not fulfil its various commitments were it not for government support. In return, it has been expected to achieve certain objectives in keeping with the broader aspirations of the Swedish Model.

In line with the aspirations of those who constructed the Swedish Model, RF has tried to promote sporting efficiency, an aim that is testified to by the existence of a number of elite sports schools. At the same time, great emphasis has been placed on the need to maximize the number of people having access to sporting activity so that the principle of "sport for all" never becomes an empty slogan. The status of sport in welfare democracies such as Sweden has clearly owed a great deal to the contribution it is believed to make to the general well-being of the population. As Norberg (1998) observes, "With its physical and moral enhancing qualities sport became a matter of public politics and moved into the public sphere of responsibility" (131). This resulted in both increased financial support and growing political interest. As we shall see, the extent to which "sport for all" has resulted in true sporting equality is open to question (Schelin 1985). In general, however, Swedish sports policy throughout most of the twentieth century has clearly reflected the ambitions of the Swedish Model as a whole. Indeed, arguably, sporting organizations have been recruited to the effort to realize a wider political project (Norberg 1998). Thus, sport has developed in ways that are consistent with the political strategies underpinning that wider social experiment—combining private and public and making the most of high levels of cooperativeness and public-spiritedness. Furthermore, by seeking to export ideas about sport as well as by organizing international tournaments at home, RF has done much to complement the outward-looking policies that have characterized Swedish politics for many decades. In sum, therefore, during the period in which the Swedish Model can be said to have been in existence, a particular form of Swedish national identity was constructed around the themes of equality, efficiency, cooperation, and internationalism and the sports movement can be seen not only to have reflected developments in that direction but also to have played a major role in constructing and consolidating that version of Swedishness. As the twentieth century draws to a close, however, Swedish society is confronted with new challenges and it is conceivable that an altogether different national identity may be constructed, with sport again playing its part.

SPORT IN A CHANGING SWEDEN

The problems currently facing RF and the Swedish Model as a whole have both economic and political origins. With reference to economic developments, because egalitarianism has been a key feature of Swedish identity during much of this century, any threat to that principle will make Sweden a very different place. Critics have questioned the extent to which the Swedish Model ever achieved proper equality either in terms of economic differentiation or of gender relationships. Indeed, it has been suggested that the failings of the Swedish Model are readily apparent in the realm of sport. Schelin (1985), for example, is in no doubt that "Swedish sport is socially stratified" (178). Moreover, "An unfortunate effect of existing sport stratification is that the sports which allow life-long involvement are restricted to the higher social classes" (180). Even those who admire what has been achieved in Swedish sport and in Swedish society more generally fear that future governments, particularly of the center right, would weaken egalitarianism further, in sport as elsewhere.

The Moderate Party, for example, has argued for more private funding of sport and leisure and less public support as well as less governmental interference in the way in which money is to be used by RF (Moderata Samlingspartiet 1995). Against these proposals, the Social Democrats, supported by the Left Party, take the view that overreliance on private funding would inevitably endanger the "sport for all" principles which are fundamental to Swedish sport and to its contribution to social improvement more generally (Socialdemokraterna 1994). Private funding, they argue, seeks out elite performers and events, leaving other parts of the sports movement to fend for themselves in a hostile economic environment. Only a substantial public subvention can guarantee the future of the weaker elements of Swedish sport and, thus, the fundamental values of the sports movement as a whole.

One element of Swedish sport that might be affected by changes to the way in which sport is funded is women's sport. Like the other Nordic countries, Sweden has an enviable reputation in terms of female empowerment. More than 40 percent of RF's active members, at present, are women and girls, and the extent of female participation in sports may be even greater than that figure indicates because many equestrian and aerobic clubs, which are particularly popular with women, have tended to operate outside of RF's sphere of influence (Riksidrottsförbundet 1994a). In spite of these positive indicators, disquiet has been expressed concerning the far lower level of female involvement in the actual running of sport. This discrepancy between image and actuality can be traced right back to the turn of the century when, as Meinander (1998) records, "although the social emancipation of women had gone far further in the Nordic countries than in central Europe, sport was still strongly maledominated" (62). It has been suggested that the fact that sport remains heavily influenced by patriarchal power relations is reflective of more general problems in a variety of sectors of Swedish society (Riksidrottsförbundet 1994b). It is undeniably a deficiency in terms of the sports movement's contribution to equality. But, even more seriously, it is now being argued that, while it is unlikely that Swedish women, or indeed most Swedish men, would agree to a reduction of women's access to sport, social developments may yet limit the opportunities open to women in a whole range of activities, sport included (Hirdman 1994; Jenson and Mahon 1993). For its part, RF continues to struggle for greater female involvement in the organization and administration of Swedish sport. But as with its quest for equal access to sport in general, its capacity to promote change is necessarily constrained by developments in the wider realm of economics and politics. However, even if the Swedish sports movement and, indeed, the Swedish Model never quite managed to achieve the levels of equality admirers of the Swedish way have claimed, it is undeniable that much was achieved in that respect and that, as a consequence, a predisposition toward equality became established as one of the main characteristics of Swedish identity. But if, as some have suggested, the Swedish Model is now in a state of terminal decline, what new version of Swedishness might emerge? Furthermore, in what ways might sport contribute to the construction of a new style of Swedish nationalism for the twenty-first century?

For the first time in decades, Swedes have become directly concerned with their national identity (Ehn 1993). Immigration, membership in the European Union, and the process of globalization are all felt to threaten a longstanding certainty about what it means to be Swedish. Given its importance in Sweden, sport will inevitably play a part in offering Swedes opportunities to respond to new challenges and to construct identities that shall carry them into the next century.

Right-wing nationalists in Sweden, particularly a small but growing body of neo-Nazis, are fearful that traditional Swedish national identity is being put at risk by immigration and European Union membership. However, as far as immigration is concerned, it has been argued that sports represents a particularly helpful vehicle for the integration of immigrants into Swedish society (Järtelius 1982). Indeed, according to Ehn (1993), "For many immigrants sport is one of the most flexible ways of 'becoming Swedish,' even if it can lead to conflicts of loyalty when Swedes compete with their former homeland" (215). Certainly sporting personalities such as Martin Dahlin, in football, and the athlete Maria Akraka have been important role models for young immigrants to follow, although with reference to Akraka it has to be said that RF has continued to experience major difficulties in trying to involve immigrant girls and women in sporting activity (Järtelius 1982).

In seeking to maintain what they regard as authentic Swedishness, the extreme Right, far from welcoming integration through sport, have shown an interest in turning sport into an arena for the expression of racist and xenophobic nationalism. Some football supporters, especially those who follow the leading Stockholm clubs, have been willing channels for this kind of nationalism. It is no accident that the most notorious of these, AIK's Black Army, have been styled, "the Last Swedes" (Sännås 1998; Tamas and Blombäck 1995). More insidiously, however, the nationalism of groups such as the Black Army has been given tacit support from within the more formal structures of Swedish sport, with far more flag waving than in the past, for example, and the playing of the national anthem before all elite series ice hockey matches (Ehn, Frykman, and Löfgren 1993).

Arguably, expressions of patriotism by the overwhelming majority of Swedes owe far less to racism in the face of large-scale immigration than to a vague feeling that Swedish identity has been eroded by a number of recent developments, most notably membership in the European Union. In terms of sport, this type of nationalism could presumably be served simply by Sweden's being successful at universally popular sports such as association football. Ironically, however, the problem with such sports for the extreme Right in Sweden is that they are every bit as accessible to immigrants as they are to "real Swedes." To look to the restoration of more traditional Nordic pastimes, which formed part of Sweden's national identity in the nineteenth century, might seem unfeasible, however, in the era of global sporting experience. It is worth noting that the fastest growing sport in Sweden at the present time is the indoor version of the old Nordic game of bandy. But it is highly unlikely that its growth owes anything to the demands of neo-Nazis for Swedish sporting purity.

Swedish Sport, Globalization, and Identity

In terms of sport, and many other activities, Sweden has of course been exposed to global pressures resulting in a multiplicity of similarities with other parts of the world. The dispute between Balck and his followers on the one hand and the advocates of Ling gymnastics on the other was largely occasioned by the British sporting revolution and subsequent export of British games to various parts of the world, the Nordic region included. In the first quarter of the twentieth century, moreover, the influence of American thinking about society and sport was beginning to be felt throughout Scandinavia. Artur Eklund, a Finnish journalist of Swedish origin, was typical of those who expressed an enthusiasm for the vibrancy of contemporary American society. Eklund's analysis, as Meinander (1998) suggests, indicated " a world of speed as a symbol of vitality that was typical of modern thinkers in the 1910s as an expression of the maximization of all forms of human sensation" (58). These, of course, included sport. As in the past, some Swedes were less eager to embrace such outside influences. The fact remains, however, that the development of Swedish sport has never been a wholly autonomous affair.

At the same time, as Maguire (1994) points out with reference to the applicability of globalization theory to sport, it is important to recognize that diminishing contrasts are frequently accompanied by increasing varieties. As a result, though global forces may well threaten the viability of existing nation states, they may also provide space for the expression of previously submerged national, ethnic, or local identities. In Sweden, for example, as Hellspong (1989) observes, the revival of traditional games in recent years has been an important element in the movement of Gotland islanders to express their cultural identity in the face not only of global forces but also in response to an all-encompassing Swedishness. According to Hellspong (1998), "Today Gotland cherishes them as symbols of the island's individual culture and they still exist, though in more organized forms than in the past" (14).

Americanization of a sort has taken place. Indeed, as Meinander (1998) argues, Sweden, like all of the Nordic countries, was very responsive to American influences from a fairly early stage. One reason for this, he contends, "was apparently that during the preceding decades the Nordic countries had experienced faster social and cultural change than the rest of Europe" (65). This coincided with a belief that "the Nordic countries and North America, from a cultural point of view, were both European 'border' countries that developed quicker than the centre of their civilization . . ." (Meinander, 65). An enthusiasm for Americana (cars, music, fast food) is palpable throughout Sweden. Nevertheless, as we have already seen in earlier chapters, nations receive the cultural products of the global process in their own particular ways. Two excellent

Swedish examples of this globalization phenomenon relate to American football and hockey, a sport that has been most professionalized in North America but has longstanding roots in Sweden itself. At the Swedish American football final, a very low key equivalent of the Super Bowl (as well as at Elite Series hockey matches), the author has listened to the Swedish national anthem being played and sung. Clearly the example of playing national anthems when the national team is not involved comes from the United States and one might take these developments as exemplary of the impact of Americanization on Swedish sport. The fact remains, however, that the anthem being played is that of Sweden. When one considers how few opportunities exist for citizens to sing their national anthem, it is clear that this particular innovation, although American in origin and increasingly globally audible, has at least as much to do with confirming specific national identities than testifying to the globalization of sport.

The other example concerns the sportswear that is favored by young people in every continent. In Sweden countless sports fans, young and old, wear North American–style caps, jackets, and so on. As in other European countries, however, these often feature the names and logos of local soccer teams. Thus, the baseball cap is employed to recognize a different sport from baseball (as it is in the United States, indeed, when it is linked to an American football or basketball franchise). This is not to deny that Swedes, like people throughout the world, also wear baseball caps and jackets that are produced on licence to the major American league and franchises. What is locally specific in Sweden, however, is the fact that the league most recognized in this way is the NHL. Numerous Swedes wear clothing that indicates an affinity to major hockey franchises. This certainly indicates some commitment to the American way of playing sport. But what should be kept in mind is that the "American" sport most commonly saluted in this way is also a Swedish sport and many of the franchises being advertised employ Swedish players. Indeed, one can reasonably assume that the popularity of certain hockey teams in Sweden will be related to the numbers of prominent Swedes, past and present, who have played for them. The Swedes have certainly not embraced the American project fully, and, arguably, there was never any likelihood that they would do so. As Meinander (1998) claims, "Despite an infatuation with the United States and a worship of machines the Nordic people were bound by the European custom to discuss and plan the future with the help of myths and messages from the past" (66).

It is impossible to predict how Swedes shall be viewed or indeed how they shall view themselves in the next century. It is also impossible to know the precise role that sport shall play in the future construction of Swedish identity. But perhaps this uncertainty is itself significant. In the

earlier periods discussed in this chapter, it appears to have been easier for
Swedes, or at least for Swedish opinion formers, to construct a coherent
national identity, and sport clearly played an integral part in underlining
their certainties. First, sport was used for the purposes of promoting
romantic, conservative nationalist ideas. Thereafter, it was part of the
process whereby a national identity based on social democratic principles, including, paradoxically, internationalism, was developed. The fact
that the sport-national identity nexus in the years to come may point in a
variety of directions—right-wing xenophobia, multiculturalism, region-
alism—illustrates the degree to which there is now far less certainty
about what it means to be Swedish. It would be premature and dangerous, however, to promote the idea that soccer fan culture in Sweden is
inevitably drawn to right-wing politics and that this, in turn, indicates a
dangerous development in terms of Swedish sporting nationalism as a
whole (Andersson and Radmann 1998a). Certainly members of the Black
Army appear less interested in reactionary politics than in the past.
According to Andersson and Radmann (1998b), "The Scandinavian supporter culture is predominantly positive in its nature" (155). This claim is
predicated on the belief that fans in the Nordic countries have adopted
the carnival spirit that is also a feature of support for the national teams
of Scotland and the Republic of Ireland. As regards such behavior, it is a
matter of supreme irony that so many young Swedish fans chose to
attend a variety of international events wearing imitation Viking helmets
given the importance of "Gotian" ideas in the formative years of their
country's sporting development. As has been argued in earlier chapters,
however, the paraphernalia of carnival can often simply conceal those
less positive aspects of the relationship between sport and nationalism
and it is perhaps too early to say that the neo-Nazi element of Swedish
soccer fandom has gone forever. The signs, however, are promising.

In any case, despite a serious weakening of support for the ruling
party in the 1998 general election, who is to say that the old social democratic identity is inevitably doomed? After all, a major beneficiary of the
social democrats' loss of votes was the Left Party (formerly the Communist Party), which was clearly helped by a nostalgic mood in certain
sections of the population for the good old days of the Swedish Model in
its prime. Perhaps a commitment to combining efficiency with equality,
both in sport and elsewhere, may yet sustain Swedish identity into the
next century. One thing is certain. Whichever option comes to dominate
debates about the nature of Swedishness, sport will continue to be an
important element in the construction of the identity that is chosen.
Writing in the *Observer* (4 October 1998), Jon Henderson comments that
"Sweden deserves recognition as the best [sporting nation on the planet]

because success in many ways is against their nature." In that respect, as in many others, of course, Sweden is changing. Indeed, it would have been foolish to imagine that it could resist with complete success developments in the global sporting culture. But the Swedish approach to sport remains distinctive in certain crucial ways.

Compared with the other peoples examined in this book, the Swedes have traditionally adopted a fairly restrained attitude toward the issue of sport and nationalism. Swedish fans with painted faces and wearing imitation Viking helmets have long been a feature of major sporting occasions. But there has consistently been a benign aspect to this kind of sporting nationalism not unlike the nationwide predilection for flying the Swedish flag outside homes, even on the remotest islands of the Stockholm archipelago. The Swedes are proud of their nation but usually in a relatively gentle manner. This is largely due to the fact that nationalism in general, at least of the overtly political variety, has been of only limited importance to Swedes in the modern era. If new forms of political nationalism grow in Sweden, one can confidently predict that these will impact on sport. If, on the other hand, the Swedish system is able to withstand emergent, exclusive nationalism, it is likely to be the case that Sweden, of all the countries studied here, will continue to be the one which is most characterized by true "sportive nationalism," as opposed to political nationalism by other, in this case sporting, means. To make any definitive statements, however, about the links between sport and national identity in the contemporary world, it is necessary to revisit the themes that were introduced in chapter 1 and to look again at theories of nationalism, national identity, and globalization in the light of what has been uncovered by the case studies.

chapter eight

Sporting Nationalism and National Identities

A THEORETICAL DISCUSSION

SPORT AND NATIONAL IDENTITY

Despite the lingering protestations of sports people themselves, there is little dispute among those who study sport in the modern world that it is political to the extent that it not only reflects social divisions but also frequently exacerbates these. As a result, sport has been discussed at length in terms of ethnicity, gender, race, sexuality, age, social class, and so on. It has also been identified as being related to questions of nationality. However, while the linkage of sport and nationalism is now widely accepted, there has been a lack of precision in terms of the types of nationalism involved and the precise ways in which they interact with sport.

For those who adhere to a simplistic view of globalization this lack of precision would scarcely constitute a problem. If the world is becoming homogenised, then nationalism or national identities in all of their manifestations are rapidly losing their social significance. If, however, one adopts the more sophisticated approach, as outlined in chapter 1 of this book, then it becomes obvious that nationalism coexists alongside globalization and is at times strengthened by it. There is a growing body of literature on the precise relationships between sport and nationalism. Some studies have concentrated on specific sports, most notably soccer (Duke and Crolley 1996; Sugden and Tomlinson 1994; Wagg 1995). In particular, this can be attributed to soccer's global appeal and the fact that it is regarded as the national game in so many countries. As shall be revealed later in this chapter, however, the precise meaning of the concept of a "national game" itself needs closer scrutiny. Indeed, it is valuable in this respect, that other studies of the relationship between sport and national identity have dealt with particular types of society rather than specific sports. For example, there are examinations of sport in multilingual societies such as Switzerland (Tomlinson 1999), ethnically divided societies, including Belgium (Vanreusel et al. 1999), historic nations that have been submerged within larger nation states, such as Catalonia (Duke and Crolley 1996), and multiracial nations such as Brazil (Lever 1983; Leite Lopes 1997). Valuable work has also been done on states and societies that were the product of colonization and subsequent struggles for independence. These include South Africa (Nauright 1997) and the West Indies (Beckles and Stoddart 1995), for which area studies have been combined with analyses of particular sports, rugby and cricket respectively. In some instances, the analysis has concentrated on the relationship between national identity and other sources of identity formation such as gender. Interesting examples of this approach are provided by Archetti (1994; 1996; 1999) in his studies of soccer and masculinity in Argentina. What each of these studies reveal, as do many others that have not been mentioned here, is that issues of national identity vary considerably from one social formation to another.

Indeed, it is important to remember that nationalism itself is multifaceted. There is a very real difference between the nationalism of a well-established world power and that of a submerged people, albeit that certain shared characteristics may also be discernible. Inevitably there will also be a marked variation in the manner in which sport is used in such different contexts to promote the nationalist cause. In some societies sport has clearly been employed as a means whereby rival identities are transcended in the interests of establishing national solidarity. Elsewhere, however, sport is in the forefront of efforts to foment division within empires or even established nation states. The case studies discussed in this book have provided examples of a variety of ways in which sport has been linked to nationalist ideology and politics. They have also revealed the degree to which sport has greatly assisted national endeavors to resist or, at the very least, to domesticate globalizing impulses.

None of this is to suggest that identities are indivisible. All human beings are characterized by a multiplicity of identities of which nationality is only one. Gender, sexuality, social class, and so on also help to make us the people we are. National identity is certainly of importance to most human beings, albeit to greater and lesser degrees. Yet even in purely spatial terms, attachment to a particular region, city, town, or village may take precedence over any affinity with the nation. This is equally true of gendered and sexualized identities. This is an important part of the problem when we try to conceptualize the relationship between sport and national identity. Even as regards sport, the nation may simply not matter as much to some people as do other allegiances. I am in no doubt that if faced with the choice between unparalleled achievement by Dunfermline Athletic Football Club on the one hand and by Scotland's national soccer team on the other, I would choose the former. This does not make me any less Scottish and proud to be so. Rather, it serves to illustrate just one aspect of a multidimensional structure of identity. Furthermore, it is conceivable that a father could transfer his allegiance from a soccer club he has supported all his life to one for which his son has been signed to play even when the two teams are in opposition. In this instance, a new sports-based identity centered around being a parent transcends another, earlier sporting identity.

It should also be noted that team sports have tended to dominate much of the foregoing discussion. One justification for this is the fact that these activities enjoy high levels of participation. More important, however, is their capacity to attract large audiences, for it is undeniable that it is usually in the behavior and attitudes of fans rather than those of participants that the relationship between sport and identity becomes most apparent. Participants are frequently able to ignore rival pulls on their emotions as they pursue a sporting career. This explains why professional soccer players are able to move more easily from one team to another than is the case for most fans. It also helps us to understand why a francophone from Quebec can represent "federal" Canada in the Olympic Games regardless of separatist sympathies and how a Catholic from the north of Ireland can come to be playing for Northern Ireland's soccer team despite having no respect for the political entity that team represents. Shortly before his death, the notorious Ulster loyalist prisoner, Billy Wright, told me that anyone who puts a sporting career ahead of loyalty to his or her identity deserves no respect. But this again was to make the mistake of assuming that each of us possesses a single identity. In fact, Wright himself had problems with trying to reconcile his violence, which he regarded as politically necessary, with his Christian faith, which taught him that killing is wrong. In the end, he allowed the former to take precedence over the latter and, in so doing, he followed a similar path, albeit one with more deadly ramifications, as those who have put their sporting ambitions ahead of their feelings of loyalty to other social constructions. Fans, however, are less likely to regard this as a realistic choice.

FANDOM AND IDENTITY IN THE GLOBAL ERA

As the global media bring events from all parts of the world into people's living rooms, the nature of sports fandom has certainly evolved. Thirty years ago, it would have been unthinkable for a youngster living in

Liverpool or Leeds to become a fan of a major Italian soccer club such as Juventus or Inter Milan far less an American sports franchise such as the Chicago Bulls or the San Francisco 49ers. As surprising, if not more so, is that fact that someone growing up in either Liverpool or Leeds can become a supporter of Manchester United or even one of the big London soccer teams. There are undoubtedly soccer clubs (and Manchester United is an excellent example) and other sports franchises that draw their following from throughout the world. All this having been said, however, the fact remains that support for Juventus and Inter is at its densest in the cities of Turin and Milan respectively and for the Bulls and the 49ers in their own home towns. In addition, the child from Liverpool, while identifying with a foreign soccer team or a franchise in a different sport entirely, is still most likely to be a fan of either Everton or Liverpool football clubs and the young fan in Leeds is almost certain to favor Leeds United. Moreover, once these choices have been made, they are difficult to overturn.

With the yuppification of English soccer has come a consumerist culture that has permitted new fans to choose their teams in the same way that they would select a car or even an item from the supermarket shelf. Most traditional supporters, however, are in a position where the choice is virtually made for them on the basis of locality, family influence, or (as for example in the case of fans of Celtic and Rangers who travel from all over Scotland and beyond to support their favourite team) some additional identity factor. Similarly it is quite possible, as was suggested in the Canadian case study, for a francophone to support the Toronto Maple Leafs and for an anglophone Canadian to follow the fortunes of the Montreal Canadiens. At the level of symbolism, however, the two franchises continue to represent the collective interests of two competing nationalities.

As far as national teams are concerned, the situation is even clearer. Few people support national sides for reasons other than their own national identity. Most fans no doubt have second and third favorites—Brazil in soccer for example—and wearing the shirts of some of the world's great soccer nations (or, if one's instincts are toward retro images, of the former Soviet Union) has become something of a fashion statement in recent years. But it would be odd to hear from someone who had grown up with Scottish parents in Glasgow or Edinburgh that he was a Brazilian fan in any meaningful sense. However, we have seen in most, if not all, of the preceding chapters how the construction of identity through sport (in Ireland, for example, or in Canada) can create difficulties that are themselves a reflection of more general problems of nationality.

NATIONAL SPORTS

If each nation in the world possessed its own unique sporting culture, the relationship between sport and national identity would be largely uncontentious. The fact is, however, that the concept of "the national sport" is a slippery one. Most societies do have their own peculiar traditions as regards sport and leisure activities. In general, however, these are regarded as having little more than antiquarian interest. On the other hand, in certain places, traditional pastimes have acquired much greater contemporary resonance. Of the case studies examined in this book, for example, Ireland provides the perfect illustration. Gaelic football, hurling, and the like are clearly national sports inasmuch as they are bound up with a specific idea of Irishness. Moreover, they are played and watched by large numbers of people throughout Ireland. To that extent they differ markedly from shinty, which is peculiar to Scotland and, thereby, evokes an idea of Scottishness but has limited popular appeal. Similarly, lacrosse is a "Canadian" sport only if one adopts a rather arcane definition of a national sport. However, despite the manifestly stronger claims of Gaelic games in this respect, it should not be forgotten that, although they are undeniably popular, unlike shinty in Scotland and lacrosse in Canada, so too are other sports which are certainly not peculiar to Ireland but which are arguably at least as important in terms of national sporting pride.

The point is that national sports take different forms and, in so doing, they provide us with important insights into the character of particular nations. Some national sports are peculiar to specific nations. As such they either confirm the exclusive character of the nation or, more commonly, reflect a contest between ethnic and civic representations of the nation. Ironically, however, those sports that are defined as national but are actually shared by countless other nations are arguably more successful at uniting the people of particular nations. Thus, soccer in the Irish Republic or in Scotland can be recognized as the national sport of the civic nation whereas native Gaelic games are inevitably linked to narrower definitions of the respective nations. The fact remains, however, that people are willing, in varying degrees, to lend their support to their sporting representatives regardless of which conception of nationhood a particular activity appears to endorse. For most sports fans, the nation that deserves their support is a given and in following their national teams they underline their sense of identity while simultaneously reflecting its complex character.

ON SPORTING NATIONALISM AND NATIONAL IDENTITY

The representation of the nation through sport, however, can differ considerably from one nation to another. Thus, American sporting nationalism puts relatively little emphasis on international success. Indeed, much of the affection for sports such as baseball, American football, and basketball is owed to the fact that they provide arenas in which the Americans remain supreme. "Playing with themselves" genuinely amounts to world-class sporting action. In any case, given the sheer size of the nation as a whole and of its great cities, contests between rival franchises assume a quasi-international status. Americans do, of course, root for their nation's representatives in events such as the Olympic Games and golf's Ryder Cup but, while these events give competitors the opportunity to fly the flag, for most sports fans domestic competition in "American" games is what really counts.

In Ireland and Canada, the situation is slightly different. Although both countries can claim that certain sporting activities support the idea of national distinctiveness, they do not have sufficient prestige to permit the belief that "playing with themselves" is adequate for the promotion of the nation. Thus, producing a great many hockey players and seeing the game promoted as something intrinsically Canadian is all well and good, but it is as important, if not more so, to be able to beat other nations, and not only at hockey. As a result, the Canadians in general arguably take the Olympics more seriously than do most Americans and they are even supportive of far less prestigious events such as the Commonwealth Games. Similarly, Irish sporting nationalism, while maintaining a strong interest in Gaelic games as the sporting guarantors of a distinctive national identity, is equally, and in some instances more, committed to those sports, such as soccer and rugby union, that provide the Irish with opportunities to take on the world. Ironically, Ulster union-ists have chosen to play "British" games as part of their national heritage, yet frequently find themselves playing and watching these games not as British nationals but as Irish men and women. In addition, those who have sought a more precise sense of who they are by way of the exploits of the Northern Ireland soccer team have been obliged to come to terms with the twin paradox, namely of Irish nationalists playing for Northern Ireland and of the English being regarded as detested opponents in the eyes of people who regard themselves as loyal to the United Kingdom. In another context, the relationship between Scotland and England has been such that sporting nationalists have been more likely to choose playing (and hopefully beating) the old enemy at their own games than to seek comfort in native pastimes. More secure in themselves and their own identity, on the other hand, the Swedes have combined the global and the local quite successfully and thereby constructed a relatively mature sporting nationalism.

SPORT AND CONTESTED NATIONAL IDENTITY

Even in the examples discussed in this book and referred to above, there is the additional problem that sport has not been wholly successful in any of them in uniting the entire nation or nationality. In each instance, in addition to contributing to the construction of a single national identity, sport has also been implicated in the creation and perpetuation of divisions centered around questions of identity—between different sorts of Irish nationalists and Ulster unionists, between francophone and anglophone Canadians as well as between both groups and First Nations peoples, between "old" Swedes and "new" Swedes, lowland and Highland and Catholic and Protestant Scots, and so on. Furthermore, in all of these examples, perhaps above all in the United States, and indeed in most countries where sport is played, there are also divisions based on race, gender, and social class, which sport can sometimes help to heal but more often merely serves to exacerbate. This obviously impacts upon sport's relationship to national identity in specific social formations.

We should always bear in mind that in many nation-states, nationality itself remains contested terrain. Tebbit's cricket test represented a somewhat offensive attempt to tease out this issue. When someone of Pakistani origin but living in England chooses to support the Pakistan cricket team against England's cricketers, he or she may be indicating a continued preference for Pakistani national identity despite, or arguably because of, British citizenship and English residence. On the other hand, it might be dangerous to read too much into such an expression of sporting nationalism. It may indicate little more than a nostalgic sentiment for the "old country," which does little or nothing to undermine that individual's sense of being a British citizen, happy to pay British taxes, willing to serve in the British armed forces, and so on. To infer political disloyalty from a simple expression of sporting nationalism, as Tebbit did, may be foolish at best and reprehensible at worst. However, we should not ignore the fact that in most nation-states there exists a hegemonic national identity that is not necessarily inclusive. In such instances, some citizens may well choose to celebrate an alternative national identity, with sport playing an important part in their activities.

For example, when Turkey beat Germany in the qualifying stage of soccer's European Championship on 10 October 1998, there was almost as much celebration in the streets of Germany's major cities as there was in Turkey itself. In the context of Tebbit's cricket test, here was evidence that the Turkish immigrants and their German-born families had not become real Germans. But to what extent had hegemonic representations of German nationalism encouraged these Turks (and other immigrant groups) to become Germans? Denied full citizenship, members of ethnic minority groups have found it difficult to represent their "new" country at sport (Merkel 1998). In circumstances such as these, it is scarcely surprising that the achievements of the nation that continues to provide them with a national identity, although not a home, become the focus of a sporting nationalism that has broader political implications. As the example of France reveals, there is no guarantee that, by allowing members of immigrant groups to represent their adopted nation, racism will abate and all immigrants will begin to strongly identify with the national identity of their hosts. But there is certainly little point in complaining when people seek alternative outlets for the expression of nationalism if it is clear that they have been excluded from embracing fully the hegemonic national identity of their places of residence.

As regards competing nationalities within nation-states, it should also be noted that when new states emerge and are recognized by the United Nations, this need not indicate that a single identity, national or otherwise, has been put in place. Sport has been used in many of the nation-states of sub-Saharan Africa to assist in the construction of civic nationalist identities. But these have only been partially successful in societies where tribalism remains a major cultural signifier. Similarly, when the state of Bosnia emerged out of the wreckage caused by the 1992–1995 war, this did not mean that a cohesive Bosnian national identity had been formed. The national soccer team, for example, consists mainly of Muslim players and there are currently three Bosnian leagues in operation, each dominated by one of the three main ethnic groups (*Independent*, 13 October 1998). Thus, sport is as likely to play a part in undermining the cohesive potential of certain national identities as in ensuring their emergence and subsequent resilience.

There is an added difficulty, however, in that sport plays little or no part at all in the construction of many people's identities. For a variety of reasons that lie beyond the scope of this particular study, only a small minority of women through the years have been a position to draw upon sport in the construction of their identities. In addition, and in order to avoid stereotyping, it should be added that not all men seek part of their identity in a relationship with sport either.

REFLECTIONS ON SPORT AND NATIONALISM IN EUROPE AND NORTH AMERICA

The case studies in this book were selected in part on the basis of the author's own personal interests but also because sport is phenomenally popular within each of the nationalities discussed. Arguably, the same could be said about virtually every nation in the world today. But it is undeniable that sport provides the people examined in this study with important symbols to the extent that sport and national identity are inextricably linked. If we were asked to list things we associate with the people involved, we would almost certainly mention sport at some stage. Were we required to identify famous people from the various nationalities discussed here we would probably name a sports personality or two along the way. In part, this tells us a lot about the omnipresence and ready accessibility of information about sport in the contemporary world. But this is not to deny that sport is accorded high levels of respect in the societies discussed in this study.

Consider, for example, the T shirt legend—"Canada Is Hockey." This is only a figure of speech perhaps and not meant to be taken too seriously. But that is doubtful. In fact, something very serious is being stated even if tourists who buy the T shirts are largely unaware of their deep significance. The meaning of this statement, however, is highly illuminating. On one hand, it identifies who the true Canadians are, i.e., the hockey players and fans. On the other hand, by implication, it is also transmitting a message about those who are not true Canadians, that is to say, those who are less than captivated by hockey's charms. Among the latter group are many women. Are they less Canadian than their hockey-playing brothers and sons? Moreover, what about the boy who has been sexually abused by his coach? What does the linkage of hockey and identity mean to him as he matures into adulthood? The other difficulty with the words— "Canada Is Hockey," is that it leaves open the questions, "whose Canada?" "which Canada?," for, as we have seen, the world of Canadian hockey is by no means homogeneous. The "national" sport is played throughout the "nation" but the nation itself remains contested terrain and hockey reflects and contributes to this contestation. That sport is important in the construction of Canadian national identity, however, remains irrefutable and the same holds true, in varying degrees, as regards national identity formation in Scotland, Sweden, and the United States as well as among the divided peoples of Ireland. So what does a study that includes these examples tell us more generally about the relationship between sport and national identity? Are sporting nationalism and political nationalism simply two sides of the same coin? Or are we speaking about two distinct phenomena?

It is crucial that any observations about sporting nationalism take full account of the peculiarities of the situation in which specific nationalities are operating. There is little point in simply stating that all nations celebrate the achievements of their sports people and, as a result, sport can be said to play a vital role in the construction and reproduction of the national identities involved. How people celebrate sporting performances will vary markedly from one situation to another and, indeed, from one sports contest to another. To understand why this is so, a detailed knowledge of the political context is required. What then are the salient points concerning the nationalities examined in this book?

The national identity of the Ulster unionists is problematic. They are British but in a peculiar way. Part of their Britishness, indeed, is simply non-Irishness. But the Irish identity to which they stand opposed is only one of a number of possible representations of what it means to be Irish and, according to other criteria, the Ulster Protestants are themselves Irish. These dilemmas are manifested quite clearly in the world of sport, as indeed are divisions within the two main traditions in Ireland in terms of national identity. The British (or English) sporting culture has been enthusiastically embraced by a majority of Protestants. Yet one odd consequence of this has been the fact that Ulster unionists have consistently represented Ireland in sports such as cricket and rugby union. They have eschewed Irish games but they have not made a fundamental break with Irish sport. One exception to this rule is soccer, the organization of which follows the contours established by partition. As a result, the national team provides a focus for a form of national (or quasi-national) identity that is neither British nor Irish but which actually addresses the unique character of the Ulster unionist people. The sporting nationalism of Northern Ireland's Protestants is a complex affair, therefore, for the very reason that the relationship between this particular group of people and the concept of nationalism is itself problematic.

On the face of it, the Scots have no such difficulties with the concept of nationalism in general and sporting nationalism in particular. Scotland's nationhood is not in doubt unless one cares to argue that a nation without a state is unworthy of the name. Despite superficial coherence, however, Scots remain divided as to what their nationalism requires at the level of politics and the resultant debate is reflected in the construction of sporting nationalism. In addition, the latter cannot disguise the internal divisions within the country, which are reflected and, arguably, deepened in the world of sport. For many years, therefore, a degree of unity in both political culture and sporting nationalism has been secured by way of anti-Englishness. Arguably, however, this sentiment has been consistently stronger in sport than in politics. Whether or not this remains the case will be crucial as far as further moves toward Scottish independence are concerned. Conversely, it is at least possible that, with the arrival of a separate assembly and some degree of self-government, the Scots will have far less need of sporting nationalism than in the past. Once again, the complex relationship between the people and nationality is reflected in the world of sport.

With the Irish case, it might be reasonable to anticipate a far greater degree of unanimity than in Ulster unionist or even Scottish identity formation. But in this example too, sport reflects complexity and, in particular, provides a window through which we can observe the division between exclusive ethnic and inclusive civic nationalisms. Is true sporting nationalism only to be constructed around the edifice of the GAA? Or is it possible to be an Irish sporting nationalist committed to so-called foreign games. The answer, of course, is that both types of sporting activity contribute to Irish sporting nationalism and this, in turn, reflects the different shades of political and cultural opinion that constitute Irish nationalism more broadly. In the case of Irish nationalism too, it is essential to get beyond the homogeneous facade, and sport allows us to gain valuable insights into the complexities that will be revealed.

Unlike Ireland, the United States do not figure prominently in studies of nationalism and nationality. But the analysis in this book indicates that there are serious questions to be asked about the national identity of Americans. Furthermore, sport has not only been in the forefront of attempts to construct a cohesive national sentiment but has also performed a prominent role in highlighting some of the main reasons why such cohesion has proved difficult to attain. With the development of a unique sporting culture, Americans from a multiplicity of different racial, ethnic, and national backgrounds have become "Americanized" through playing and watching sport. But this process has not been without its difficulties and, in any event, this basis for the creation of a national identity excludes many for whom sport is of little importance. Moreover, just because people become sporting Americans has never been a guarantee that they come to be regarded as real Americans in other spheres of human activity. Similarly, while sport has made the realization of the American Dream a reality for many, it has also been involved in cruelly dashing the hopes of many more.

Canadians, for their part, have been faced with similar problems—to decide what it means to be Canadian and to confront divisions that undermine the search for a unified national identity. Sport is deeply implicated in both issues. Meanwhile, Canada has also been faced with the additional problem that with the United States as a neighbor, a distinctive national identity in sport and more generally has been particularly hard to maintain.

Finally the book examined the case of Sweden, where both political and sporting nationalism have been relatively insignificant forces. The weakness of the latter is a manifest product of the undeveloped state of the former. Yet this is not to suggest that the Swedes are wholly without a sense of sporting nationalism. Indeed, as was suggested earlier, because it exists in an environment where political nationalism has traditionally been of little importance, Swedish sporting nationalism is arguably the only example of true (as opposed to quasi-political) sporting nationalism discussed in this work.

Three general points emerge from all of this. First, sporting nationalism is closely linked to political nationalism in each case. Second, neither political nor sporting nationalisms are ever as homogeneous as superficial readings might suggest. Third, by examining the links between sport and the formation of national identities, we are able to get a clearer understanding of the complex character of nationality. For instance, it is of particular importance when the links between sport and national identities are being studied that attention is paid to the key concepts of civic and ethnic nationalism.

CIVIC AND ETHNIC SPORTING NATIONALISMS

So long as the nation-state remains the most common form of political organization, it is vitally important that the citizens of each state are permitted, if it is their wish, to feel part of the nation upon which that state has been constructed. Indeed, the whole principle of citizenship is tarnished if it is not accompanied by a sense of real belonging. Sport can play a vital role in this respect. If the sporting culture of a particular nation or nationality is organized and presented in an exclusive manner, an important point of access to the national community is inevitably denied to large numbers of citizens. Naturally, this type of social exclusion does not relate to the issue of nationality alone. When sport is deeply embedded in patriarchy, women are either denied access completely or offered only restricted opportunities to participate in this particular element of the national culture. A sporting culture that celebrates the virtues of youthful vitality, at the expense of other human qualities, is equally likely to be discriminatory. For the purposes of this book, however, the central concern is with exclusion centered around understandings of national identity.

In those circumstances in which sport becomes linked to expressions of ethnic nationalism, the dangers of exclusion are palpable. Nationalism, in any setting, runs the risk of being indistinguishable from the worst excesses of chauvinism. This can be as true of civic nationalism as it is of ethnic nationalism. However, where nationalist politics are based almost entirely upon ethnic exclusion, the risk becomes virtually unavoidable. Of course, ethnic nationalism is never solely the product of the human will. It emerges as a response to specific politico-cultural and material circumstances. Thus, there is a degree of inevitability about the way in which it has impacted on the sporting experiences of certain nations and nationalities. To recognize its existence and potential harm, however, is to go some way at least toward negating its pernicious influence. All of those who are involved with sport whether as participants, fans, administrators, journalists, and even sports sociologists might be well advised to advance the cause of civic sporting nationalism since the emotions this inspires are frequently at worst relatively harmless (except from the standpoint of international harmony, and even in that context sporting rivalry may well have a beneficial, cathartic effect) and, at their best, may possess an integrative potential that helps people to live together more harmoniously. However, it is equally important to recognize the short-comings of civic nationalism, which at times can be no less problematic. For example, the kind of civic nationalism that has been practised in the United States has a long history of forcibly incorporating nationalist and ethnic minorities. For those members of the latter who become "real" Americans, there may be great rewards to be won. But what happens to the sensibilities of the Native American, for example, who cannot endorse the civic nationalism of a country in which the representation of his people through the Chief Wahoo logo of the Cleveland Indians is still regarded as acceptable? With reservations about civic nationalism in mind, therefore, one is tempted to argue that sport as well as society in general would benefit to a considerable extent if nationalism in whatever guise was allowed to disappear. The inherent danger in such an approach, however, could be to leave the way clear for the ultimate triumph of the homogenizing tendencies of globalization.

Sport, Nationality, and the Resistance to Globalization

In addition to the fact that a close relationship between sport and national identity is discernible in each of them, another reason for choosing the case studies for this book was the fact that Western societies might be regarded as being particularly susceptible to the homogenizing process. This book began with an examination of the concepts of globalization and nationality and discussed, at the level of theory, the extent to which nationalism is capable of resisting the pressures toward global conformity. It was pointed out, at the outset, that one can, and indeed should, adopt an approach to global forces that stops short of stating a case for Americanization or even greater homogenization more generally. The case studies confirm this theoretical proposal. In each case, other than that of the United States, it is clear that while general global trends and the cultural influence of the United States in particular have impacted in different ways on the sporting experience, the local or perhaps the glocal remain of paramount importance in terms of how sport is played and watched. As a result, sport continues to play a greater role in the maintenance of distinctive national identities than in the construction of some uniform global identity. In the United States, moreover, there is also evidence of the influence of cross-fertilization of sporting cultures while the national identity, which is rooted in a distinctively American sports culture, is still as strong as ever.

It is undeniable that in virtually every society in the world the number of sports people are able to play and watch has increased dramatically. Limitations persist as regards such crucial factors as gender, race, and social class. But there are few restrictions that originate from the exigencies of particular national sporting cultures. Even if specific sports predominate in given social formations, it is almost certain that most other sports are played even if only by relatively small numbers of participants. This confirms the assessment of globalization put forward by Maguire (1994). The various societies of the world have become increasingly similar to one another. Soccer is played in the United States and American football in Sweden. Gaelic games are played beyond the shores of Ireland, albeit mainly by members of the Irish diaspora. Cricket is relatively popular in Canada for the first time in well over a century. The pattern that emerges reflects what Maguire (1994) refers to as "diminishing contrasts." The result, however, is also to confirm the value of his concept of "increasing varieties." Each country may more closely resemble every other country far more than in previous years and yet each country, as a consequence, affords its inhabitants far greater choice in terms of what sports to play and watch.

That, then, is the main way in which globalization has impacted on sport and there are lessons to be learned here as regards the nature of the entire globalization project. To speak in terms of homogenization is to do a disservice to the multifaceted cultural impact of what has actually happened. Moreover, to refer to the process as one that has resulted in something called "Americanization" is to distort reality to an even greater extent. Even when American sports have been introduced to other countries, the process has often developed in such a way as to confirm national distinctiveness. Glocalization as opposed to global conformity has frequently been the most common result. That said, however, there is little point in seeking to deny the extent to which global capitalism has affected the ways in which sport is played, administered, packaged, and watched throughout the world. This has clearly compressed the distance between the sporting nations of the world both physically and metaphorically. Indeed, as far as the most popular sports are concerned we can actually recognize the emergence and consolidation of a global sporting political economy involving the sale of merchandise, sponsorship, labor migration, and so on. In creating this particular sporting world, however, the same global forces have kept alive the possibility of international competition. Indeed, events such as the Olympic Games and soccer's World Cup are the flagships of the global sporting economy. In turn, these events ensure that far from being submerged, national sporting identities remain to the fore. It is for this reason that we can talk about nationalism having successfully resisted the encroachment of globalization's homogenizing tendencies. Or, to put it another way, sport and globalization have become accomplices in a process whereby the importance of national identity has been ensured despite, or arguably because of, supranationalist tendencies.

CONCLUSION

Sport and national identity, no matter how complex the specific relationships, are inextricably linked. Global forces have affected the nature of their relationship to varying degrees from one place to the next. But through sport, nationalism and nationalities have successfully resisted globalization unless we adopt a very weak definition of the latter. It looks as if national flags will be on show at sports stadia throughout the world for a very long time to come. To understand what this means to the people waving the flags, however, it will be essential that each particular context is explored. It is hoped that when other researchers take up the baton, some of the ideas explored in this book will help them on their way.

According to Cronin and Mayall (1998), "Sport cannot win territory or destroy an opposing ideology or religion which the nation seeks to demonise" (2). Perhaps not. But bearing in mind Hoberman's (1984) description of sports people as "proxy warriors," the fact is that, throughout the twentieth century, sport has been one of the most valuable weapons at the disposal of nationalists, whatever their situation and respective aspirations. This book has focused on societies that might appear to be susceptible to a changing geopolitical environment in which national identity is thought by some to be increasingly unimportant. However, the evidence uncovered on the basis of a study of sport in a selection of North American and European countries indicates that cultural convergence is still some way off. Sport and nationalism will remain intimately linked at least for the forseeable future. Their relationship, however, will be considerably more complex than a superficial reading might suggest. Certainly sport will play a part in allowing nations to resist global homogenization. At the same time, however, it will also continue to reflect the fact that national identity is a contentious and contested issue even in stable Western democracies.

bibliography

Adelman, M. L. 1988. "The First Modern Sport in America: Harness Racing in New York City 1825–1870." In P. A. Zingg (ed.), *The Sporting Image: Readings in American Sport History*. Lanham, MD: University Press of America, pp. 107–138.

Aldskogius, H. 1993. *Leksand, Leksand, Leksand! En studie av ishockeyns för en bygd.* Hedemora, Sweden: Gidlunds.

Allison, L. 1986. "Sport and Politics." In L. Allison (ed.), *The Politics of Sport.* Manchester, United Kingdom: Manchester University Press, pp. 1–26.

Anderson, B. 1991. *Imagined Communities: Reflections on the Origin and Spread of Nationalism, Revised Edition.* London: Verso.

Andersson, J. 1991. *Turbulens i Rörelsen: Sju Perspektiv På Idrottens Fframtid.* Farsta, Sweden: Riksidrottsförbund and SISU.

Andersson, T., and A. Radmann. 1998a. *Från Gentleman till Huligan? Svensk Fotbollskultur förr och nu.* Stockholm: Brutus Östlings Bokförlag Symposion.

———. 1998b. "Football Fans in Scandinavia: 1900–1997." In A. Brown (ed.), *Fanatics! Power, Identity, and Fandom in Football.* London: Routledge, pp. 141–157.

Appadurai, A. 1990. "Disjuncture and Difference in the Global Cultural Economy." *Theory, Culture, and Society* 7 (2–3), Special Issue: pp. 295–310.

Archard, D. 1995. "Myths, Lies, and Historical Truth: A Defence of Nationalism." *Political Studies* 43 (3), September: pp. 472–481.

Archetti, E. P. 1994. "Argentina and the World Cup: In Search of National Identity." In J. Sugden and A. Tomlinson (eds.), *Hosts and Champions: Soccer Cultures, National Identities, and the USA World Cup.* Aldershot, United Kingdom: Arena, pp. 37–63.

———. 1996. "The Moralities of Argentinian Football." In S. Howell (ed.), *The Ethnography of Moralities.* London: Routledge, pp. 98–123.

———. 1999. *Masculinities: Football, Polo, and the Tango in Argentina.* Oxford: Berg.

Aughey, A. 1989. *Under Siege: Ulster Unionism and the Anglo-Irish Agreement.* Belfast, United Kingdom: Blackstaff Press.

Bairner, A. 1994a. "Football and the Idea of Scotland." In G. Jarvie and G. Walker (eds.), *Scottish Sport in the Making of the Nation: Ninety Minute Patriots?* Leicester, United Kingdom: Leicester University Press, pp. 9–26.

———. 1994b. "Sweden and the World Cup: Soccer and Swedishness." In J. Sugden and A. Tomlinson (eds.), *Hosts and Champions: Soccer Cultures, National Identities, and the USA World Cup*. Aldershot, United Kingdom: Arena, pp. 195–217.

———. 1996a. "Ireland, Sport, and Empire." In K. Jeffery (ed.), *"An Irish Empire"? Aspects of Ireland and the British Empire*. Manchester, United Kingdom: Manchester University Press, pp. 57–76.

———. 1996b. "Sportive Nationalism and Nationalist Politics: A Comparative Analysis of Scotland, the Republic of Ireland, and Sweden." *Journal of Sport and Social Issues* 20 (3), August: pp. 314–334.

———. 1996c. "Fields of Dreams and Nightmares: Images of the Sports Fan in the Universal Baseball Association, inc. J. Henry Waugh, PROP, and Shoeless Joe." *Irish Journal of American Studies* 5: pp. 59–76.

———. 1997. "'Up to Their Knees?' Football, Sectarianism, Masculinity, and Protestant Working-Class Identity." In P. Shirlow and M. McGovern (eds.), *Who Are "The People"? Unionism, Protestantism, and Loyalism in Northern Ireland*. London: Pluto Press, pp. 95–113.

———. 1999a. "Civic and Ethnic Nationalism in the Celtic Vision of Irish Sport." In G. Jarvie (ed.), *Sport in the Making of Celtic Cultures*. London: Leicester University Press, pp. 12–25.

———. 1999b. "Soccer, Masculinity, and Violence." *Men and Masculinities* 1 (3): pp. 284–301.

Bairner, A., and P. Darby. 1999. "Divided Sport in a Divide Society: Northern Ireland." In J. Sugden and A. Bairner (eds.), *Sport in Divided Societies*. Aachen, Germany: Meyer and Meyer, pp. 51–72.

Bairner, A., and P. Shirlow. 1998. "Loyalism, Linfield, and the Territorial Politics of Soccer Fandom in Northern Ireland." *Space and Polity* 2 (2): pp. 163–177.

Beckles, H. McD., and B. Stoddart. 1995. *Liberation Cricket: West Indies Cricket Culture*. Manchester, United Kingdom: Manchester University Press.

Bergin, S., and D. Scott. 1980. "Cricket in Ireland." In E. W. Swanton (ed.), *Barclay's World of Cricket*. London: Collins.

Blain, N., and R. Boyle. 1994. "Battling Along the Boundaries: The Marking of Scottish Identity in Sports Journalism." In G. Jarvie and G. Walker (eds.), *Scottish Sport in the Making of the Nation: Ninety Minute Patriots?* Leicester: Leicester University Press, pp. 125–141.

Blom, K. A., and J. Lindroth. 1995. *Idrottens Historia: Från Antika Arenor till Modern Massrörelse*. Farsta, Sweden: SISU Idrottsböcker.

Bradley, J. 1995. *Ethnic and Religious Identity in Modern Scotland*. Aldershot, United Kingdom: Avebury.

Bradley, J. M. 1998. *Sport, Culture, Politics, and Scottish Society: Irish Immigrants and the Gaelic Athletic Association*. Edinburgh: John Donald.

Bryson, L., and C. McCartney. 1994. *Clashing Symbols: A Report on the Use of Flags, Anthems, and Other National Symbols in Northern Ireland*. Belfast, United Kingdom: Institute of Irish Studies, Queen's University.

Burnett, J. 1995. *Sporting Scotland*. Edinburgh: National Museums of Scotland.

Campbell, J. 1997. "Female Gaels," unpublished B.A. (Hons.) dissertation, University of Ulster, Jordanstown, Northern Ireland (UK).

Campbell, K. 1994. "Ode to Canada: Hockey Central." *Hockey News* 20, May.

Canovan, M. 1996. *Nationhood and Political Theory.* Cheltenham, United Kingdom: Edward Elgar.

Carter, G. L. 1988. "Baseball in Saint Louis, 1867–1875: An Historical Case Study in Civic Pride." In P. A. Zingg (ed.), *The Sporting Image: Readings in American Sport History.* Lanham, MD: University Press of America, pp. 195–208.

Churchill, W. 1993. *Indians Are Us? Culture and Genocide in Native North America.* Monroe, ME: Common Courage Press.

Coover, R. 1992. *The Universal Baseball Asssociation, inc. J. Henry Waugh, PROP.* London: Minerva.

Cosentino, F. 1989. "Football." In D. Morrow et al., *A Concise History of Sport in Canada.* Toronto: Oxford University Press, pp. 140–168.

Cosgrove, S. 1991. *Hampden Babylon: Sex and Scandal in Scottish Football.* Edinburgh: Canongate Press.

Coulter, C. 1994. "The Character of Unionism." *Irish Political Studies* 9: pp. 1–24.

Coyle, P. 1999. *Paradise Lost and Found: The Story of Belfast Celtic.* Edinburgh: Mainstream.

Crepeau, R. C. 1980. *Baseball: America's Diamond Mind 1919–1941.* Orlando: University Presses of Central Florida.

Cronin, M. 1994. "Sport and a Sense of Irishness." *Irish Studies Review* 9, Winter: pp. 13–17.

———. 1996. "Defenders of the Nation? The Gaelic Athletic Association and Irish Nationalist Identity." *Irish Political Studies* 11: pp. 1–19.

Cronin, M., and D. Mayall, eds. 1998. *Sporting Nationalisms: Identity, Ethnicity, Immigration, and Assimilation.* London: Frank Cass.

Dagg, T. S. C. 1944. *Hockey in Ireland.* Tralee, Ireland: Kerryman Limited.

Daiches, D. 1952. *Robert Burns.* London: G. Bell and Sons.

———. 1987. *Two Worlds: An Edinburgh Jewish Chidhood.* Edinburgh: Canongate Press.

Daily Record. 13 August 1998.

Daun, Å. 1994. *Svensk Mentalitet: Ett Jämförande Perspektiv, Revised Edition.* Stockholm: Rabén Prisma.

DeLillo, D. 1986. *End Zone.* Harmondswoth, United Kingdom: Penguin Books.

Dimeo, P., and G. P. T. Finn. 1998. "Scottish Racism, Scottish Identities." In A. Brown (ed.), *Fanatics! Power, Identity, and Fandom in Football.* London, Routledge, pp. 124–138.

Donnelly, P. 1996. "The Local and the Global: Globalization in the Sociology of Sport." *Journal of Sport and Social Issues* 20 (3), August: 239–257.

Dryden, K. 1993. *The Game, Revised Edition.* Toronto: Macmillan Canada.

Dryden, S. 1996. "New Reality Setting in for Canadian Fans." *Hockey News,* 27 September.

Drysdale, N. 1994. "Spreading the Gospel." *Scotland on Sunday,* 11 September.

———. 1995a. "Bordering on the Precipice." *Scotland on Sunday,* 1 October.

———. 1995b. "People's Palace of Holyrood." *Scotland on Sunday,* 10 September.

————. 1995c. "Marr Lodge Their Claim to a Giant-Slaying Victory." *Scotland on Sunday*, 1 October.

Duke, V., and L. Crolley. 1996. *Football, Nationality, and the State.* Harlow, United Kingdom: Longman.

Dunn, J. 1994. "Crisis of the Nation State?" *Political Studies* 42, Special Issue: pp. 3–15.

Dunning, E. 1999. *Sport Matters: Sociological Studies of Sport, Violence, and Civilization.* London: Routledge.

Dyreson, M. 1995. "The Emergence of Consumer Culture and the Transformation of Physical Culture: American Sport in the 1920s." In D. K. Wiggins (ed.), *Sport in America: From Wicked Amusement to National Obsession.* Champaign, IL: Human Kinetics, pp. 207–223.

Ehn, B. 1993. "Nationell Inlevelse." In B. Ehn et al., *Försvenskningen av Sverige.* Stockholm: Natur och Kultur, pp. 203–265.

Ehn, B., J. Frykman, and O. Löfgren. 1993. *Försvenskningen av Sverige.* Stockholm: Natur och Kultur.

Eichberg, H. 1989. "Editor's Introduction." *Scandinavian Journal of Sports Science* 11 (1), October: pp. 1–2.

Elklit, J., and O. Tonsgaard. 1992. "The Absence of Nationalistic Movements: The Case of the Nordic Area." In J. Coakley (ed.), *The Social Origins of National Movements: The Contemporary West European Experience.* London: Sage, pp. 81–94.

Featherstone, M. 1993. "Global and Local Cultures." In J. Bird, B. Curtis, T. Putnam, G. Robertson, and L. Tickner (eds.), *Mapping the Futures: Local Cultures, Global Change.* London: Routledge, pp. 169–187.

Featherstone, M., and S. Lash. 1995. "Globalization, Modernity, and the Spatialization of Social Theory: An Introduction." In M. Featherstone, S. Lash, and R. Robertson (eds.), *Global Modernities.* London: Sage, pp. 1–24.

Feldreich, S. 1993. "Svenska Modellen på Export." *Svensk Idrott* 65 (12), December: pp. 20–23.

Finn, G. T. P., 1994. "Faith, Hope, and Bigotry: Case Studies of Anti-Catholic Prejudice in Scottish Soccer and Society." In G. Jarvie and G. Walker (eds.), *Scottish Sport in the Making of the Nation: Ninety Minute Patriots?* Leicester: Leicester University Press, pp. 91–112.

Finn, G. T. P., and R. Giulianotti. 1998. "Scottish Fans, Not English Hooligans! Scots, Scottishness, and Scottish Football." In A. Brown (ed.), *Fanatics! Power, Identity, and Fandom in Football.* London: Routledge, pp. 189–202.

Fischler, S. 1996. "Bettman's NHL Reign Far from Perfect." *Hockey News*, 2 February.

Forsyth, R. 1990. *The Only Game: The Scots and World Football.* Edinburgh: Mainstream.

————. 1992. "Sport." In M. Linklater and R. Denniston (eds.), *Anatomy of Scotland.* Edinburgh: Chambers, pp. 334–353.

Gannon, M., and H. Kanafani. 1994. "American Football." In M. Gannon et al., *Understanding Global Cultures.* Thousand Oaks, CA: pp. 302–320.

Garvin, T. 1981. *The Evolution of Irish Nationalist Politics.* Dublin, Ireland: Gill and Macmillan.

Gibson, W. H. 1988. *Early Irish Golf: The First Courses, Clubs, and Pioneers.* Nass, Ireland: Oakleaf.

Giddens, A. 1990. *The Consequences of Modernity.* Cambridge, United Kingdom: Polity Press.

————. 1991. *Modernity and Self-Identity: Self and Society in the Late Modern Age.* Cambridge, United Kingdom: Polity Press.

Giulianotti, R. 1995. "Football and the Politics of Carnival: An Ethnographic Study of Scottish Fans in Sweden." *International Review for the Sociology of Sport* 30 (2): pp. 191–219.

————. 1996. "'All the Olympians: A Thing Never Known Again?' Reflections on Irish Football Culture and the 1994 World Cup Finals." *Irish Journal of Sociology* 6: pp. 101–126.

Globe and Mail. 10 November 1997.

Goksøyr, M. 1998. "The Popular Sounding Board: Nationalism, 'the People,' and Sport in Norway in the Inter-war Years." In H. Meinander and J. A. Mangan (eds.), *The Nordic World: Sport in Society.* London: Frank Cass, pp. 100–114.

Gorn, E. J., and W. Goldstein. 1993. *A Brief History of American Sports.* New York: Hill and Wang.

Gramsci, A. 1971. "Selections from the Prison Notebooks." Q. Hoare and G. Nowell Smith (eds.). London: Lawrence and Wishart.

Gruneau, R., and D. Whitson. 1993. *Hockey Night in Canada: Sport, Identities, and Cultural Politics.* Toronto: Garamond Press.

Guardian. Various Dates.

Guttmann, A. 1994. *Games and Empires: Modern Sports and Cultural Imperialism.* New York: Columbia University Press.

Hall, A., T. Slack, G. Smith, and D. Whitson. 1991. *Sport in Canadian Society.* Toronto: McClelland and Stewart.

Hargreaves, J. 1986. *Sport, Power, and Culture.* London: Routledge and Kegan Paul.

————. 1992. "Olympism and Nationalism: Some Preliminary Consideration." *International Review for the Sociology of Sport* 27: pp. 119–137.

Harvey, J. 1999. "Sport and Québec Nationalism: Ethnic or Civic Identity?" In J. Sugden and A. Bairner (eds.), *Sport in Divided Societies.* Aachen, Germany: Meyer and Meyer, pp. 31–50.

Harvie, C. 1994. "Sport and the Scottish State." In G. Jarvie and G. Walker (eds.), *Scottish Sport in the Making of the Nation: Ninety Minute Patriots?* Leicester, United Kingdom: Leicester University Press, pp. 43–57.

Healey, P. 1998. *Gaelic Games and the Gaelic Athletic Association.* Cork, Ireland: Mercier Press.

Hedlund, S. 1984. "Pompa och Ståt När Tanzaniaprojekt Invigdes." *Svensk Idrott* 56 (2), February: pp. 16–17.

Hellspong, M. 1989. "Den Gotländska Idrotten." *Idrott, Historia och Samhälle*, pp. 79–94.

————. 1998. "A Timeless Excitement: Swedish Agrarian Society and Sport in the Pre-Industrial Era." In H. Meinander and J. A. Mangan (eds.), *The Nordic World: Sport in Society.* London: Frank Cass, pp. 11–24.

Henderson, J. 1998. "It's Sweden." *Observer*, 4 October.

Hill, C. R. 1992. *Olympic Politics*. Manchester, United Kingdom: Manchester University Press.

Hirdman, Y. 1994. "Women—from Possibility to Problem? Gender Conflict in the Welfare State—the Swedish Model." *Arbetslivscentrum Research Report*, p. 3.

Hoberman, J. 1984. *Sport and Political Ideology*. London: Heinemann.

————. 1993. "Sport and Ideology in the Post-Communist Age." In L. Allison (ed.) *The Politics of Sport*. Manchester: Manchester University Press, pp. 15–36.

————. 1997. *Darwin's Athletes: How Sport Has Damaged Black America and Preserved the Myth of Race*. Boston: Houghton Mifflin Company.

Hobsbawm, E. J., and T. Ranger, (eds.). 1983. *The Invention of Tradition*. Cambridge: Cambridge University Press.

Hockey News. Various Dates.

Holmäng, P. O. 1988. *Idrott och Utrikespolitik: Den Svenska Idrottsrörelsens Internationella Förbindelser, 1919–1945*. Gothenburg, Sweden: Meddelande från Historiska Institutionen.

Holmes, M. 1994. "Symbols of National Identity and Sport: The Case of the Irish Football Team." *Irish Political Studies* 9: pp. 81–98.

Holt, R. 1989. *Sport and the British*. Oxford: Clarendon Press.

————. 1994. "The King over the Border: Denis Law and Scottish Football." In G. Jarvie and G. Walker (eds.), *Scottish Sport in the Making of the Nation: Ninety Minute Patriots?* Leicester, United Kingdom: Leicester University Press, pp. 58–74.

Holton, R. J. 1998. *Globalization and the Nation-State*. Basingstoke, United Kingdom: Macmillan.

Hone, W. P. 1956. *Cricket in Ireland*. Tralee, Ireland: Kerryman Press.

Horne, J. 1995. "Racism, Sectarianism, and Football in Scotland." *Scottish Affairs* 12, Summer: pp. 27–51.

Horney, N. 1960. "Hjalmar Branting och Idrotten." Stockholm: Sveriges Centralförening för Idrottens Främjande Årsbok, pp. 58–62.

Houlihan, B. 1994. *Sport and International Politics*. Hemel Hempsted, United Kingdom: Harvester Wheatsheaf.

Hutchinson, R. 1989. *Camanachd! The Story of Shinty*. Edinburgh: Mainstream.

Illmarinen, M., ed. 1982. *Sport and International Understanding*. Berlin: Springer-Verlag.

Independent. Various dates.

Independent on Sunday. 11 August 1991.

Irish Times. 29 September 1998.

Jackson, S. J. 1994. "Gretzky, Crisis, and Canadian Identity in 1988: Rearticulating the Americanization of Culture Debate." *Sociology of Sport Journal* 11 (4): pp. 428–446.

————. 1998. "A Twist of Race: Ben Johnson and the Canadian Crisis of Racial and National Identity." *Sociology of Sport Journal* 15 (1): pp. 21–40.

Järtelius, A. 1982. *Invandrare och Idrott*. Stockholm: Sveriges Riksidrottsförbund and Tidens Förlag.

Jarvie, G. 1991. *Highland Games: The Making of the Myth*. Edinburgh: Edinburgh University Press.

———. 1993. "Sport, Nationalism, and Cultural Identity." In L. Allison (ed.), *The Changing Politics of Sport*. Manchester, United Kingdom: Manchester University Press, pp. 58–83.

Jarvie, G., and J. Maguire. 1994. *Sport and Leisure in Social Thought*. London: Routledge.

Jarvie, G., and G. Walker. 1994. "Ninety Minute Patriots? Scottish Sport in the Making of the Nation." In G. Jarvie and G. Walker (eds.), *Scottish Sport and the Making of the Nation: Ninety Minute Patriots?* Leicester, United Kingdom, Leicester University Press, pp. 1–8.

Jeffery, K. 1996. "Introduction." In K. Jeffery (ed.), "An Irish Empire"? *Aspects of Ireland and the British Empire*. Manchester: Manchester University Press, pp. 1–24.

Jenson, J., and R. Mahon. 1993. "Representing Solidarity: Class, Gender, and the Crisis in Social-Democratic Sweden." *New Left Review* 201, September/October: pp. 76–100.

Johansson, A. 1986. "Tanzaniaprojekt Har Gett 493 Nya Klubbar." *Svensk Idrott* 56 (2): October, pp. 14–20.

Johansson, L. 1998. *Många Mål—Många Planer*. Halmstad, Sweden: Sportförlaget.

Jones, S. G. 1988. *Sport, Politics, and the Working Class: Organised Labour and Sport in Inter-War Britain*. Manchester: Manchester University Press.

Jørgensen, P. 1998. "From Balck to Nurmi: The Olympic Movement and the Nordic Nations." In H. Meinander and J. A. Mangan (eds.), *The Nordic World: Sport in Society*. London: Frank Cass, pp. 69–99.

Kamenka, E. 1993. "Nationalism: Ambiguous Legacies and Contingent Futures." *Political Studies* 41, Special Issue: pp. 78–92.

Karowski, J. 1995. "I Had a Rainy Night in Georgia on My Mind." *Scotland on Sunday*, 16 April.

Keating, F. 1999. "Ulster Unites for 'Our Boys.'" *Guardian*, 29 January.

Kellas, J. G. 1991. *The Politics of Nationalism and Ethnicity*. Basingstoke, United Kingdom: Macmillan.

Kidd, B. 1992. "The Culture Wars of the Montreal Olympics." *International Review for the Sociology of Sport* 27 (2): pp. 151–164.

———. 1996. *The Struggle for Canadian Sport*. Toronto: University of Toronto Press.

Kiernan, V. 1993. "The British Isles: Celt and Saxon." In M. Teich and R. Porter (eds.), *The National Question in Europe in Historical Context*. Cambridge: Cambridge University Press, pp. 1–34.

Kimmel, M. 1990. "Baseball and the Reconstitution of American Masculinity, 1880–1920." In M. A. Messner and D. F. Sabo (eds.), *Sport, Men, and the Gender Order: Critical Feminist Perspectives*. Champaign, IL: Human Kinetics Publishers, pp. 55–65.

King, S. J. 1998. *A History of Hurling, Revised Edition*. Dublin: Gill and Macmillan.

Lane, J.-E. 1993. "The Twilight of the Scaninavian Model." *Political Studies* 41 (2), June: pp. 315–324.

Lawton, W. 1995. "Worn Themes and New Developments in Quebec and Canadian Politics." *Politics* 15 (3): pp. 167–174.

Leite Lopes, J. S. 1997. "Successes and Contradictions in 'Multiracial' Brazilian

Football." In G. Armstrong and R. Giulianotti (eds.), *Entering the Field: New Perspectives on World Football*. Oxford: Berg, pp. 53–86.

Lever, J. 1983. *Soccer Madness*. Chicago: Chicago University Press.

Liljegren, L., and B. Wallin. 1985. *Idrott i Rörlese: Inlägg inifrån*. Malmö, Sweden: Liber Förlag.

Lindroth, J. 1974. *Idrottens Väg till Folkrörelse: Studier i Svensk Idrottsrörelse till 1915*. Uppsala, Sweden: Acta Universitatis Upsaliensis.

————. 1977. "Unionsupplösninger 1905 och Idrotten: Den Svenska Idrottsrörelsen i en Utrikespolitisk krissituation." Stockholm: Sveriges Centralförening för Idrottens Främjande Årsbok, pp. 50–68.

————. 1981. "Viktor Balck Som Idrotts Ideolog—Ett Föredragsmanuskript Utgivet Med Inledning och Kommentarer." Idrott, Historia och Samhälle, pp. 107–129.

————. 1987. *Idrott Mellan Krigen: Organisationer, Ledare och Idéer i den Svenska Idrottsrörelsen, 1919–1939*. Stockholm: HLS Förlag.

Lowerson, J. 1994. "Golf and the Making of Myths." In G. Jarvie and G. Walker (eds.), *Scottish Sport in the Making of the Nation: Ninety Minute Patriots?* Leicester, United Kingdom: Leicester University Press, pp. 75–90.

Lynch, M. 1992. *Scotland: A New History*. London: Pimlico.

————. 1993. "Scottish Culture in Its Historical Perspective." In P. H. Scott (ed.), *Scotland: A Concise Cultural History*. Edinburgh: Mainstream, pp. 15–45.

MacClancy, J., ed. 1996. *Sport, Identity, and Ethnicity*. Oxford, United Kingdom: Berg.

MacGregor, R. 1997. *The Home Team: Fathers, Sons, and Hockey*. Toronto: Penguin Books.

Macintosh, D., et al. 1988. *Sport and Politics in Canada: Federal Government Involvement since 1961*. Kingston, Canada: McGill-Queen's University Press.

Macintosh, D., and D. Whitson. 1990. *The Game Planners: Transforming Canada's Sport System*. Montreal, Canada: McGill-Queen's University.

Maguire, J. 1994. "Sport, Identity Politics, and Globalization: Diminishing Contrasts and Increasing Varieties." *Sociology of Sport Journal* 11 (4), December: pp. 398–427.

————. 1999. *Global Sport: Identities, Societies, Civilizations*. Cambridge, United Kingdom: Polity Press.

Malamud, B. 1963. *The Natural*. London: Eyre and Spottiswoode.

Mandle, W. F. 1987. *The Gaelic Athletic Association and Irish Nationalist Politics, 1884–1924*. London: Gill and Macmillan.

Mangan, J. A. 1987. "Ethics and Ethnocentricity: Imperial Education and British Tropical Africa." In W. J. Baker and J. A. Mangan (eds.), *Sport in Africa: Essays in Social History*. New York: Holmes and Meier, pp. 138–171.

————, ed. 1996. *Tribal Identities: Nationalism, Europe, Sport*. London: Frank Cass.

Maolfabhail, A. 1973. *Camán: Two Thousand Years of Hurling in Ireland*. Dundalk, Ireland: Dundalgan Press.

Markovits, A. S. 1988. "The Other 'American Exceptionalism': Why Is There No Soccer in the United States?" *Praxis International* 8 (2), July: pp. 125–150.

Marks, J. 1999. "The French National Team and National Identity: 'Cette France d'un bleu métis.'" In H. Dauncey and G. Hare (eds.), *France and the 1998 World Cup: The National Impact of a World Sporting Event.* London: Frank Cass, pp. 40–57.

Marr, A. 1992. *The Battle for Scotland.* Harmondsworth, United Kingdom: Penguin.

Mason, T. 1988. *Sport in Britain.* London: Faber and Faber.

McCarra, K. 1993. "Sport in Scotland." In P. H. Scott (ed.), *Scotland: A Concise Cultural History.* Edinburgh: Mainstream, pp. 279–290.

McCrone, D. 1992. *Understanding Scotland: The Sociology of a Stateless Nation.* London: Routledge.

McElligott, T. 1984. *Handball: The Game, the Players, the History.* Dublin, Ireland: Wolfhound Press.

McKenzie, B. 1997a. "Zero Tolerance Learning Starts Now." *Hockey News,* 28 November.

———. 1997b. "Hurtful Slurs Now Thorny NHL Issue." *Hockey News,* 12 December.

Meidner, R. 1993. "Why Did the Swedish Model Fail?" *Socialist Register,* pp. 211–228.

Meinander, H. 1992. "Towards a Bourgeois Manhood: Nordic Views and Visions of Physical Education for Boys, 1860–1930." *International Journal of the History of Sport* 9 (3), December: pp. 337–355.

———. 1998. "The Power of Public Pronouncement: The Rhetoric of Nordic Sport in the Early Twentieth Century." In H. Meinander and J. A. Mangan (eds.), *The Nordic World: Sport in Society.* London: Frank Cass, pp. 47–68.

Merkel, U. 1999. "Sport in Divided Societies—The Case of the Old, the New and the 'Re-united' Germany." In J. Sugden and A. Bairner (eds.), *Sport in Divided Societies.* Aachen: Meyer and Meyer, pp. 139–165.

Messenger, C. K. 1990. *Sport and the Spirit of Play in Contemporary American Fiction.* New York: Columbia University Press.

Messner, M. A. 1992. *Power at Play: Sport and the Problem of Masculinity.* Boston: Beacon Press.

Messner, M. A., and D. Sabo, eds. 1990. *Sport, Men, and the Gender Order: Critical Feminist Perspectives.* Champaign, IL: Human Kinetics Books.

Metcalfe, A. 1987. *Canada Learns to Play: The Emergence of Organized Sport, 1807–1914.* Toronto: McClelland and Stewart.

Miller, D. 1995. *On Nationality.* Oxford: Clarendon Press.

Milner, H. 1990. *Sweden: Social Democracy in Practice.* Oxford: Oxford University Press.

Moderata Samlingspartiet. 1995. "Bättre villkor för idrotten." *Motion till Riksdagen* (by B Lundgren and S Bertilsson), m 340, January.

Moorhouse, H. F. 1986. "Repressed Nationalism and Professional Football: Scotland versus England." In J. A. Mangan and R. B. Small (eds.), *Sport, Culture, Society: International Historical and Sociological Perspectives.* London: Spon, pp. 52–59.

———. 1991. "On the Periphery: Scotland, Scottish Football, and the New Europe." In J. Williams and S. Wagg (eds.), *British Football and Social Change.* Leicester, United Kingdom: Leicester University Press, pp. 201–219.

———. 1994. "From Zines Like These? Fanzines, Tradition, and Identity in Scottish Football." In G. Jarvie and G. Walker (eds), *Scottish Sport in the Making of the Nation: Ninety Minute Patriots?* Leicester, United Kingdom: Leicester University Press, pp. 173–194.

Morrow, D. 1989. "Baseball." In D. Morrow et al., *A Concise History of Sport in Canada.* Toronto: Oxford University Press, pp. 109–139.

Morrow, D., M. Keys, W. Simpson, F. Cosentino, and R. Lappage. 1989. *A Concise History of Sport in Canada.* Toronto: Oxford University Press.

Mrozek, D. J. 1983. *Sport and the American Mentality, 1880–1910.* Knoxville: University of Tennessee Press.

———. 1995. "The Cult and Ritual of Toughness in Cold War America." In D. K. Wiggins (ed.), *Sport in America: From Wicked Amusement to National Obsession.* Champaign, IL: Human Kinetics, pp. 257–267.

Murray, B. 1984. *The Old Firm: Sectarianism, Sport, and Society in Scotland.* Edinburgh: John Donald.

———. 1994. *Football: A History of the World Game.* Aldershot, United Kingdom: Scolar Press.

Nairn, T. 1981. *The Break-Up of Britain, Second Edition.* London: Verso.

———. 1991. "Scottish Identity? A Cause Unwon." *Chapman* 67, Winter: pp. 2–12.

Nauright, J. 1997. *Sport, Cultures, and Identities.* London: Leicester University Press.

Nilsson, T. 1979. *Fotbollens Kval och Lycka: En Läsebok om Fotboll.* Uddevalla, Sweden: Semic Förlags.

Norberg, J. R. 1998. "A Mutual Dependency: Nordic Sports Organizations and the State." In H. Meinander and J. A. Mangan (eds.), *The Nordic World: Sport in Society.* London: Frank Cass, pp. 115–135.

Observer. Various dates.

O'Connor, F. 1993. *In Search of a State: Catholics in Northern Ireland.* Belfast: Blackstaff Press.

O'Hagan, A. 1994. "Scotland's Fine Mess." *Guardian,* 23 July.

O'Halloran, C. 1987. *Partition and the Limits of Irish Nationalism: An Ideology Under Stress.* Dublin: Gill and Macmillan.

Oliver, G. 1992. *The Guiness Record of World Soccer: The History of the Game in over 150 Countries.* Enfield, United Kingdom: Guiness Publishing, Ltd.

Orange Standard. September, 1998.

ÓRiain, S. 1994. *Maurice Davin 1842–1927: First President of the GAA.* Templeogue, Ireland: Geography Publications.

Oriard, M. 1982. *Dreaming of Heroes: American Sports Fiction, 1868–1980.* Chicago: Nelson-Hall.

———. 1993. *Reading Football: How the Popular Press Created an American Spectacle.* Chapel Hill: University of North Carolina Press.

Paterson, L. 1981. "Scotch Myths—2." *Bulletin of Scottish Politics* 2: pp. 67–71.

———. 1993. "Scottishness." *Scottish Affairs* 4, Summer: pp. 1–4.

———. 1994. *The Autonomy of Modern Scotland.* Edinburgh: Edinburgh University Press.

Patriksson, G. 1973. *Idrottens Historia i Sociologisk Belysning.* Stockholm: Utbildningsförlaget.

Perkin, H. 1986. "Sport and Society: Empire into Commonwealth." In J. A. Mangan and R. B. Small (eds.), *Sport, Culture, Society: International Historical and Sociological Perspectives*. London: Spon, pp. 3–5.

Phillipson, N. T. 1969. "Nationalism and Ideology." In J. N. Wolfe (ed.), *Government and Nationalism in Scotland*. Edinburgh: Edinburgh University Press, pp. 167–188.

Pieterse, J. N. 1995. "Globalization as Hybridization." In M. Featherstone, S. Lash, and R. Robertson (eds.), *Global Modernities*. London: Sage, pp. 45–68.

Pope, S. W. 1997. *Patriotic Games: Sporting Traditions in the American Imagination, 1876–1926*. New York: Oxford University Press.

Poulin, D. 1992. *Lindros: Doing What's Right for Eric*. Markham, Canada: Panda Publishing Inc.

Preston, P. W. 1997. *Political/Cultural Identity: Citizens and Nations in a Global Era*. London: Sage.

Puirseal, P. 1982. *The GAA in Its Time*. Dublin: Purcell.

Purdie, B. 1991. "The Lessons of Ireland for the SNP." In T. Gallagher (ed.), *Nationalism in the Nineties*. Edinburgh: Polygon, pp. 66–83.

Rader, B. G. 1988. "The Quest for Subcommunities and the Rise of American Sport." In P. A. Zingg (ed.), *The Sporting Image: Readings in American Sport History*. Lanham, MD: University Press of America, pp. 139–154.

———. 1996. *American Sports: From the Age of Folk Games to the Age of Televised Sports, Third Edition*. Englewood Cliffs, NJ: Prentice-Hall.

Richards, D. A. 1997. *Hockey Dreams: Memories of a Man Who Couldn't Play*. Toronto: Doubleday.

Richler, M. 1992. *Oh Canada! Oh Quebec! Requiem for a Divided Country*. Toronto: Penguin Books .

Riess, S. A. 1988. "Race and Ethnicity in American Baseball." In P. A. Zingg (ed.), *The Sporting Image: Readings in American Sport History*. Lanham, MD: University Press of America, pp. 247–266.

Riksidrottsförbundet. 1994a. *Swedish Sports Pocket Book*. Farsta, Sweden: Riksidrottsförbundet.

Riksidrottsförbundet. 1994b. *Sport in Sweden*. Farsta, Sweden: Riksidrottsförbundet.

Robertson, R. 1990. "Mapping the Global Condition: Globalization as the Central Concept." *Theory, Culture, and Society* 7 (2–3), Special Issue: pp. 15–30.

———. 1995. "Globalization: Time-Space and Homogeneity-Heterogeneity." In M. Featherstone, S. Lash, and R. Robertson (eds.), *Global Modernities*. London: Sage, pp. 25–44.

Robinson, L. 1998. *Crossing the Line: Sexual Assault in Canada's National Sport*. Toronto: McClelland and Stewart.

Roth, P. 1973. *The Great American Novel*. New York: Farrar, Straus and Giroux.

Rouse, P. 1993. "The Politics and Culture of Sport in Ireland: A History of the GAA Ban on Foreign Games 1884–1971. Part One: 1884–1921." *International Journal for the History of Sport* 10 (3), pp. 333–360.

Ruane, J., and J. Todd. 1996. *The Dynamics of Conflict in Northern Ireland: Power, Conflict, and Emancipation*. Cambridge: Cambridge University Press.

Sage, G. H. 1990. *Power and Ideology in American Sport*. Champaign, IL: Human Kinetics Books.

Sandblad, H. 1984. "1800—talets idrotts tävlingar på Sannahed—Legend och Verklighet." Idrott, Historia och Samhälle, pp. 79–83.

———. 1985. Olympia och Valhalla: Idéhistoriska Aspekter av den Moderna Idrottsrörelsens Framväxt. Stockholm: Almquist and Wiksell International.

Sännås, P.-O. 1998. Black Army. Södertälje, Sweden: Action Bild.

Schelin, B. 1985. Den Ojämlika Idrotten: Om Idrottsstratifiering, Idrottspreferens och val av Idrott. Lund, Sweden: Lunds Universitet.

Scotland on Sunday. Various dates.

Scott, P. H. 1993. "Introduction." In P. H. Scott (ed.), Scotland: A Concise Cultural History. Edinburgh: Mainstream, pp. 9–14.

Simpson, W. 1989. "Hockey." In D. Morrow et al., A Concise History of Sport in Canada. Toronto: Oxford University Press, pp. 169–229.

Smith, A. D. 1995. Nations and Nationalism in a Global Era. Cambridge, United Kingdom: Polity Press.

Smout, T. C. 1994. "Perspectives on Scottish Identity." Scottish Affairs 6, Winter: pp. 101–113.

Socialdemokraterna. 1994. "Alla ska Platsa: Idrottspolitiska Riktlinger." Politisk Redovsning 22, August.

Sörlin, S. 1996. "Nature, Skiing, and Swedish Nationalism." In J. A. Mangan (ed.), Tribal Identities: Nationalism, Europe, Sport. London: Frank Cass, pp. 147–163.

Spiers, G. 1994. "Cadette Has the Perfect Answer." Scotland on Sunday, 9 January.

Spirit of the West. 1996. "Open Heart Symphony." Scarborough, Canada: Warner Music Canada Ltd.

Standeven, J. 1994. "Games, Culture, and Europeanization." In R. C. Wilcox (ed.), Sport in the Global Village. Morgantown, WV: Fitness Information Technology, pp. 235–242.

Stewart, A. T. Q. 1977. The Narrow Ground: Aspects of Ulster, 1609–1969. London: Faber and Faber.

Stoddart, B. 1988. "Sport, Cultural Imperialism, and Colonial Response in the British Empire." Comparative Studies in Society and History 30, pp. 649–673.

Story, R. 1995. "The Country of the Young: The Meaning of Baseball in Early American Culture" In D. K. Wiggins (ed.), Sport in America: From Wicked Amusement to National Obsession. Champaign, IL: Human Kinetics, pp. 121–132.

Sugden, J. 1994. "USA and the World Cup: American Nativism and the Rejection of the People's Game." In J. Sugden and A. Tomlinson (eds.), Hosts and Champions: Soccer Cultures, National Identities, and the USA World Cup. Aldershot, United Kingdom: Arena, pp. 219–252.

———. 1996. Boxing and Society: An International Analysis. Manchester: Manchester University Press.

Sugden, J., and A. Bairner. 1986. "Northern Ireland: Sport in a Divided Society." In L. Allison (ed.), The Politics of Sport. Manchester: Manchester University Press.

———. 1993a. Sport, Sectarianism, and Society in a Divided Ireland. Leicester, United Kingdom: Leicester University Press.

———. 1993b. "National Identity, Community Relations, and the Sporting Life in

Northern Ireland." In L. Allison (ed.), *The Changing Poltics of Sport*. Manchester: Manchester University Press, pp. 171–206.

————, eds. 1999. *Sport in Divided Societies*. Aachen, Germany: Meyer and Meyer.

Sugden, J., and A. Tomlinson, eds. 1994. *Hosts and Champions: Soccer Cultures, National Identities, and the USA World Cup*. Aldershot, United Kingdom: Arena.

————. 1998. *FIFA and the Contest for World Football: Who Rules the Peoples' Game?* Cambridge, United Kingdom: Polity Press.

Sunday Times Magazine. 3 October 1998.

Sunday Tribune. 11 October 1998.

Tamas, G., and R. Blombäck. 1995. *Sverige, Sverige, Fosterland: Om Ungdom, Identitet och Främlingskap*. Stockholm: Kombinera—Röda Korsets Ungdomsförbund.

Telfer, H. 1994. "Women and Sport in Nineteenth-Century Scotland." In G. Jarvie and G. Walker (eds.), *Scottish Sport in the Making of the Nation: Ninety Minute Patriots?* Leicester, United Kingdom: Leicester University Press, pp. 27–42.

Therborn, G. 1991. "Sweden." In A. Pfaller (ed.), *Can the Welfare State Compete? A Comparative Study of Five Advanced Capitalist Countries*. London: Macmillan, pp. 229–269.

Time Magazine. 27 July 1998.

Todd, J. 1987. "Two Traditions in Unionist Political Culture." *Irish Political Studies* 2: pp. 1–26.

————. 1990. "Northern Irish Nationalist Political Culture." *Irish Political Studies* 5: pp. 31–44.

Tomlinson, A. 1999. "Sport, Cultural Diversity, and National Identity: The Swiss Case." In J. Sugden and A. Bairner (eds.), *Sport in Divided Societies*. Aachen, Germany: Meyer and Meyer, pp. 113–137.

Tomlinson, J. 1991. *Cultural Imperialism—A Critical Introduction*. London: Pinter.

Tranter, N. 1994. "Women and Sport in Nineteenth-Century Scotland." In G. Jarvie and G. Walker (eds.), *Scottish Sport in the Making of the Nation: Ninety Minute Patriots?* Leicester, United Kingdom: Leicester University Press, pp. 27–42.

Tully, J. 1994. "The Crisis of Identification: The Case of Canada." *Political Studies* 42, Special Issue: pp. 77–96.

USA Today. 26 August 1998.

Vanreusel, B., R. Renson, and J. Tolleneer. 1999. "Divided Sports in a Divided Belgium." In J. Sugden and A. Bairner (eds.), *Sport in Divided Societies*. Aachen, Germany: Meyer and Meyer, pp. 97–111.

Verducci, T. 1995. "In the Field of Nightmares." *Independent on Sunday*, 26 March.

Wagg, S. 1995. "The Missionary Position: Football in the Societies of Britain and Ireland." In S. Wagg (ed.), *Giving the Game Away: Football, Politics, and Culture on Five Continents*. London: Leicester University Press.

Wakefield, W. E. 1997. *Playing to Win: Sports and the American Military, 1898–1945*. Albany: State University of New York Press.

Walker, G. 1990. "'There's Not a Team Like the Glasgow Rangers': Football and Religious Identity in Scotland." In G. Walker and T. Gallagher (eds.), *Sermons and Battle Hymns: Protestant Popular Culture in Modern Scotland*. Edinburgh: Edinburgh University Press, pp. 137–159.

———. 1994. "Nancy Riach and the Motherwell Swimming Phenomenon." In G. Jarvie and G. Walker (eds.), *Scottish Sport in the Making of the Nation: Ninety Minute Patriots?* Leicester, United Kingdom: Leicester University Press, pp. 142–153.

———. 1995. *Intimate Strangers: Political and Cultural Interaction between Scotland and Ulster in Modern Times.* Edinburgh: John Donald.

Waters, M. 1995. *Globalization.* London: Routledge.

Webb, K. 1978. *The Growth of Nationalism in Scotland.* Harmondsworth, United Kingdom: Penguin.

West, T. 1991. *The Bold Collegians: The Development of Sport in Trinity College, Dublin.* Dublin: Lilliput Press.

Wilcox, R. C. 1994. "Of Fungos and Fumbles: Explaining the Cultural Uniqueness of American Sport, or a Paradoxical Peek at Sport." In R. C. Wilcox (ed.), *Sport in the Global Village.* Morgantown, WV: Fitness Information Technology, pp. 73–102.

Yttergren, L. 1994. "The Nordic Games: Visions of a Winter Olympics or a National Festival." *International Journal of the History of Sport* 11 (3), December: pp. 495–505.

Zingg, P. A. 1988. "Myth and Metaphor: Baseball in the History and Literature of American Sport." In P. A. Zingg (ed.), *The Sporting Image: Readings in American Sport History.* Lanham, MD: University Press of America.

index